POETRY AND CONTEMPLATION
IN ST. JOHN OF THE CROSS

POETRY AND

CONTEMPLATION

IN ST. JOHN OF

THE CROSS

GEORGE H. TAVARD

OHIO UNIVERSITY · ATHENS

Library of Congress Cataloging-in-Publication Data

Tavard, George H. (George Henry), 1922–

Poetry and contemplation of St. John of the Cross.

Includes index.

1. John of the Cross, Saint, 1542–1591—Criticism and

interpretation. I. Title.

PQ6400.J8Z87   1988   861'.3   87-28169

ISBN 0-8214-0893-3

CONTENTS

Introduction / vii

Chapter 1. Before the Jail / 1

Chapter 2. The Daughter of Babylon / 15

Chapter 3. The First Canticle / 37

Chapter 4. The Night / 53

Chapter 5. The Contraries / 75

Chapter 6. Faith / 93

Chapter 7. The Second Canticle / 117

Chapter 8. The Beloved / 137

Chapter 9. Sparks of Love / 159

Chapter 10. The Living Flame of Love / 181

Chapter 11. The Divine Being / 193

Chapter 12. The Third Canticle / 217

Chapter 13. The Threshold of Eternity / 229

Conclusion / 247

Notes / 251

Index / 283

A Note about the Author / 289

INTRODUCTION

One day in early November five years ago I traveled by train from Madrid to the Escorial monastery for what was meant to be a diversion from my visit of the various places where John of the Cross had spent the first part of his life, before the events of the quarrel between the Calced and the Discalced forced him to move to Andalusia. In fact, however, this visit turned out to be much more than a distraction. Leaving the train at the station of Escorial, I met with the first snow of the season, which soon melted on the ground while it changed to rain in the air. Under a heavy downpour I saw the austere walls of the monastery erected by Philip II (1527–98, king in 1556) to the glory of God in thanksgiving for his victory over the French army at St. Quentin (1556). Although all such victories have been short-lived, the monument remains, a moving testimony to both royal grandeur and monastic austerity. Where did the king of Spain, three times widowed—all the more famous for his second wife, the unhappy Queen Mary of England, married for reasons of state and religion, whom he never could love—draw inspiration for such a project? The majestic and yet tranquil overall plan of the building, the dark tones of the stone, the stark simplicity, even the emptiness, of the main church—a lesson in contrast with the rococo churches that Catholic central Europe was soon to build—the unpretentiousness of the small apartment that Philip reserved to himself in this immense palace, are marked by a profound and sober piety. The king whose dominion extended across the Atlantic, who had effectively halted the spread of Protestantism in the Iberian peninsula, projected to spend his last days within these walls in silence, meditation, and simplicity. The neighboring apartment of his favorite daughter, Isabella, was no larger and no more luxurious, unlike the apartments later created and used by the next dynasty, the Bourbons. These evoke the royal palace in Madrid and even, on a smaller scale, the archetypal model of Versailles, the architectural crown of the Bourbons' senior line.

Philip II, aware of his religious duties, heir to the one who has been called "the only adversary of Luther who showed some grandeur,"[1] himself anxious for the proper reform of the church and its orders—yet who did not act when Teresa of Avila begged him to find where John of the Cross was jailed and to free him—showed a kinship to the mind of John of the Cross. The place chosen for his palace was called *escorial* long before the construction of Philip II took the name to itself. An escorial is a dump, a slagheap, a place for refuse and waste. Such a place King Philip decided to transform into a house of prayer and meditation at the very time when John was singing the transformation of human misery, of the human dump and waste, into God's bride and temple. Indeed, Philip II must have been affected by the signs of the times. Such were, along with the Spanish Inquisition and its well-meant horrors (which he had inherited) a remarkable group of saints: after Ignatius Loyola (1491–1556) and the saints of Carmel, above all Teresa of Avila (1515–82) and John himself, the Jesuit Francis Borgia (1510–72), Peter of Alcantara (1499–1562) among the Franciscans. Yet what seemed, under a November rain, to come the closest to the intended meaning of the stone buildings of the aging Philip II, were the spiritual constructions, filled with beauty and youth, of John of the Cross.

Writing a new book on St. John of the Cross is a hazardous enterprise since the bibliography of the Mystical Doctor has already reached nearly three thousand titles.[2] The chance is slim that an additional title will add something really new to the current knowledge and appreciation of John of the Cross's writings. Works on the Bible, however, escape counting, yet recent studies have indeed brought up new points of view. A slightly different vantage point may suffice to let a new light shine on the topic. Yet, as one may well object, to speak of John of the Cross requires certain qualifications that are bound to be rare: he was a poet, a mystic, a theologian of the mystical experience, a saint. Ideally, one ought to be all that to understand him and to speak of him. Or at least one should belong to the spiritual tradition that carried him and that, in a sense, he brought to its perfection. Yet a list of the major volumes published on John of the Cross in this century would show that some of the most important ones were not composed by authors of the Carmelite Order. Besides, there are links between the contemplative tradition of Carmel and some other, more recent, spiritual lines recognized in the Catholic Church. The influence of John of the Cross has extended outside the Carmelite friaries and nunneries.

Now, I consider that I belong, in different ways, to two such lines of spirituality that were both marked, at a major point of their development, by the reading of John of the Cross's major writings. On the one hand, Emmanuel d'Alzon (1810–80), vicar general of Nîmes in southern France, founder, in 1845, of the Augustinians of the Assumption (Assumptionists), the order to which I belong, recommended to his followers, in an admittedly eclectic way, familiarity with "several ascetic authors, St. Bonaventure, St. John of the Cross, St. Francis of Sales. . . ."[3] I have myself noted this point in my study, *The Weight of God. The Spiritual Doctrine of Emmanuel d'Alzon* (Rome: Centennial series, 1980). On the other hand, I have consecrated two volumes to the spiritual experience and doctrine of a mystic of the eighteenth century, beatified by Pius XII in 1954, and to whom I am related by blood through my paternal grandmother: *L'Expérience de Jean-Martin Moye. Mystique et mission* (Paris: Beauchesne, 1978); *Lorsque Dieu fait tout. La Doctrine spirituelle du Bienheureux Jean-Martin Moye* (Paris: Le Cerf, 1984). Jean-Martin Moye (1730–93), of the Foreign Missions of Paris after being a priest of the diocese of Metz in Lorraine, should be ranked among the adepts of the "French school" of spirituality, influenced by Bérulle, but he also belongs, directly by his readings, indirectly by some typical aspects of his own experience, to the filiation of John of the Cross.

Let me add that I did not wait to join the Augustinians of the Assumption and, later, to read Moye's printed and manuscript works, before obtaining some initiation into the thought of John of the Cross. I started reading his works in my first year at the diocesan seminary of Nancy (France), in 1940–41. Read in time of war and even of national despair, John of the Cross speaks with a special voice: hope is founded on nothing other than God! Since that time, if there has been an author whom I have never left unread for a sizable time, it has been the Mystical Doctor. Having read his works first in several French translations, I read them later, during a three-year stay in England, in the classical English text of Allison Peers, then, some years later, in the more recent American rendering of Kieran Kavanaugh and Otilio Rodriguez.[4] Finally, I used part of a sabbatical year to read the works in Spanish. In so doing I discovered John of the Cross anew, in ways that no translation conveys. Being already acquainted with some of the secondary literature, I found that some of my ideas and understandings were not to be found in print.

Apart from purely historical or textual studies, most works on John of the Cross easily fall into two categories. First, there is the category, by far the larger one, of studies of his theology and spirituality; written chiefly by specialists, these books usually pay little attention to the properly poetic or literary dimensions of John of the Cross. Second, there is the category of literary and poetic studies, which generally pay little attention to the properly theological dimension. This separation I would like to bridge. As a theologian I believe I can do justice to the theological form of John's experience and doctrine. Moreover, having published several volumes of poetry,[5] I believe I can also read John of the Cross's works in their strictly poetic dimension. In addition, most previous studies of his poetry have focused all but exclusive attention on John's major poems, those for which he himself provided commentaries. A certain number of so-called minor poems have been neglected, except by the few historians of Spanish literature who have attempted to find their sources and antecedents in medieval folksongs. Yet these secondary poems also should be studied theologically, for they have a theological dimension, like all the writings of the Mystical Doctor. I have wished to fill this gap.

I have followed a chronological order. Admittedly, the exact date of most of the Johannist writings is not absolutely certain.[6] When opinions vary I have chosen to follow the Spanish edition of Simeon de la Sagrada Familia (*Juan de la Cruz. Obras Completas*, 2d ed. [Burgos: Monte Carmelo, 1982]), which I have used mostly on account of its practical dimensions. The dates generally agree with those of the critical edition made by Silverio de Santa Teresa (*Obras de San Juan de la Cruz*, 5 vols. [Burgos: Monte Carmelo, 1929]). In the main I have followed the practice of borrowing the English translation of John's works from the Kavanaugh-Rodriguez edition, except for version (A) of both the *Spiritual Canticle* and the *Living Flame of Love*, which is not in that translation, and which I have therefore borrowed from the older and less fluent translation of Allison Peers. In many cases, however, especially for the poems, I have more or less thoroughly modified the translation to bring it closer to the flavor of the original.

The overall plan consists in taking one poem, or even several, as leading to some theological themes highlighted in the commentaries. After a first look at the poems composed before John of the Cross was kidnapped and imprisoned (chap. 1), I have studied the minor poems of captivity (chap. 2), the version of the *Spiritual Canticle* that John brought out of jail when he escaped (chap. 3), and next the poem of the *Dark Night* and the theme of the "night" in the *Ascent of Mount Carmel* and the commentary of the *Dark Night* (chap. 4). The theme of the "contraries," which complements that of the night, constitutes the heart of the next chapter (chap. 5), leading to the theme of "faith" (chap. 6). The second form of the *Canticle*, usually called version (A), is then examined (chap. 7); it leads to the theme of the "Beloved" (chap. 8). Chapter 9 studies the secondary poems composed during the Andalusian period of John's life, along with the shorter spiritual tractates and collections of maxims. The poem of the *Living Flame of Love* (chap. 10) introduces a study of the divine attributes and Being (chap. 11). Finally, version (B) of the *Spiritual Canticle* (chap. 12) leads to a focus on the "threshold of eternity" as adumbrated in version (B) of the commentary (chap. 13).

An investigation of this kind cannot be made without incurring many debts to many people: the colleagues and a niece who welcomed me in Spain, librarians, students in a course on "The Christian Mystics' Experience of God," relatives and friends, who have assisted or encouraged me. Among the many persons who could be mentioned, I will choose only two: the late abbé André Gircourt (1907–85), of my home diocese of Nancy (France), who drew my attention to John of the Cross during my first year in seminary; and an unforgettable student, whose name need not be divulged, who shone like a brief light in a professor's life and now lives in a Carmelite nunnery in South Korea, her country.

CHAPTER 1

BEFORE THE JAIL

he experience of John of the
Cross in the improvised jail where he was locked up by the Carmelite
friars of the Observance raises questions that have not yet been
answered. It has been possible approximately to describe the place,
in this friary that no longer exists, but that is known to have been
located at the edge of the town, just within the walls from which
Toledo dominates the curve of the river Tagus. One has been able
to describe in detail the sufferings of the prisoner, his perpetual
fast, the weekly scourgings to which he submitted on Friday, the
lack of air and of light in the sort of closet where he spent his days
and his nights, the cold he felt, since, having been kidnapped in
Avila on 2 December 1577, he arrived in Toledo some days later
after crossing the mountains and avoiding the city of Madrid, the
heat also, since he escaped only in the octave of the feast of the
Assumption, shortly after 15 August 1578. But only the imagination
of his biographers has reconstructed what John of the Cross felt in
the depths of his soul.

The fact is that John of the Cross remained surprisingly quiet
concerning his experience in Toledo. Presumably out of charity for
his gaolers in particular and for the Calced Carmelites in general,
he said little about the painful aspects of his enforced captivity. We
know more about the joys, since that is where he composed and
probably wrote several of his poems: among those he was to com-
ment upon at a later time, the *Spiritual Canticle* as far as stanza
31 (perhaps also, though I doubt it very much, the *Dark Night*);
among the minor poems, which he did not comment upon, the
"romances" on the Incarnation, the paraphrase of Psalm 137, *Super*

flumina Babylonis, and the short poem on the "Fountain": *For I know well the spring.* . . . The prisoner successfully occupied his time, devoting himself not only to prayer but also to poetic seeking in the lengthy days and nights when he was so cold. For it seems that a goodly part of these poems, perhaps even the whole, was composed in his mind and kept in his memory when, in the sixth month of his captivity, he asked his new guardian for some writing implements.

There undoubtedly was, the entire experience of John of the Cross is witness to it, a profound spiritual experience during these months of imprisonment. It was first a passage through the active night, even though this night may have started earlier, the modalities of which were imposed on him by the decisions of the General Chapter of Piacenza, Italy, in 1575,[1] and by the concrete circumstances of his jailing at the hands of a ruthless prior. Above all, it was an experience of the passive night, the work of divine grace as it shapes the soul in preparation for union with God. All this at the two levels of sense and spirit. This experience is known to us: it forms the central theme of the theological commentaries that John of the Cross later wrote on his major poems. The demands of the active night and the impositions of the passive night, as these are analyzed in the *Ascent of Mount Carmel,* must be quite particularly referred, in the author's life, to what he himself suffered in his prison, when, humanly speaking, he faced the prospect of an indefinite night of captivity that, under the conditions of hygiene and nourishment that were imposed on him, could easily have taken him to a premature death. No doubt this journey to the end of night was accompanied by the lights that are preparatory to union with God. It did happen in Toledo between December 1577 and August 1578: John of the Cross was raised by grace to the highest union with God, as described in the commentaries on the *Canticle* and the *Living Flame of Love,* where they are identified with the spiritual espousals and the spiritual marriage.

John of the Cross himself links together his properly mystical experience and the composition of his poems, at least of the *Canticle.* This is clear in the prologue to his commentary, in which it is stated that the stanzas of the *Canticle* "were obviously composed with a certain burning love of God."[2] This love of God includes in itself an immense wisdom and love. Thus, continues John of the

Cross, the soul that "is informed and moved by it bears in some way this very abundance and impulsiveness in his words." What does he mean? This is no less than a transformation of human language by divine love: "It would be foolish to think that expressions of love arising from mystical understanding, like these stanzas, are fully explainable." And again: "Since these stanzas, then, were composed in a love flowing from abundant mystical understanding, I cannot explain them adequately."[3]

Thus John of the Cross affirms that the language of the *Spiritual Canticle* is inspired. Undoubtedly, he does not take the inspiration of prophets as the model of such inspiration. The model is rather the prayer of the Spirit in the depths of the soul, as suggested in chapter 8 of the epistle of St. Paul to the Romans. But one may wonder about the exact mode of this inspiration. Is it simply a poetic inspiration, similar to that of poets of all lands and times? Or is there something in the highest mystical experience that is able to transform the language of the mystic? The second case corresponds better to the clear sense of the text. John of the Cross does not propose a theory on poetic inspiration in general or on his own poetic inspiration in particular. He speaks of the effects of mystical experience upon the language that attempts to express it. Like the experience, the language is inspired by the Spirit to the extent that it is "informed and moved" by mystical love of God. The Spirit "gives understanding . . . experience . . . desires."[4] And no one, not even the one who receives these gifts, has the capacity to enclose in formulas such understanding, experience, or desires. This is why the language involved has recourse to an indirect mode, which is made of "figures and similes." Through a process that is not described here, these symbols place the reader on the way to grasp what has been experienced. This is the foundation for the symbolism of the *Spiritual Canticle*.

Yet one may wonder if what is presented as a language transformed by grace would not be simply, despite the Mystical Doctor's own conception, the poetic dimension as such, that John of the Cross shares with many other poets. For his interpretation was conceived after the fact. The prologue to the Commentary was composed along with the Commentary itself, in Granada in the years 1582–84, at the request of Anne of Jesus, the prioress of the Carmelite sisters of the city.[5] John of the Cross tells us, equivalently, that mystical experience made him, in his prison at Toledo, the poet that he became as he wrote the stanzas of the *Spiritual Canticle*. Yet seven years later memory may have transformed the impression originally received. Or also, theological interpretation may have affected the very form of remembrance.

John of the Cross was no doubt a poet before he was kidnapped. He had already composed, it would seem, the stanzas of *I live, but not in myself,* and some other pieces in a manner that was proper to the Spain of his times, and that consisted in rewriting in a pious or religious vein some originally profane or secular poem. As he was suffering cold and heat, fasts, and public flagellations while on his knees in the middle of the friars' refectory, something transformed the poetic capacity of John of the Cross. Was it the mystical grace? Did the overflowing of his heart suffice for the Reformer of the Carmel to take hold of the images, the comparisons, the similes mentioned in the prologue? Was it enough to lead the desire to speak, in the silence of his gaol, toward the structure of his stanzas, toward the shape of his verses, toward his abundant biblical allusions, toward the remembrance of literary studies of former years, toward echoes of religious readings of more recent days? Something else must have been present, an "I-know-not-what": grace indeed[6]; yet, in the Thomism that John of the Cross as theologian generally followed, "Grace does not take away nature, but makes it perfect."[7] Grace did transform something in the nature of John of the Cross so that he could become the sublime poet who escaped from gaol with the *Spiritual Canticle* in his heart. This something we should hope to find as we study the poetry of John of the Cross before he was captured and confined in Toledo.

Nature never goes without culture. Between the nature of John of the Cross and divine grace, there was the culture in which he lived, and which provided him with the intellectual air that he breathed in his soul and in his thought.

The influence of the popular poetry of Old Castile on John of the Cross, especially of the forms known as romances and *villancicos,* has often been noted.[8] A *romance* was a very simple narrative poem, with a rhyme that often remained unchanged throughout, and that usually tells a love story. The *villancico* was a poem with a refrain, often sung, the theme of which was formulated in an envoy, the envoy reappearing, at times in slightly different forms, as refrain. In all the popular literatures of the feudal age, the theme of love recurred the most frequently. And for a long time the lyrical tradition of Spain made use of secular songs and poems to celebrate divine love. Alphonsus X the Wise (1221–84), king of Castile and Léon,[9] who welcomed Christian troubadours as well as Jewish and Muslim singers at his brilliant court, had collected hundreds of popular religious compositions in honor of the Virgin Mary, the *Cantigas de Santa Maria* (songs of St. Mary), which were modeled on profane *Cantigas de amigo* (songs of my friend).[10] It is well known that the poets and singers of Spain, in the medieval period, had favored the dialect of Galicia as the poetic tongue *par excellence.* Not only did the Galicians use it, but also the Portuguese and Castilians. It is also known that mozarabic Spain had mixed together Spanish and Arabic in its popular poetry. The *kharja* was a poem of some five stanzas, each ending on a refrain; Spanish and Arabic words appeared side by side, as presumably in the daily language of the market place and of many homes. Yet the origin of these poems is not to be found in Islamic poetry. Scholarship is generally agreed that the Muslim and Jewish poets of Spain were in fact influenced, in their compositions in Arabic or in Hebrew, by a powerful romanesque poetic tradition. Such compositions did not entirely vanish from common practice with the reconquest of the Muslim kingdoms by the Christian knights. Romanesque poetry, now at home in the Castilian dialect, enriched with the traditions of Arabic poets, was still in favor at the end of the medieval period, and remained so at the time of John of the Cross. It is all the more important to appreciate the place of the Mystical Doctor in the poetry of Spain as he had lived his adolescence in the city of Medina del Campo before joining the Carmelite friars.

The very name of Medina del Campo is reminiscent of Arabic occupation.[11] It was a crossroads of commerce when Juan de Yepes lived in it alongside his mother and his older brother Francisco. Annual fairs brought to it visitors from all over Spain and even from beyond the borders. Undoubtedly, sellers and buyers were not the only ones who came: all kinds of entertainers, singers, dancers, animal trainers, fortune tellers, contortionists, fire swallowers, and story tellers must have come along, too. If Juan de Yepes became familiar with the *villancicos* in the ancient tradition of popular poetry, the occasion must have been found for this in the fairs of Medina del Campo and in the occasional evenings during which, presumably, the city dwellers shared the songs they had learned and improvised additional stanzas. The *villancico* is the first form of the poetry of John of the Cross, a form he never abandoned, and which was transformed in the fire of his experience in Toledo.

In order better to understand the art of John of the Cross one could study the Latin hymns in use in the liturgy of the hours in the Carmelite friaries of Spain.[12] One could also study the mozarabic liturgy of the times, which John of the Cross certainly knew during his childhood at Fontiveros, Arévalo, and Medina del Campo, the hymns of which may have provided John of the Cross with certain rhythms and certain themes. Yet it is particularly difficult to determine which version of the Carmelite liturgy was in use at Medina del Campo and Salamanca.

If the study of possible literary sources for John of the Cross, outside of the Bible, has not yet been carried out exhaustively, the study of his Spanish sources is well advanced. It is admitted that John of the Cross drew, not only on the *Song of Songs*, in the commentary which the Augustinian friar, professor in Salamanca, Luis de Léon (1528–91) began in 1554, but also on the secular poetry of Garcilaso de la Vega (1504–36) and on its transformation *a lo divino* that Sebastián de Córdoba (d. 1603) published in 1575.[13] The elegies of Garcilaso generally feature an artificial bucolic landscape borrowed from the Italian Renaissance, in which shepherds and shepherdesses sigh after one another. Rather sad, they evoke arcadian scenery in which friends attempt in vain to console one another for their unrequited or unfortunate loves. One is floating between seasons and between worlds; it is neither day nor night, neither summer nor winter, neither here nor there. Cloudy landscapes feed misty dreams. The soldier in Garcilaso (he was an officer in the armies of Charles V) dreams, during campaigns in Austria, Tunisia, Italy, and southern France, of a peaceful home, of a deep and lasting love, of a faraway friend, of everything that he cannot have.

John of the Cross himself notes, in his commentary on the *Living Flame*, that he imitated one of the poetic forms used by Sebastián de Córdoba,[14] who had rewritten in a pious vein the works of two poets, Boscán (d. 1542) and Garcilaso. Sebastián modified the texts in order to apply to divine love what they said of human love. The first edition of this pious fraud saw the light in 1575; a second one appeared in Saragossa two years later. Since reminiscences from *Boscán a lo divino* (as John of the Cross calls the work of Sebastián) are interspersed through the stanzas of the *Canticle* that were written in Toledo, it seems probable that, shortly before his arrest, while he was chaplain to the monastery of the Incarnation in Avila, John of the Cross had read this book. Practically all the allusions contained in the poems written in Toledo were made from memory, since the entire library of John of the Cross in his gaol consisted in his breviary, so that the reader of Garcilaso-Sebastián must have spontaneously assimilated certain cadences, some bits and pieces of verses, a few key words, perhaps some entire sequences. Such reminiscences, sparked in his memory by some aspect of his painful existence, came back to him in the form of an inner music. And it must have been spontaneously, without trying to imitate anyone, yet without the false pride of one who would use only his own original discoveries, that the prisoner gave his words shapes that had become familiar to himself. And so he borrowed, consciously or inadvertently, directly or through Sebastián, images, words, expressions, from Garcilaso de la Vega.

Between the early learning of *villancicos*, done during his adolescence, and the poetry he took with him when he fled his jail, John of the Cross had read Garcilaso. First, it must have been as secular literature, presumably as he was studying at the Jesuit College of Medina del Campo in the years 1556 to 1563. Then it was in the *Boscán* of Sebastián de Córdoba, shortly before his capture by the friars of the Observance. All this was still alive enough in his heart for John of the Cross to draw from it in his captivity, as he tried to occupy his time and his mind in order to survive.

How much of a poet was John of the Cross before his Toledan night? Let us examine the stanzas that begin with "I live, but not in myself." The works of Teresa of Avila contain a poem with the same refrain.[15] The two compositions must have been made at the same time, when Teresa and John were near to each other, that is, between April 1572 and December 1577. John of the Cross was then living with another friar, German de St

Matthias, next to the Convent of the Incarnation in Avila. He acted as chaplain to the sisters. Teresa was the prioress. It is likely that the two poems of John of the Cross and of Teresa were written around a refrain or envoy that was already known to them, being borrowed from a popular song.[16] Such an exercise was not unknown in religious communities. It could serve both to entertain the sisters at recreation time and to teach them some points relating to the spiritual life. After a three-verse envoy, there are eight stanzas of the form known as a *lira:* six verses lead to a last one which is in principle identical with the third verse in the envoy. The rhyme follows the rhythm, *abbaabb,* the rhyme *a* varying from one stanza to the next, the rhyme *b* remaining, by and large, the same. In fact, neither poet keeps strictly to this cadence: with both of them, the same rhyme recurs only in the last two verses of each stanza. The theme, which had been frequent in the love poetry of the Spanish troubadours, evokes death in the midst of life:

> I live, but not in myself,
> And I have such hope
> That I die because I do not die.

This envoy is common to the two saints. But the treatment of its theme has been transposed in diverse ways; and this undoubtedly highlights the poetic superiority of John of the Cross. Teresa's poem is honest and prosaic; stanza after stanza, without progression, it repeats the dialectical opposition of death and life, with a strongly sentimental accent, and without changing in any way the last verse, "That I die because I do not die." On the contrary, John's poem vibrates. It moves as a succession of waves that intersect at various points. Within each stanza the orientation of the first four verses, which are descriptive, is reversed in the last three. In stanzas I to 3, the absence of God is described, as nonlife, as death, and as distance; but a contrast immediately follows, in the last three verses, that stresses hope, prayer, and perseverance. Stanza 4 cuts through the movement of the whole poem by universalizing the perspective. Until this moment the poet has spoken of his own experience; he has desired God in God's absence. Now, however, the absence of God is extended to the entire horizon of creaturely life through a metaphor: life away from God is compared to the life of a fish without water. The concrete scope of the metaphor broadens the perspective indefinitely, as it allows each reader to identify with the fish without water.[17] The resulting break in the descriptive movement is followed, in the last three verses of this stanza 4, by a stop in the movement of hope that has hitherto marked the second part of each stanza. The poet poses the question, How deep and universal is death? This ultimate interrogation brings to its climax a wave of questioning that started at the first stanza. From the beginning John of the Cross has contrasted the life that is really death with the death that is really life: "What will life be?" (st. 1). "What life can I have / Except to endure / The bitterest death known?" (st. 3). This leads to the most profound query, which is also the last:

> What death can equal
> My pitiable life,
> For the longer my life the more drawn out my dying?

In stanzas 1 and 2, the question emerged from the affirmative form of the description. In stanza 4 it takes the place of the theme of hope that previously characterized the last three verses.

After being thus broken at several levels, the movement of the first part of the poem starts again on a new note. In stanzas 5 to 7, the theme of hope comes at the beginning, in the first four verses. This theme dominates the picture. The poet seeks for the divine presence in the eucharist (st. 5), in his expectation of the vision (st. 6), in his desire for the true life, far from the present death (st. 7). The second side of each stanza still stands in contrast with the first. But now the contrast is born of hope itself and of the impossibility of hope to fill the void left in desire: from the eucharist a deep sorrow is born (st. 5), from the expectation of the vision a fear (st. 6), from the desire for the vision of God a pain which is, this time, all-invading (st. 7).

Then the last stanza arrives. One discovers the reason for the distance of God from the present death-life: it lies in the author's own sinfulness. His life is kept away by his sin, though one does not discern too clearly which life is thus kept away: Is it the unhappy life here below? Or is it rather the true life to come, which is somehow impeded by sin from finally breaking through? This very ambiguity of the poet's language brings in the final question, which is in fact, in spite of its question form, a profession of hope. It ends the movement of the preceding stanzas as with a clasp:

> O my God, when will it be
> That I can truly say:
> Now I live because I do not die?

In its main devolution, the poem takes the shape of an inversed sequence, *ab ab ab cd ba ba ba ef,* in which stanza 4 acts as the central hinge, and 8 as the closing of the gate. If we take note of the insertion of an interrogative mode at several points, we obtain a more subtle movement: *a?b ab a?b cd? ba ba ba ef?* Compared to this Teresa's poem is no more than a monotonous repetition, scarcely altered by a few interrogation and exclamation marks: *aa aa a!a a!a aa aa aa a!a.* Besides this John of the Cross does not keep the strict form of the refrain, "That I die because I do not die." This form recurs three times, at stanzas 2, 3, 7. The other stanzas more or less alter the form, leading finally to its opposite: "Now I live because I do not die."

Thus John of the Cross remains free from the very form that he uses. He becomes creative and imaginative, showing himself to have mastered his tool, being at the same time less sentimental and more theological than Teresa of Avila. Far from simply repeating the dialectical opposition of life and death, he uncovers its cause. The very shape of the poem points to the locus of hope and therefore of the true life to come: it coincides with that of the false life, in which the true life is absent. The four-cornered structure of the present life in the absence of God (where one may sense a reminiscence of the four elements that are constitutive of the material world in the physics of the ancients)[18] leads to the ternary structure of hope, which is itself obviously modeled on the Trinitarian life. Then, after the universalizing image of the fish without water (and is not the fish also the *Ichtus* that symbolized Christ in early Christian iconography?), the quaternary structure of the present hope helps the reader to gauge the threefold, Trinitarian, depth of the absence of God.

As regards the doctrine of mystical experience, we do not find here, evidently, the equal of the great poems that will invite John's own commentary. The language is not yet that of the night. Yet the contents are not far from this. From the life that implies death and the death that implies life to the light-filled night and the nocturnal light there will be a transition, a passage. John of the Cross will acquire and unfold a new image, both in his poetry and in his commentaries. The basic image will be deepened by experience. But the new image will emerge in the line of the life-death and the death-life of the present poem.

The stanzas of "I live, but not in myself" may be compared with those of another *villancico* which also most probably belongs to the pre-Toledan period of the saint's life: "I entered where I knew not."[19] The theme is that of the "learned ignorance," which has been illustrated in western European literature since the first Latin translations of the works of Denys the Areopagyte (also known as Pseudo-Denys). Exploited chiefly during the Renaissance, especially by Nicholas of Cusa (1401–64), some of whose writings may have been known to John of the Cross, it had been featured in the fourteenth century in the works of the anonymous English author of *The Cloud of Unknowing*. It also occupied a central place in the spiritual doctrine of the Rhineland mystics. The poem is similar in form to the previous one, although the eight stanzas end on two verses from the envoy rather than on one: the last but one varies slightly, the last, "Transcending all knowledge," remains the same but for one slight variation in stanza 7.

The text is divided in two clearly distinct sections. Stanzas 1 to 3 soberly describe a personal experience. John of the Cross has entered he knows not where, and he has heard ineffable words (st. 1). He has thus acquired a most secret knowledge, of which he can only babble (st. 2). He found himself so absorbed in this knowledge that he lost all personal feelings and all clear understandings (st. 3). From this point on, the poet tries to instruct others by universalizing this experience. Such a knowledge, as he explains, forces one out of oneself and of all that has been hitherto known (st. 4). Like a dark cloud that illuminates the night (st. 5), it is higher than what all wisdom can say (st. 6), and it cannot be learned (st. 7). The last stanza (st. 8) identifies this knowing that is unknowing with a sudden prehension of the divine essence.

Were there no critical consensus dating this poem from the time spent by the author in Avila, one would be tempted to read it, on account of its topic and especially of its first line, as though written either in prison or shortly after the escape: it would primarily evoke the night of his dark cell.[20] Led blindfolded through back alleys after passing into the city, John of the Cross entered he knew not where. There he learned a hidden wisdom, as the *Spiritual Canticle* testifies. Moreover, both the darkness and the night are mentioned. This could be the poem of his captivity, in parallel to that of his escape: "In a dark night." Yet this poem does not lose its value if one does not change the usually received date. It even acquires a unique dimension of anticipation. Did John of the Cross foresee what was going to happen to him? Once already, at the beginning of the year 1576, he had been forcibly removed from his dwelling by order of the prior of the Calced friars in Avila. He had then been led, along with his companion at the time, Francisco de los Apóstoles, to Medina del Campo. The two of them had been released a short time later on order from the Apostolic Nuncio. It would therefore seem that "I entered where I knew not" could be the poem of his first imprisonment, in which, presentiment being added to remembrance, the second imprisonment would be adumbrated.

However this may be, "I entered where I knew not" relates to "I live, but not in myself," like experience to the theory that precedes or follows it, like the reality of a play to the last rehearsal of it, even though the chronological order of the two poems is not absolutely certain. Indeed, from the standpoint of music and rhythm, this piece is inferior to the other. But its text takes value from its promises concerning at least two points, thanks to which it lies in fact closer to the major poems.

In the first place, it already alludes to the night. Admittedly, the image of the night is not as rich as it will become in the darkness of the Toledo jail. It is the night of this life, the living death, or the dead life, that is already featured in "I live, but not in myself." A "dark cloud" throws light over it, a cloud that becomes darker as one ascends into unknowing. Thus, the light that illumines the night is itself night. This echoes the foundational language of Exodus 14: 19–20. It may also have been inspired by Psalms 18: 10–12: "He inclined the heavens and came down, with dark clouds under his feet . . . And he made darkness the cloak about him; dark, misty rain-clouds his wrap."

In the second place, one of the most powerful verses of the *Canticle* is already hinted at. Later, when John of the Cross will write "Of an I-know-not-what which they keep stammering,"[21] he will be rewriting a more modest verse of the present *villancico*: "That I was left stammering." This verse already refers to an "I-know-not-what," to something felt, yet not known, of which one can only babble.

Indeed, John of the Cross was a poet before his experience in Toledo. Yet the poet he was had not quite found his way. Truly, he never practiced the prosaic versifying of which the Great Teresa never rid herself. Already his poetry was filled with undeniable breadth and power. The theological dimension of his experience lay just under the surface of what he wrote. But as he had not yet entered the great sea of suffering, likewise John of the Cross had not yet penetrated very far into the symbolic dimension of language. It will be an original feature of his poetic works that he will enter jointly these two distinct worlds. Before Toledo, one cannot yet state that the stanzas of John of the Cross are composed "in a love flowing from abundant mystical understanding," as he himself will affirm it of the *Spiritual Canticle*.[22] Yet, as he arrived at the threshold of the highest contemplation, John of the Cross also reached the entrance to a deeper poetry.

CHAPTER 2

THE DAUGHTER OF BABYLON

mong the poems that saw the light in Toledo, the one on the "fountain" or "spring" conveys an impression of in-between, as though one were caught in a migration. Admittedly, one cannot know for certain in what chronological order the poems from prison were composed. Yet the logical order that emerges from their contents places the stanzas on the spring in the first place. This is clear from Dámaso Alonso's demonstration that this poem results, once again, from a transformation *a lo divino* of a popular theme,[1] which is summed up in the two verses of the envoy:

> For I know well the spring that flows and runs,
> Although it is night.

No concrete instance of such a refrain in popular literature has in fact come down to us. Yet Alonso finds sufficient evidence in the numerous *villancicos* that begin with those very words: *Que bien* . . . (For . . . well . . .). And he suspects that the primitive form may have contained three verses, with an assonance in *o-e:*

> For I know well the spring
> that flows and runs,
> although it is night.

Noting that the normal form of the word for "fountain" in the Castilian dialect would be *fuente*, Alonso explains that the poem begins with the Galician form, *fonte*, this being due to the influence of the Galician dialect on the early poetry of Christian Spain.[2] He also remarks that, if the poem of John of the Cross has a certain kinship with Galician, it nonetheless belongs to the Castilian favorite form of the *villancico:* an initial envoy provides a refrain, the last verse of which recurs at the end of each stanza. It also follows a movement of progressive flow, as is the wont of early Castilian poetry, the poets of Portugal and Galicia preferring to use parallelisms. Besides, the poem also reflects, in its choice of a verse of eleven syllables, the influence of the Italian Renaissance, which was known to John of the Cross through Garcilaso de la Vega.

The outcome of this association of several styles is a poem of great originality. All is harmonized in it. Even the passage from *fonte* to *fuente,* each form appearing twice after the initial envoy, pertains so deeply to the deeper rhythmic context of the poem that it seems to be perfectly natural. That John of the Cross, in the horrible conditions of his imprisonment, was able to effect such a perfect synthesis of styles need not throw doubt on his authorship of the poem. It should rather suggest that as he entered the tiny confines of his gaol he also took a decisive step across the threshold of great poetry. The eleven stanzas of the "Fountain" are far superior to the previous transpositions *a lo divino.* Yet one may still wonder why this is so and how it was done.

The reader who is already acquainted with the two poems of the *Canticle* and the *Dark Night,* and who therefore knows details of John of the Cross's later experience that he himself did not know at the time, will undoubtedly think that the night that is mentioned at the end of each stanza of the "Fountain" is not yet the great mystical night that will be described later. As a poem of the night, which it certainly is, the "Fountain" brings to mind the material darkness of an obscure closet and, more symbolically, the darkness of the present world, the night of ignorance and unknowing. Such a night invades everything, haunts everything. But it is not described here at any length or in any detail. It is simply the night in which the poet finds himself. It hides in its darkness the deeper theme of remembrance. In his night, John of the Cross remembers. His true theme is that in the night, despite the night, he knows. And what he knows is not something that he would have discovered in his jail, as it will be in the case of the two longer poems. He does not speak here of a recent enlightenment, of a light in his darkness. He rather speaks of a peaceful possession; he speaks of what he knows because he already knew it before being locked up. He writes a poem of memory.

In this perspective the Galician form of the word for fountain, *fonte*, makes perfect sense, even without recourse to popular poetry.[3] *Fonte* appears three times: in the envoy and in the first and ninth stanzas. The first six stanzas, with the envoy, are those of the *fonte*; the five others alternate between *fonte* and *fuente*, ending on the latter.

Now the fountain as *fonte-fuente* evokes no less than the divinity of the Father.[4] From this fontal fullness, to borrow a term from the Trinitarian theology of St. Bonaventure, there proceeds the twofold movement that, in God, results in the Word-Son and in the Spirit.[5] One cannot know if John of the Cross, while studying at the University of Salamanca, where there was a chair of Scotist theology, had been initiated to the doctrines of the Franciscan schoolmen. Yet, on the one hand, having studied Thomism he knew that St. Thomas, although denying fontal fullness as the positive aspect of the innascibility of the First Person, nonetheless called fontality the Father's prerogative of being, in the Trinity, the source of origination of the other Persons.[6] On the other hand, all his thought and experience being oriented toward his contemplative vocation, John must had read some of the mystical opuscula of Bonaventure. Precisely, in the "Tree of Life" Jesus is called fontal ray, the superessential radiance that comes directly from the Father as its source; as it follows Jesus is himself source (*fons*) of life and light for those who believe.[7] Thus, Latin reminiscences from the mystical literature of the Middle Ages may have guided John of the Cross toward a preference for the Galician form of the word, *fonte*.

There is more. The *fons* that, in the Father, is the source, not only of the creative act, but also, and before all else, of the divine life identified with the two Persons of the Son and the Spirit, could easily, for the prisoner, evoke his own origin. The village where Juan de Yepes was born was called *Fontiveros*. This name certainly meant, in its remote origin in the Roman occupation of Spain, "Iberian fountain," from the old Greek name of the area around the valley of the Ebro, the great river of northern Spain that flows into the Mediterranean. The name had come to designate the entire peninsula. Yet John of the Cross, who presumably had not studied the etymology of the word, must have been led by the sound of the name to take it as tantamount to *fons verus*, the true fountain, or the fountain of truth. This is all the more likely as the street where his parents had their small house was the *calle de Cantiveros*, "Cantiveros street," from the name of the neighboring village to which it eventually led. This must have suggested, again by its very sound, "the true song."

Indeed, the poet in his gaol knows well where he comes from; he remembers the village where he was born, the *fons* of his life. Is that not where, since 1545, the father whom he has hardly known, Gonzalo de Yepes,[8] has been buried in the central nave of the large church? The very origin of the life of John of the Cross joins together knowledge and night: knowledge of the place, night as to the person of his father. And so, in the night that is now his, and that unexpectedly prolongs the night of his unknowing, he knows well the place of his origin.

This is the start of the contrast between "For I know well," and "Although it is night." The dialectic of knowing and unknowing, of light and night, is, at this poetic and mystical moment in John of the Cross's existence, a dialectic of time and venue. The night is no other than time at its most negative point; it is the trajectory of the creature in its downward curve. Such a movement takes paradoxically the form of inertia: the refrain repeats, without variation, without change of tone, monotonously: "Although it is night."

Over against ignorance of time, there is acquaintance with place: "For I know well the spring. . . . " The place in question, contrasted with the night, which is a symbol of inertia, of creaturely passivity, is first of all the absolutely stable, the eternal fount. The place of origin, the true fount, the *fontiveros*, is no other than what provides stability to every place; it is the place that is identical with eternity.

Yet it also is, in the progression of the poem, movement at its most absolute: the Trinitarian movement of the divine life. This movement is suggested in two ways. After stating in the first stanza that the fountain is hidden, and yet that he knows well where it is, John of the Cross explains in the three next stanzas that the fountain has no origin, that nothing is more beautiful, that its light never fades. But this negative mode of knowing, this unknowing, runs along a positive affirmation: John of the Cross knows where to find the fountain; he knows that all has its origin in it; he knows that heaven and earth drink from it, that no one can cross it, so wide is it, and that all light ultimately derives from it.

This twofold, contrasted movement between affirmation and negation corresponds, in light of the contents of these verses, to the absolute transcendence of the Father. In the last six stanzas it is followed by a double affirmation, or a double and parallel positive movement. This underlies in the first place the wealth of the source as the origin of the processions of the Son and of Spirit. With a bold theological leap, since the incarnation has not been mentioned, the poet finds this eternal fountain, still hidden, where faith discovers it in the living bread of the eucharist. It attracts to it all the faithful, who in darkness drink of its water. And finally the poet, who desires to drink from this living fountain, sees it in the bread of life. This time, the originally one fountain (*fons, fonte*) has divided itself on the model of the two eternal streams that flow from it: it has become *fuente* at the precise moment of the first procession. Being again *fonte* when the poet speaks of its hidden dwelling in the eucharistic bread, it again becomes *fuente* at the moment when John of the Cross contemplates it in the living bread. For no one sees the Father but through the Son in the Spirit.

Thus one may perceive how the Toledan night of John of the Cross began to let in some rays of light. Just as water reflects the sky and its brightness, the fountain also becomes, in the course of this *villancico*, a symbol of light. The Trinitarian and eucharistic light has pierced the inertia of darkness and has illuminated the time of night with the light of the origin. As he dreamt of his childhood in an attempt to escape temporarily the horror of his present condition, John of the Cross discerned, in the absence of his earthly father, the eternal radiating presence of the Father in heaven.[9] The movement that is inseparable from this unique locus broke the dark obstacle of time.

The romance is another type of popular poetry in Spain. It is quite different in form from the *villancico*.[10] Featuring eight-syllable verses and assonances with little variety, it can be easily improvised, added on to, sung, and danced. Simple in its movement, somewhat monotonous in its form, it runs the danger of falling into sheer repetition, even though the Spanish romance, unlike the French one, does not hinge around a recurring refrain. It is rather a story told in very simple verses. In its secular form it usually tells a love story.

John of the Cross's romance on the Incarnation is a long poem of one hundred and twenty-eight verses, divided in nine sections of unequal lengths. It is also a love story. The poet tells how the Father's love is expressed in the nuptials between the Son and the creatures. Before describing this nuptial union, the poet leads up to it with a tale of the divine Trinitarian life. Thus his nuptial song goes from the eternal birth of the Word in God to his earthly birth, and it successively passes through an account of the life of the three Persons (I), a dialogue between the Father and the Son concerning the Love that unites them (II), the projected nuptials with the creatures (III), the creation of the world as the palace of the bride, with the creation of the bride herself, one entity made of angels and men, who received from the beginning the promise of the Incarnation (IV), the long, at times painful, wait for the coming of the Bridegroom (V), the preannunciation found in the words of the Holy Spirit to old Simeon (VI), the dialogue of the Father and the Son concerning the Incarnation as the work of their love, and the human destiny of the Son who will take on himself the sufferings of the bride and will die for her in order to bring her back to the Father (VII), the mission of the archangel Gabriel and the annunciation to Mary (VIII), and finally the birth of the Incarnate Son, which brings about the song of angels and men and the admiration of Mary (IX). In its central content this poem evidently fills the gap left in the poem on the "Fountain": between the Holy Trinity and the eucharist, there have to be creation and the Incarnation.

This contemplative romance is couched in a biblical framework: it begins with a paraphrase on the first chapter of the Gospel of John, and ends with chapter 1 of the Gospel of Luke (the annunciation), after introducing chapter 2 of Luke (Simeon in the Temple). These episodes are placed in alternating expositions and dialogues. This is not without resemblance to the liturgical or paraliturgical dramas of the Middle Ages. It also echoes the canticles of St. Mary (*cantigas de Santa Maria*) in the collection of Alphonsus X the Sage.[11] Raymon Lull (1235–1316) had adapted the forms of the latter to his own poetic piety. But the *cantigas* often celebrated extraordinary, even fantastic, miracles; they clearly belonged to the hagiographic genre. The art of John of the Cross, however, is sobriety itself. Being neither a personal overflow of feeling as with Lull, nor an appeal to the extraordinary as in the *cantigas*, the romance on the Incarnation opens the mind and heart to the divine purpose by raising the reader to the level of pure faith. The poet lets the mystery speak for itself; he enters the intra-Trinitarian dialogue, the principle of which he outlines in the first section, and afterwards applies, through an imagination that remains utterly simple and unpretentious, to the Incarnation. Is it presumptuous to suggest that these lines were composed to celebrate the mystery of Christmas? John of the Cross, after all, entered Toledo in mid-December. It would have been quite natural for him to see his pilgrimage into jail as a journey to Bethlehem. He sang, soon after his arrival, a poem of light and quiet joy.[12]

This is a song of serenity rather than of exuberance. It introduces an unexpected contrast between the theme, which is of love and of joy, and the tone, which remains subdued and is not exempt of sadness. Admittedly, the author means to speak of God's joy in the Trinitarian love, and of the joy of the creature when it learns of its coming nuptials with the Son. He mentions the "happiness," the "glory" of the Word, the "profound delight" that fills the words of the Father to the Son; yet a note of sadness underlies the entire romance. One may sense it, still discrete, in the Trinitarian apophatism of the poet. There is indeed divine light, the divine being of each Person, united "in an ineffable knot / one beyond words."[13] There are

> Words of great power . . .
> Of such profound delight
> That no one understood them.[14]

If the bride herself, in her angelic condition, knows "the Bridegroom she had"; if "those higher ones possessed / the Bridegroom in gladness, / the lower, in hope, founded / on the faith which he infused in them."[15] Thus the sadness of waiting is written within the human condition. The promised joy is for later. The bride will, some day, share the very life of God. Although she still waits, she bemoans her condition; even her desire wearies her:

So, with prayers,
And sighs and suffering,
With tears and moanings,
They asked night and day
That now he would determine
To grant them his company.[16]

Both angels and men express the sorrow of waiting with accents partly inspired by the Old Testament. And even the response of the Son to the Father is not devoid of nostalgia:

I will go seek my bride
And take upon myself
Her weariness and labors
In which she has suffered so.
And that she may have life
I will die for her,
And, lifting her out of that deep
I will restore her to You.[17]

The last section of the poem speaks of the song of humankind and the angelic melody. Yet it is still on a lingering note of sadness that the romance comes to an end:

But God there in the manger
Cried and moaned;
And these tears were jewels
the bride brought to the wedding.
The Mother gazed in sheer wonder
On such an exchange:
In God, man's weeping,
And in man, gladness,
To the one and to the other
Things usually so strange.[18]

The underlying sadness of the poem is stressed by its monotonous rhymes. On the one hand, the same assonances recur without variations: all the verses end in *a, ía, o, e,* with a few *an, os, en, es,* which do not break the haunting repetition of the sound. On the other hand, some expressions often come back: *decía* (4 times), *se decía* (4 times), *de esta manera decía* (twice). *Unos decían* balances *otros decían*. This standard introduction of the words that are being said relates to scriptural simplicity: "He said to them" is a frequent expression in the Gospels. But it also points to a renunciation of vivacity of expression, and to the priority of words over actions. It suggests the predominance of speech and hearing over imaging and depicting.

The variety in the tenses of the verbs is astonishing when contrasted with the recurrence of the same vowels. The text is generally put in the past; but the present keeps breaking in. Thus, the Trinitarian life is generally described in the past tense, in keeping with the rhyme in *ía* as found in the Spanish imperfect,[19] yet three verbs are also in the present tense:

> For the being that the Three possess,
> Each of them possessed,
> And each of them loves
> the one who bore this being.[20]

And again, further down:

> Thus it is a boundless
> Love that unites them,
> For the Three have one love
> Which was called their essence.

This interjection of a few present tenses in a discourse in the past (more exactly in the imperfect) introduces a note of present participation in an eternal or a past event. This very day, in the misery of his prison, the poet celebrates the expectation and the birth of the Word.

At the same time as his discourse passes from past to present before returning to the past, it goes from the masculine to the feminine, even though one cannot always discover the proper antecedent that would justify the grammatical gender used:

> Three Persons, and One Beloved
> Among all Three there was.

And one Love among them all,
And this made them one Lover.

This last "them" is in the feminine. "Them all" designates the Father, the Son, the Spirit. The "being" is of course divine Being, which may be designated in the feminine as well as the masculine, since, in the scholastic adage, it lies "beyond all genus": In Spanish, as a matter of fact, the Persons are always feminine, but the Being and the usual names of the Persons are masculine. Thus the two grammatical genders connote one identical reality. The two genders, as John of the Cross uses them here, create the effect of some sort of wave. The language swings between the two poles of grammatical gender. (A third gender, neuter, does exist in Spanish but is not in use at this point.) The romance waves back and forth like a lullaby. This is not out of place, since the poet is celebrating a birth, and since through this celebration he is himself being reborn. The language gains from this a note of sweet quiet, which helps to soften the sharp edges of the dogmatic formulae to which it is connected and which serve as framework for the poet's own faith.

Sadness and peace are accompanied by joy. This joy is discrete; it surfaces when the poet sings of what he knows of the divine life and the lofty dwelling place of angels. As soon as he turns to humankind, John of the Cross, who at that moment is experiencing an inhuman human condition, allows an abyss of sadness to show, however soberly. This is all the more striking as he seems to be entirely oblivious to sin, which is the true source of human sadness. Likewise, the Cross is not mentioned in the romance. The death of the Lord is only briefly alluded to. What serves as focus for the poet's sadness is the coming of the Word into the flesh, for this was also a taking over of all the pains of humankind. One wonders if John of the Cross had seen some of those oriental icons of the nativity, where the crib where the child lies has been shaped like a coffin.[21] Whether he has or not, his insight converges on that of the icon painters: Christmas already takes the colors of Good Friday; the birth of the Word already reveals something of his future death. The power of what is said and suggested and the impact of what remains unsaid, yet is implied, provide the romance on the Incarnation with a tone of peaceful resignation that is unique in the poetic works of John of the Cross. One has to wait until 1582–84, with the short poem on the *Pastorcico* (the Little Shepherd), to find a similar tone again.[22]

From a strictly doctrinal standpoint, the ballad on the Incarnation reveals the originality of John of the Cross. Though he had studied Thomism, which he usually followed in his didactic writings, he occasionally adopted theses that were not those of St. Thomas, even on important questions of doctrine. What was the purpose of the creation of this world? It was the Incarnation of the Word of God, since the world was created to provide the Son with a bride. The Incarnation is the very mode of the nuptials of the divine Word.[23] Its purpose is the exchange of love between God and the creature. There is no trace here of the idea, which prevailed in scholasticism before John Duns Scotus (c. 1265–1308), that the sin of Adam and the promise of Redemption were preliminary conditions leading to the Incarnation. Furthermore, the angels, according to John of the Cross, who differs in this from the teaching of Thomas Aquinas,[24] constitute with humankind one body, that would have, so to say, two levels, the upper one being that of angels, the lower one that of humankind. All together, both constitute the body of the bride. The Virgin Mary is not herself the bride, except insofar as she belongs within humanity: in herself she is, in keeping with the archangel's words at the Annunciation, the Mother.

The Trinitarian doctrine of the poem deserves careful attention. For one of the strong points of John of the Cross's spiritual teaching will relate to the relevance of Trinitarian life to mystical experience. Here, the poem follows the Gospel of John: it opens on a paraphrase of the first chapter of this gospel.

> In the beginning the Word
> Was; he lived in God
> And possessed in him
> His infinite happiness.[25]

The word "beginning" connotes the absolute starting point of all creatures. But "beginning" also designates God, and, in God, the Father:

> That same Word was God,
> Who is the Beginning;

> He was in the Beginning,
> And had no beginning.
> He was himself the Beginning
> And therefore had no beginning.
> The Word is called Son;
> He was born of the Beginning.

In this way the poet points out both the total unity and equality of the Father and the Son, and the origin of the latter in the former. Such an origin entails neither separation nor chronological succession or loss of substance on the part of the Father,

> Who has always conceived him
> And was always conceiving him,
> He gives him always his substance
> And He always possessed it.

The glory of the Son lies in the Father, and that of the Father in the Son. They are each in the other like beloved and lover, and their mutual love is equal to themselves:

> And the Love that unites them
> Was one with them,
> Their equal, excellent as
> The One and the Other.

"Love" is, in this context, the name of the Holy Spirit, whom eastern theology since St. Augustine has often identified as the mutual love, the link, between Father and Son. John of the Cross leads us here to the heart of his understanding of the Trinity.

I do not think that John of the Cross identifies the Father, the Son, the Spirit respectively as the Lover, the Beloved, and the Love between them, although the text that was quoted above may conceivably be read in this way. I rather think that it is the divine being or essence that is identified here as being all at the same time lover, beloved, and love.[26] The divine Being is Love exhaustively, in its threefold dimension:

> For the being that the Three possess

Each of them possessed,
And each of them loves
Her who bore this being.
Each one is this being
Which alone unites them,
In an ineffable knot
That could not be said.

Such a love is no other than the divine essence:

Thus was infinite
The love that united them,
For Three have One love,
Which was called their essence.

Yet, John of the Cross knows it well, if the Scriptures, in the First Epistle of John, allow us to identify the divine Essence as Love,[27] the Augustinian tradition, of which he himself had inherited in his scholastic days, also regards the Third Person as being the mutual Love of the Father and the Son. These two traditions join hands in the Trinitarian poetry of John of the Cross, by virtue of the principle,

That the more love is one
The more love it became.

Thus the Third Person is entitled to be called Love by its procession from the first two Persons as loving each other:

In that immense love
Proceeding from the two . . . .[28]

This is made possible precisely by the divine being's identification with loving.

It may be admitted that the poetic form of the romance did not easily lend itself to theological nuances. In the parameters of the style he had chosen, the poet has succeeded in formulating the heart of his Trinitarian theology. In this context the dialogue that the poet imagines between the Father and the Son touching the Incarnation takes the aspect of a contemplative participation in the divine life. Is it truly an anticipation of the Trinitarian experience sung in the *Spiritual Canticle* and the *Living Flame of Love* and explained later in their commentaries? Is it already such an experience, couched in simpler terms? Or would it be only an exercise on the part of the prisoner, who might have tried in this way to while the time and to forget for a few moments his present miserable condition? The existential interpretation makes the better sense. John of the Cross expresses at this point an experience he has or has had. As he found himself raised to a certain level of sharing in the divine life, he understood the Trinitarian context and the purpose of the Incarnation of the Word. By the same token, he understood also the Trinitarian dimension of creation.

However this may be (and the point remains debatable), these pages clearly show that John of the Cross's own religion and theology, at a period which is also that of the composition of most of the stanzas of the *Canticle,* leave no room for an unhealthy cult of suffering. Sin even has no place in the poet's vision of the created world and the Incarnation of the Word. Indeed, Salvation and Redemption are implied, since it is said that the Son will die for humankind. Yet Redemption is not presented as a sacrifice for sin. Nothing in the ballad on the Incarnation suggests that the child, playing the part of a substitute victim, will some day have to be nailed to a cross. The theory of St. Anselm of Canterbury (c. 1033–1109) concerning divine justice and the conditions it has imposed on Christ for its own satisfaction has left no trace in John of the Cross's imagination, even though it did enjoy considerable popularity, and its influence has even perdured into our own days, both in piety and in theology. The Mystical Doctor opens another avenue. His horizon makes his thought germane to that of a few medieval authors, such as Honorius of Autun (c. 1080–1137) and Rupert of Deutz (c. 1170–1230), who themselves paved the way for John Duns Scotus's later position on the Incarnation in a sinless world.[29] And yet, at the very moment when he is composing this romance, John suffers in his flesh and spirit. A dolorous version of the Incarnation and the Redemption might have helped alleviate his pains and brought him some spiritual comfort. However, the prisoner finds his consolation not in remembering the passion of Our Lord, but rather in viewing the Incarnation as the converging point of the created world and the transcendent Trinity. The Incarnation is both the fruit of grace and the flower of the earth. Thus one prayed under the Old Covenant:

> Oh clouds, rain down from your height
> As the earth besought you;
> And open itself the earth,
> Which used to produce thorns,
> And let it produce this blossom
> With which it would flower![30]

The Incarnate Word, Son of the Father, is also the flower of the earth. The land of thorns and sufferings, where the poet lives, is destined to contemplate, in the Son, the Father's own beauty. As John of the Cross will make it clearer in his more famous poems and their commentaries, this will entail a new knowledge of the divine attributes. Accordingly, the Son foresees in the dialogue that precedes the Incarnation, that

> . . . in this way
> Your goodness would be the more seen,
> Your great power will be seen,
> And your justice and your wisdom;
> I will go and tell the world,
> And the news I would give it
> Of your beauty and your sweetness
> And of your sovereignty.[31]

In John's vision the divine attributes are seen better in the light of the Incarnation; they belong integrally to the good news. In the structure of the poem, the preannunciation to Simeon crowns the messianic expectation of the Old Covenant. But the Annunciation to Mary, which has been prepared by a dialogue between the Father and the Son, inaugurates the opening of the mysteries: participation in the Trinitarian life, unveiling of the divine attributes, nuptials of the Son with the creature, union in Love.

John of the Cross is well acquainted with Psalm 137 (136 in the Latin Vulgate). It is the psalm of prisoners and people in exile. In Babylon a Hebrew poet sings of his exile. Like prisoners the world over, he refuses to sing for the victors, he practices nonviolent protest, he opposes his "no" to their request that he sing for them. In Babylon he will not sing one of the hymns of Sion. At what moment of his captivity did the prisoner in Toledo turn to the psalmist, borrow the words of this psalm of contestation, listen to its echo in his heart, and create new accents out of this age-long theme? One cannot know, yet it is not without significance that John's version of the psalm starts with a mention of the rivers of Babylon. The Tigris and the Euphrates of the land and history of Abraham the Patriarch, father of the faithful, have become the rivers of his own exile, the symbols of estrangement:

> By the rivers
> Of babylon
> I sat down weeping,
> There on the ground,
> And remembering you,
> O Sion, which I loved.[32]

Did the rivers of Babylon constitute, at the instant when the poem was born, a counter symbol of the two streams that had been featured in the stanzas on the Fountain? On the one side, two well-known, rich streams enwrap the universe; each is distinct; yet both are joined as originating in the same spring. On the other side, two rivers are there, imposing their presence on the prisoner who does not wish to know them; they trace the borders of his exile, like, in modern days, the barbed wires of concentration camps. John of the Cross does not speak much of them. Yet the two streams remain present throughout his poem. They identify the *alli* (over there) where the poet is weeping, where his tears wet the ground. Their substance brings green to the willows where he hangs his musical instrument, and to the twigs and branches that Babylon extends toward him. The idea that the romance on Babylon has reversed the poem on the Fountain by using the same basic symbol negatively, is attractive. It is only a hypothesis, but one that opens up a way of reading the poem: the verses may be connected, not only with the concrete, existential, context of John of the Cross's exile in his prison, where he is deprived of his liturgical food, of the bread in which, as he has said, he sees the living fount, but also with a literary context. After the hymn of the streams that he wishes to see, and that he knows how and where to see, he writes the hymn of the streams that he does not wish to see, but cannot avoid seeing. After the presence in absence of the known fountain, there is now absence in a hostile presence.

Being thus related to the *Fountain* by its point of departure, the poem on Babylon is close, by its style, to the romance on the Incarnation. It is also a romance, with eight-syllable verses, simple assonances, in which the *a*'s dominate in monotonous sequence, supported by two *ia*'s, and briefly distracted by a few *o, or, os, e, es, i*'s. At first sight three parts seem to stand out. For if the poem begins and ends in parallel with Psalm 137, the poet has inserted into it a central part (verses 15 to 28) that is new.

If one looks at the text more closely, however, five sections emerge. They are made of 14, 14, 12, 12, and 10 verses respectively. Their themes may be summarized as: (1) the contrast between Babylon and Sion, the present and the past, or rather yesterday and the day before, since this passage is put in the past, like all the poem, except in the last section; (2) a present reflection on the past: the poet, placing himself in his mind after his hoped-for liberation, reflects, as though after the fact, on the experience of exile; (3) a dialogue between the victors and the exile: they invite him to sing a song of Sion, and he refuses; (4) a curse on himself if ever he should forget Sion; (5) a curse on Babylon, which is soon changed into a blessing.

The transitions from one section to the next are noteworthy. The contrast between Babylon, the foreign land, the land of tears, and Sion, which the poet remembers and loves, is also a contrast between toil and play, between the greenness of nature and silence. These contrasts bring the poet to seek his shelter in hope only. Yet this hope flourishes, precisely, over there, in the land of exile.

"There"—the beginning of the section—the poet has been wounded by love. He describes his experience of the wound, which is both death and fire, love having caused the wound, the death, and the fire. He came too near to the fire, like the bird who died in the flames. Thus he experienced a death that coincided with life. This was already, before the time, a mystical death:

> I was dying in myself,
> Breathing in you alone;
> I died within myself for you
> And for you I revived,
> Because the memory of you
> Gave life and took it away.

"You," in this passage, is Sion, the motherland far from the exile. A delicate dialectic draws its threads between the poet, Sion, which he has been forced to leave, and love, present as a burning and killing fire, yet which also gives life and resurrects the one who throws himself into it. The bird in question is undoubtedly the phoenix, a traditional symbol for the resurrection, since legend has it that the phoenix comes alive out of the flames that have killed him. The theme of death and of life will soon be incorporated in the major works of John of the Cross. It will form the central thread in the *Ascent of Mount Carmel*. It will later be placed at the heart of the *Sayings of Light and of Love*. Without yet the vocabulary of *todo-nada* (all-nil),[33] this is already the fully developed doctrine of the Mystical Doctor.

Thus John of the Cross tells us, with the imagery of Psalm 137, that in dying he has found life. This life he has drawn from love, but also from memory. For, "over there," love carried him to Sion, a Sion that existed for him only in the oneness of hope and memory. In hope the poet anticipates the time of his recovered freedom, when he will be able to look back at the experience of prison and discover its hidden richness.

Yet John of the Cross is not analyzing a dream. His imprisonment is all too real. The memory of Sion, which ends the second section of the poem, brings about, by contrast, an anticipation of the future memory in which he will some day remember the miseries of his present condition. Hence the third section:

> The strangers among whom
> I was captive rejoiced;
> They asked me to sing
> What I sang in Sion:
> "Sing us a song from Sion,
> Let us hear how it sounded."

Having closed the parenthesis he had opened on the experience and the depth of the death and the life that will have been his "over there," John of the Cross now returns to the Psalm and its symbolization of the days of his captivity. The jailers laugh at him, invite him with irony to sing for them. John of the Cross may have thought, while composing these verses, of bits of hymns that may at times have reached him from the friary's choir. If he sang with his guardians, would he thereby renounce the reform of Carmel? The temptation may have been powerful. But would it not be a treason, an infidelity? John of the Cross has his own land, his own mountain. The name of this, for the reformer who intends to be a true son of the prophet Elijah, will soon be "Mount Carmel." But here, in an obscure corner of the unreformed Carmel of Toledo, it cannot yet have its future name; it still bears the name of its past: Sion. The poet's refusal to sing reaches further than a mere negative answer to the invitation that has been extended to him. He foresees, were he to consent, not death, which he knows to be life, but oblivion, the forgetting of Sion:

> I would be forgetting her
> If I rejoiced in a foreign land.

Oblivion is, beyond death and life, nothingness.

The oblivion that has closed up this third section tragically, by opening up the perspective of nothingness, makes the next section possible. The poet picks up the theme with a curse on himself if, which is impossible, he should happen to agree to his jailers' demand: may he forget himself, who has forgotten Sion! And may the instrument of oblivion be no other than the green boughs of Babylon, since he had loved so much the green boughs of Sion:

> Sion, by the green branches
> Babylon holds out to me,
> Let my right hand forget me
> (These are what I most loved in you)
> If I do not remember you
> In what gave me the greatest joy,
> And if I held a feast-day
> And if I feasted without you!

The false feast of Babylon, the lying celebration shared with the daughter of Babylon, brings about a dramatic reversal in the last section of the poem. The poet now evokes with pity the one who offered herself to him as a companion for a falsely good time and for sin:

> O daughter of Babylon,
> Unhappy and unfortunate!

Unlike Psalm 137, which John of the Cross still follows closely, the malediction suddenly changes into benediction. The hatred of the Hebrew psalmist is shattered by the Christian poet in a perspective of reconciliation. For it is really Christ who is declared blessed at this point. John of the Cross leaves the past tense; he turns to the future. That is to say, he speaks from his own present time in its horrid actuality.

> Blessed be He
> In whom I have trusted,
> For He will bring you the punishment
> Which I obtained from you,
> And He will unite his children
> And me, for I wept in you,
> To the rock which was Christ,
> For whom I did leave you.

This very full conclusion includes in the blessing pronounced upon Christ by the poet all those who make him suffer, the daughter of Babylon, and John himself. All will be joined to the true rock, Christ, by the action of the one who will unite them to himself. The last verse is particularly apt as a pointer to the state of mind of John of the Cross, the instrument of the Carmelite reform: it was in order to follow Christ that he abandoned the mitigated rule of the Carmel. Thus he himself testifies that his present troubles and trials, in spite of what his jailers expect from them, are confirming his calling and his determination. This poem is therefore a sort of synthesis. Steeped in Scripture John of the Cross remembers it in the new context of his present experience, with its material framework (the prison) and its interior structure (divine grace). This horizon brings together the remembrance of the past and the hoped-for future, the personal dimension as well as the community.

No other conclusion than that of the ballad on Babylon would be appropriate at this moment. The minor poems composed during the poet's captivity in Toledo were not written as introductions to the others or as part of an overall writing project. In a way they remain near to the previous poems, which like them were never commented upon by the author. Yet they may also be compared with the stanzas that the poet will transform *a lo divino* later, during his sojourn in Andalusia. Moreover, the circumstances of their composition create a unique link between these poems and the greatest of all, written also in jail, the thirty-one first stanzas of the *Spiritual Canticle*.

CHAPTER 3

THE FIRST *CANTICLE*

Interpreting John of the Cross's major poetical work, his *Spiritual Canticle,* requires making certain choices, presented to the reader by the critical study of the text. Should one opt between version (A) and version (B) of the poem? As is well known, version (A) is composed of three successive parts. The first, which includes the first thirty-one stanzas, was written in Toledo during the poet's captivity, that is, in the first six months of 1578. The second, which comprises stanzas 32 to 34, is an addition composed in Baeza or Granada, sometime between 1579 and 1582. The last part, which goes from 35 to 39, was added still later, on a few days' visit to the Carmelites of Beas de Segura, before the poet, who was then prior in Granada, had finished his commentary. This he did in 1584. It will surprise no one that a poet should rework a piece a few years after a first version. New experiences bring to mind new images. Besides, the poet is also, in this case, a theologian. His commentary on the *Spiritual Canticle* is in process, along with his book on the *Ascent of Mount Carmel:* both were started, somewhat unsystematically, when the author lived at the Calvario, in 1578–79, and gave occasional explanations of his poems to the sisters of Beas. They were finished in Granada around the same time. One cannot exclude the possibility that redacting the commentaries may have suggested some additions to the poem.[1]

I will return to the problem of the authenticity of version (B) in chapter 12. For the time being, I would posit a principle that has apparently been overlooked by the studies of John of the Cross with which I am acquainted. This is simply that it would be an error in methodology to consider version (A) as constituting the first full text of the *Spiritual Canticle.* The first text has to be the one that John of the Cross carried in his pocket and especially in his memory when he escaped from prison in August 1578. Nothing suggests that, at the time, the author believed his poem to be incomplete.[2] Not only did he wait at least one year, perhaps as many as three years, to add to it three stanzas, then, some time later, five others, but also stanza 31 provides a perfect ending to what John had composed in Toledo. The *Canticle* must have been in the same shape as the other poems of captivity: they were finished works. Being now free, their author intended to devote himself to other tasks, the nature of which would come to him through holy obedience.

I therefore start from the principle that three successive forms of the *Spiritual Canticle* are known to us. The poem of Toledo ends at verse 31; that of Baeza-Granada, so-called version (A), at stanza 39; and finally, version (B), which saw the light in Granada, or possibly during a visit to Segovia, in 1586, has forty stanzas, st. 11 being new, and many of the subsequent ones following a different order than formerly. Versions (A) and (B) were commented upon. To be exact, one could speak of a version (A-1), of thirty-one stanzas, and of a version (A-2), of thirty-nine. The first is not tied to a commentary. In the first place, John of the Cross did not start his systematic theological and mystical interpretation of his own poetry until several years after the Toledo experience. In the second he did not form the project, during his enforced stay in Toledo, of a commentary. This simple fact should have a freeing effect on our reading of John's text. For the stanzas of the first *Canticle* may then be looked at and listened to in a purely poetic perspective, without interference from the analyses that John of the Cross made of them later. These analyses pertained only to the second form of the poem (A-2). Accordingly, I intend to treat the two versions (A-2) and (B) as being other poems than the first *Canticle.* Between the three forms of the text there are obvious relationships, but no identity.[3]

The framework of the poem is borrowed jointly from the *Song of Songs* and from the Italian type of Renaissance poetry introduced into Spain and popularized by Garcilaso and Boscán. The form is that of a dialogue between bridegroom and bride, shepherd and shepherdess, the latter searching for the former, who has fled and is hiding, and appears only twice, in the middle and toward the end of the poem. A rustic, even idyllic, tone, allusions to the flock, the appeal to nature for help in searching after the spouse, delimit the general parameters of the action and place the poem in a literary genre that had been known since Roman antiquity, that of pastoral poetry. Over against the poems on the fountain and on Babylon, which directly reflect some aspects of John of the Cross's captivity, the *Canticle* immediately takes the reader to a situation that lies beyond the present straitened circumstances of the author. These are briefly indicated in the second verse: you "left me moaning. . . . " Everything else contributes to what may be called a poetry of escape, of a forward flight following after the Beloved. Thus the tone and the orientation are quite different from the other captivity poems. In the heart of the prisoner, the *Canticle* is related to a wish to escape, not to a need to complain. Naturally starting from the present situation, it leads the reader, with the author, toward something else.

Unlike the romance on the Incarnation, the *Canticle* does not stress the note of sadness. It starts from this sadness, but only to leave it behind and go forward to a point that lies nearer to an ineffable joy than to the serenity and peace of the romance. Moreover, the focus is no longer located in a divine act in the process of the incarnation, which infinitely transcends the human capacity to see; rather is it in interior movements of the poet's own being. The Beloved is no longer painted with the colors, as it were, objective, of the Word who took flesh from the Virgin, but with more subjective features as imagined by a shepherdess in love with a shepherd.

The poem is easily divided, in light of the visible progression of its fundamental theme:

—searching for the Beloved in creatures	st. 1-4
—response from the choir of creatures	st. 5
—desire for the Beloved in himself	st. 6–12
—response from the Beloved	st. 12
—song of encounter:	
—the Beloved is found in creatures	st. 13–16
—the Beloved is found in himself	st. 17–26
—the choir of creatures	st. 27
—response from the Beloved	st. 28–30
—conclusion by the bride	st. 31

The several sections of the poem are of unequal length, yet the whole is highly structured. As could be expected from the fact that the poet was without the most elementary writing material, this structure is not to be sought in literary devices. These would have required a lengthy task of correcting and rewriting the text several times. It would not have been possible without a proper supply of pens and paper. The structure in fact entirely pertains to the mutual relationships of the different sections. Both the search for the Beloved among creatures and desire for the Beloved himself announce a twofold encounter with him, among the creatures and in himself. The creatures' response to the bride's request for help unites these two sections by inviting the bride to seek further. The first response of the bridegroom, very short, implies a promise, which itself acts as a hyphen between the search-desire and the twofold encounter. His second response speaks again of the twofold encounter, but in a reversed order: starting from the lovers' loving touch, it evokes the basic meaning of creatureliness. These three answers follow one another in a progressive wave that runs parallel to the progress of the bride's search. The resulting structure may be summed up in the following schema:

Search (I)	st. 1–4
Preliminary answer (1)	st. 5
Search-desire (II)	st. 6–11
First full answer (2)	st. 12
Encounter (I), responding to search (I)	st. 13–16
Encounter (II), responding to search-desire (II)	st. 17–27
Second full answer (3)	st. 28–30
Conclusion	st. 31

It is not necessary at this point to look in detail at the language of the *Canticle*.[4] As has been pointed out by others, one finds in it a predominance of substantives, few verbs, a moderate recourse to adjectives, more plurals than singulars, a relatively high number of present participles, which usually act as qualifiers, and a postnominal rather than prenominal position for most of the adjectives (in the proportion of three to one). Were such choices spontaneous or carefully thought out? Is John of the

Cross an immediate artist, whose verses overflow from his heart, or a language crafter, who goes over the same lines time and time again until he meets the aesthetic standards that he has implicitly set for himself? One could presumably argue on behalf of both opinions; yet the circumstances of his imprisonment and the lack of writing material he then suffered would seem to point to the spontaneity of his art. This would also be suggested by comparisons of his captivity poems with the only drawing of the Crucified that has survived from his pen or brush, and with the sketch of the *Ascent of Mount Carmel,* of which we have what seems to be a faithful copy: these give the impression of being made at one swoop, with no hesitancy or false starts. Yet what may be true of drawing need not necessarily apply to speech.

Yet, whether simply chosen or carefully crafted, the linguistic options made by the poet do correspond with basic orientations of his speech, and therefore of his thought, and accordingly of some primary tendencies in his relationships to the world,[5] to self, and to God. Dámaso Alonso characterizes the result as a fresh style, the freshness of which derives from the condensation and the swiftness of thought as it goes through a string of unadorned substantives falling off like a cascade. Besides, whereas prenominal adjectives limit beforehand the meaning of the noun they affect, their postnominal position extends the meaning of the noun in connotations that emerge after it as its colored echoes. It is indeed noteworthy that, if the first ten stanzas, those of search and desire, do not contain one single adjective, these spring up in force in stanzas 13 to 15, when the bride begins singing in the joy of her first encounter with the Beloved. These last adjectives express superabundant life, a sort of surplus of life.

A certain aesthetic is undoubtedly at work in what John of the Cross composed in captivity. Adoption of the stanza called a *lira,* presumably inspired by the fifth canto, *Flor de Gnido,* of Garcilaso, ascribed strict formal boundaries within which the author had to function. The stanzas in question have five verses and two rhymes: the first one connects the first verse and the third; the second one is common to the remaining three verses. Thus the entire poem follows a double rhythm, related on the one hand to syllabic length—*abaab*—on the other to rhyme—*ababb.* The periodic recurrence of the syllabic rhythm within that of the rhymes conveys to the whole poem the appearance of light dancing. Far from being an orgiastic dance modeled on the bacchanals of Dionysian mysticism, this dance is strictly controlled. Enthusiasm is held in check by the evanescence of the rhymes. These are chiefly feminine, ending in a vowel: they open the soul at the sound of its words, yet with a certain monotony, since the Spanish language, which has few words ending in *u*, forces the poet constantly to fall back on the three basic vowels, *a, e, o*. As to the masculine rhymes, closed on a consonant, they end with *s* (mostly plural nouns, with some verbs in the second person singular), interspersed with a few *n*'s (verbs in the third person plural). In this way the simplicity of rhymes puts the brakes on the rich flow of words, as the double rhythm of the verses introduces a dancing motion into the music of the discourse.

In order to approach greater completeness, one would have to refer to John of the Cross's use of alliteration. Some verses of the *Canticle* are quite striking from this point of view. One should note, for instance:

—a scale of *a*'s, in *sali tras ti clamando, y eras ido* (v. 5),
—a clatter of *d*'s and *l*'s, in *decidle que adolesco, peno y muero* (v. 10),
     or in, *de lo que del Amado en ti concibes* (v. 45),
—the whistling of *s*'s, in *el silbo de los aires amorosos* (v. 70).

These alliterations may be related, respectively, to the bride's exit for her search after the Beloved, which is at the same time an ascent outside of herself; to the pangs of sorrow caused by the Beloved's absence; to the wounds received from the Beloved's arrows in the course of the quest; to the breath of the refreshing breeze that caressed their first encounter. . . . Above all, one should cite the famous verse 30: *un no sé qué que quedan balbuciendo* "an I-know-not-what which they keep stammering": three *que* in quick succession mime the babble of the creatures who vainly attempt to describe the One who remains ineffable in his transcendence. Dámaso Alonso speaks also of accents that accelerate or slow down the rapid march of prepositions, and of inversions, where he perceives "a subtly expressive element."[6] These are signs of an exquisite poetic sensibility and of an unusual mastery of the language. It would be fruitless to launch a debate on the origins of these capabilities in John of the Cross. Is this inborn talent? or the experience of popular poetry? or the influence of his parents, of whom we know very little in fact? or literary studies in general? or the direct impact of Garcilaso and Boscán? or the sublimation by grace of what John of the Cross already possessed from the gifts of nature and the acquisitions of culture? There is presumably a little of all that, but a full answer to such questions could only be formulated in the wake of a general theory of poetic creation. This is not the place to attempt it. At any rate John's prologue to his first commentary on the *Canticle* suggests the last perspective of grace-full transformation:

> Forasmuch as these stanzas . . . appear to be written with a certain degree of fervor of the love of God, whose wisdom and love are so vast that, as is said in the Book of Wisdom, they reach from one end to another, and the soul which is informed and moved by him has to some extent this same abundance and impetus in its words, I do not now think of expounding all the breadth and plenteousness embodied in the fertile spirit of love, for it would be ignorance to think that sayings of love understood mystically, such as those of the present stanzas, can be fairly explained by words of any kind.[7]

Clearly, John of the Cross was aware of a certain mystery in his own poetry, and he knew that this mystery was connected with mystical experience. In other words the sum total of literary effects in his work cannot account for his writing. It is the very nature of his writing that takes to itself certain virtualities of the language and actualizes them.

Several stanzas of the *Spiritual Canticle* open a window toward the process of assumption and of poetic transformation of previous experience that is at work in the poem. Take stanza 15 for instance. At face value it looks somewhat odd, and the commentary does not help very much as it shows some awkwardness and artificiality itself:

Our Bed is in flower,

Bound round with linking dens of lions,
Hung with purple,
Built up in peace,
And crowned with a thousand shields of gold.

In the structure of the poem we are now at the first level of the song of encounter. The bridegroom has just announced his coming; the bride imagines him, who is still absent, with the features of what is then missing in John of the Cross's life: mountains, valleys, islands, brooks, breezes, the quiet of night just before dawn, music, sweet solitude, banquet. Stanzas 15 and 16 operate a transition; they anticipate on the second level of the encounter, first by describing the lovers' bed, then by evoking, in a reference to the parables of the wedding feast, young girls running to welcome the bridegroom. The description of the nuptial bed would seem bizarre had one never seen, in a museum or a historic palace, a huge bed of the late Middle Ages, with four posts, colorful draperies, and a baldachino adorned with the coat of arms of the lord of the house: hence "hung with purple, . . . a thousand shields of gold. . . . "

The "dens of lions," which are unexpected in a nuptial bed, become clear if one pays attention to the coat of arms of John of the Cross's paternal ancestry.[8] The de Yepes shield features, on a central escutcheon, a lion rampant, crowned, gold on azure field. Around the central escutcheon, five smaller ones, gold, each with a transversal bar of gules, are pinned on a band of vert tincture. The dens of lions are easily recognized: they are coats of arms such as seen by a child. The child's imagination placed the lions in their dark azure, nearly sable, dens. Admittedly, we do not know whether Gonzalo de Yepes, John's father, ever used or exhibited the family coat of arms, or perhaps Catalina Alvarez, John's mother, for whom Gonzalo had exchanged the comforts of his family for her own poverty and toil, ever depicted the shield to her children so that they would be acquainted with their ancestral nobility. It is also quite possible, perhaps likely, that at some time during the disastrous journey Catalina undertook with her children to visit her brothers-in-law after Gonzalo's untimely death, the eight-year-old child who was then the future John of the Cross saw such a bed with such a coat of arms. This could have been at the residence of the archdeacon who did not receive them well in Torrejos and who sent them away empty handed, or at the home of the doctor at Galvez, who received them kindly and kept the older brother, Francisco, in his house. Possibly too, Francisco, when he returned home to Medina del Campo more than a year later,[9] may have described such a bed to his younger brother.

Furthermore, Toledo, where the poet is kept in captivity, is the city where both his parents were born. His enforced sojourn in the house of the calced Carmelites, his actual miseries, bring back to his memory the journey of so long ago and his scarcely remembered father. That the Yepes coat of arms, previously transformed by the child's imagination, should find its place in the poem John is now composing, should cause no surprise. Memory brings to the poet usable material, already reinterpreted by dreams of former years, and which his present imagination transforms once more. The four-posted bed becomes that of the bride and bridegroom, themselves borrowed from the biblical *Song of Songs*.

A symbol of love, the bed is also, in the mystical and literary tradition of the Middle Ages, identified with the "litter of Solomon" (*Song of Songs*, 3:7). Solomon is Christ, the bridegroom; the bed is the place of his nuptials with the believing soul; the steps leading up to it are the rungs of the mystical ladder, as one may see, among other writings, in St. Bonaventure's *Pilgrimage of the Soul into God.*[10] Such a bed is indeed, as in John of the Cross's *Canticle,* "built up in peace." The soul of the poet assumes to itself the past and its miseries, the present and its sufferings, all this being then fired in the encounter of the mystical espousals. The reality of the past warrants that of the present in the continuity of memory by which the poet transcends both the past and the present while he meshes them together in a new experience and a new meaning. Hope is thereby freed in view of the future.

The poem is decked with reminiscences. Recent memories provide the backdrop: the reading of Garcilaso, at least in the updating *a lo divino* that John of the Cross used when staying next to the Convent of the Incarnation in Avila, shortly before the Carmelites of the Observance arrested him. There is also, and above all, the constant, meditative reading of the *Song of Songs*, whose lyrics John has perfectly absorbed and assimilated.[11]

There are also—this was to be expected—remembrances from the countryside of Old Castile, with its hills and banks, its flowers, its animals (the stag of stanza 1, the wild beasts of stanza 3), its astonishing piles of stones and rocks, which look indeed like "forts and frontiers," its woods and groves, its flower-strewn green meadows, its mountains, valleys, creeks, the whistling of the wind on spring mornings, its calm nights, its lanes, its cool dawns, its vineyards (numerous in the Sierra de Gredos, south of Avila), its birds, its mists. Other allusions, the fruit of imagination, may also bear the marks of former readings: thus the "strange islands" of stanza 13, the lions of stanza 29. The nature that is evoked and invoked in the *Canticle* is indeed that which John of the Cross has known since his childhood, made more ethereal by the very distance that physically and morally keeps John away from it.

This nature is not described in detail. It seems quietly to glide under the light touches of the names of its varied components. This plays an essential role in the structure of the *Canticle*. In stanzas 3 and 4, the bride, who is of course the poet, ascends the scale of creatures and, at the level of stanza 5, receives their response, which invites her to go on further. The bride's complaint of longing follows: nature is featured only at the end of it, in the guise of a "spring like crystal," the waters of which give shape, in their eddies, to "eyes" that look at you. Here too the bride has continued her ascent, no longer in nature, but, according to a pattern that was well known in spiritual writings of the Middle Ages, within herself, in her own life, toward the One in whose direction nature has sent her without being able to tell her more about him.[12] Through a series of wounds, through death (st. 7), through life that is not life (st. 8), and through the special wound received from the One she seeks, the bride experiences a change in her horizon. Even when, at stanza 3, she formulated negatively her relationship to nature, "I will not gather flowers . . . ," she nonetheless felt the creatures to be a source of joy. Here, in stanzas 7 and 8, what she has hitherto experienced as joy has become sorrow, the sorrow of absence. Her life is hurt even by what is best and dearest in it, the thought of her Beloved. But if this so, it is because the Beloved himself causes her wound. The One she pursues like a stag (st. 1) has made himself hunter to wound her and to steal her heart (st. 9). From this breakdown and rebuilding of the poet's universe the image of the "spring like crystal" derives. Called for by the "eyes," the light of which is the Beloved, and which do not wish to see anyone else (st. 10), the spring, this eye of the soul,[13] gathers up at this point all the creatures that have been named so far. In her desire the bride wishes and, wishing, imagines that the source reflects, not her own eyes leaning over it, as an ordinary source would of course do, but rather "the eyes I have desired," those of the bridegroom, a reflection of which the bride already possesses "deep within" her heart. Face to face with a nature that is not merely creaturely, with so deeply transformed creatures that, instead of inviting the eyes that seek the bridegroom to look further beyond themselves, they reflect his very eyes, the bride is caught in a sort of ecstasy; she begins to soar, and, fearful in front of the extraordinary novelty of this vision of the desired eyes, she begs the Beloved to withdraw them from her.

Creatures thus belong to two levels, which may be called nature-passage and nature-reflection. Yet there is a third level. At this moment, for the first time, the bridegroom speaks. He also evokes nature. In her beginning soaring, the bride has become "dove." This biblical image is precisely, in the *Song of Songs*,[14] associated with the eyes of the bride. The Beloved is the stag—but a wounded stag, as though he were taking on himself the bride's wounds—who appears at the summit and feels refreshed by the flight of the dove. In this way the bride is brought, in stanzas 13 and 14, to identify the Beloved and the creatures. Depicting the Beloved under the features of what is missing in John of the Cross's life in his jail, these stanzas do not affirm an identity, yet they make an identification. Identity would be a primordial datum, a starting point; identification is a result: it derives from the brief encounter between the stag and the dove. The creatures are now transformed indeed. They no longer try to speak of the Beloved, muttering an I-know-not-what. They participate in the creative process. As to the Beloved, he is no longer only the stag, but he has also become mountains, valleys, islands, creeks, the whistling of breezes, music, solitude, feast. Nature-icon follows nature-passage and nature-reflection.

This metamorphosis of the universe is like a game played by the bridegroom, who puts on the creatures like a wedding garment. The encounter between the bridegroom and the bride has truly become nuptial.

Stanzas 17 to 26 constitute the
bride's nuptial song, celebrating the place of encounter, the Beloved's
"inner wine cellar." The wine, which symbolizes mystical nourish-
ment in Greek paganism,[15] keeps this symbolism in Eucharistic
sacramental practice. The entire passage abounds in biblical allu-
sions. Already the maidens of stanza 16 are the virgins who hasten
to the wedding feast (Luke 25:1–13), to the "touch of a spark" that
will light their lamps, and to the "spiced wine" of Cana. Both the
wine and the spark are "flowing from the balsam of God"; and,
contrary to the parable, there is no hint that the light may go out.
Then, through an unexpected reversal, in stanza 18 the bridegroom
gives his breast to the bride. How bold the poet for whom all is
pure! He stammers; he vainly attempts to express directly the "sweet
and living knowledge." And the bride responds through her unre-
served self-gift. Stanza 19 echoes back the theme of love. Once more
the bride turns to the creatures. For she realizes that she cannot
always remain in the inner wine cellar. When she leaves it she will
seem to be lost, yet in reality she will have been found (st. 20).
With the bridegroom she will take the creatures and make a garland
with them, which she will tie together with one of her hairs (st.
21). She then imagines the Beloved in admiration before this hair
of hers as it falls on her neck, as though wounded by one of her
eyes (st. 22). She sees him filled with admiration for her; yet, knowing
full well that the mark of his eyes is in her only because he put it
there, she also knows that not herself, but he, the bridegroom,
attracts their mutual looks (st. 23). The Beloved's own look has left
grace and beauty in her (st. 24). Let him return to the hunt; this
would not stop their vineyards from having bloomed or the roses
from being numerous enough for a nosegay.[16] No one anymore need
appear on top of the mountain, in contrast with the fleeting appar-
ition of stanza 12 (st. 25). The breeze that will refresh the bridegroom
will no longer be the weak flight of the dove or the north wind,
harbinger of the cold weather: it will be the hot south wind blowing
through the bride's garden, spreading the scents around. There,
among the flowers, it will feed the Beloved (st. 26).

To be exact the next stanza is not part of the Beloved's response.
It depicts what is now taking place. This is the choir of creatures
speaking, as in stanza 5.[17] The bride and bridegroom are no longer
in the wine cellar, but in the desired garden. No longer is the

bridegroom entangled in a single hair of the bride; it is now the bride who reclines in the gentle arms of her Beloved (st. 27). A higher degree of their encounter opens up.

The bridegroom speaks again, not from a distance and in a fleeting way as in stanza 12, but from very near. He softly murmurs to the sleeping bride. Their union under the apple tree rectifies and restores the order long ago broken when the bride's mother was raped: this bold, violent image, which sees the meeting of Eve with the serpent as a rape (Genesis, 3), would no doubt be astonishing were it not already in the *Song of Songs*, 8:5 (st. 28).[18] The bridegroom then turns to the creatures (st. 29) in a stanza that is almost entirely made of nouns falling down like a cascade, without any verbs and with only three adjectives: this is a long address in the vocative case. The verb ("I conjure you") surfaces only at the second verse of the next stanza. As formerly at the sea of Galilee, the word of the Beloved wants the creatures to end their anger. But the Beloved speaks to them softly; it is like a music of lyres or the songs of sirens: let them not even touch the garden wall, for the bride should enjoy her mystical slumber in peace (st. 30).

Analysis of stanza 31 is of special importance if, as I think, John of the Cross escaped from jail in August 1578 with his great poem finished and no project of further additions.

At the level of biblical allusions and sources, this stanza evidently paraphrases *Song of Songs*, 8:4. This is not surprising since such paraphrases abound in the *Canticle*. The "nymphs of Judea" of John of the Cross are easily recognizable as the "daughters of Jerusalem" of the Bible. But in the *Song* the injunction not to wake up the bride comes from the bridegroom. John of the Cross has reversed the perspective: the bride is now speaking. Yet how can she speak? The Beloved has just told the creatures not to awaken her. She must be asleep. But to speak in a sleep means to dream. And if one may have found it odd that the "daughters" of the biblical song should become nymphs here, this is only because this point has not been noticed. In a Christian horizon, nymphs exist only in dreams. The word of the bridegroom has entered into the bride's slumber without awakening her, and just enough to suggest to her, in her innocent subconscious, to beg the creatures for silence. As in the two preceding stanzas, the creatures are approached in their full creaturely dimensions. After being nature-passage, then nature-reflection, finally nature-icon, they have to become nature-silence. Time is no more to boisterousness, but to recollection; no more to clear affirmative knowledge, either distant, as before the reflection, or near and even immediate, as before the icon, but to negative knowledge, when nothing may be said.

In the dream of her mystical sleep, the bride sees herself in Judea, the country of her Beloved. The maidens who used to hasten to the wedding feast have been metamorphosed into nymphs, which is to say that they float in the unreal, in a universe of dreams. For, once in the arms of the bridegroom, nothing else is more real than the bridegroom himself. The bride asks the nymphs to stop running, to wait in the neighborhood, where amber gives out its perfume among flowers and rose-bushes, that is, in the gardens. Though she is not yet there, she believes herself in the gazebo, since it is in the desired garden that she has fallen asleep in the Beloved's arms. She conjures the nymphs not to knock at the threshold of the house. This, obviously, is heaven. The bride is not there, but has the impression of being in it, for her sleep brings her close to it.

In this way stanza 31 brings the *Canticle* of Toledo to a perfect conclusion. The bride is close to the last threshold, without having yet passed it, though she believes she has. Once stanza 31 is read in this fashion, it is clear that the *Canticle* is finished. Why the poet added nine more stanzas later is of course a question that must be faced. But it would not be in its right place at this point.

What relationship is there between the poet's escape and the conclusion of the poem? One should presumably not seek intrinsic connections between the dream of stanza 31 and the decision to escape. Nor do we know at what moment in his captivity John of the Cross finished composing the *Spiritual Canticle*. Yet one may think that he had finished the poem on the fountain, the romance on the Incarnation, and the romance on Babylon, before putting the last touches to the *Canticle*, perhaps even before starting it. As most readers will willingly admit,[19] the *Canticle* is not in the first place a matter of John of the Cross's creative imagination, but of the inner experience of union with God that he underwent in his Toledan jail. The mystical doctor, once he had reached stanza 31, could only wait for death where he was or, if he could, escape. He felt near to heaven. Death would have been sweet to him. But he had to do all he could to live, for above all he must follow the will of the Beloved, of the One who alone is fully living, who is the sole Lord of life and of death. And the task of the Carmelite reform had scarcely begun. John of the Cross fled into the night.

CHAPTER 4

THE NIGHT

The poetic flowering that coincided with John of the Cross's imprisonment in Toledo did not dry out with his escape. One cannot know for certain how he employed his time during the month and a half he spent in hiding at the home of don Pedro Gonzalez de Mendoza, a canon of the cathedral of Toledo who was a friend and supporter of the Carmelite sisters. Yet in all likelihood the poem of the *Dark Night*, written before the end of 1578, was composed before his departure for Andalusia, which was decided by the chapter of the discalced in Almodovar in October 1578.[1] As was apparent in the first *Canticle*, the poet willingly borrowed images from the simplest elements of his human experience in contact with nature, with his family, with people in general. He formulated his ineffable experience of God with the help of such images. Thus the poem of the *Dark Night* is a tale of his flight, in a warm August night, when he escaped through a window, lowered himself down to the wall of the city, above the river Tagus, with an improvised cord, climbed over the wall of a neighboring convent, and finally walked on top of the city wall till he was able to jump down into a dark alley.

> One dark night . . .
> I went out unseen . . .
> In darkness and secure,
> by the secret ladder, disguised . . .

Another of the so-called minor poems could well also refer to this experience of captivity. In the Sanlúcar manuscript,[2] this bears the awkward title of "stanzas concerning an ecstasy of high contemplation." More simply, one may call it, from its first words, the poem *Entréme*. There is no agreement on the probable date of this work. It has been dated from the time of the chaplaincy at the convent of the Incarnation, between 1572 and 1577, before John of the Cross was kidnapped.[3] It has been included among the writings made in Granada, between 1582 and 1584.[4] A third hypothesis may be proposed. For these stanzas start with what does sound like a scarcely veiled allusion to the author's imprisonment, with the difference that if the *Dark Night* is the poem of the prisoner's escape, *Entréme* would be the poem of his incarceration:

> I entered where I knew not . . .

> I knew not where I entered,
> yet when there I saw myself,
> without knowing where I was,
> great things I understood . . .

The theme is germane to that of the *Dark Night:* it speaks of "perfect knowledge," which is "so secret a thing," and which transcends all knowledge. It is the poem of an unknowing that is truly knowing, of a noncomprehension that is truly comprehension. It also speaks the language of the night, with its " . . . dark cloud / which lit up the night." One of its verses seems to echo the famous line of the *Spiritual Canticle,* "*un no se qué que quedan balbuciendo*" (an I-know-not-what which they keep stammering):

> It was so secret a thing
> that I remained stammering,
> transcending all knowledge.

This last verse recurs at the end of each stanza, as in the envoy. The last but one, which is equally borrowed from the envoy, is slightly modified, yet keeps the hesitant assonance that is germane to the *no se qué* of the *Canticle: que me quedé . . .* (twice), *que se queda . . .* , *queda siempre . . .* , *hace quedar. . . .* [5] Even the third stanza, as it changed the penultimate verse (*de un entender no entendiendo*), preserved the stammering effect by moving it: *que se quedo* appears in the third verse instead. Stanzas 6 and 7, which have also replaced the penultimate verse with phrases that are close to those of the third stanza, have kept the stammering by starting the verse with *que* and *quien:* there are two *que* in stanza 5, two *que,* one *quien,* one *aqueste,* and one *con* in stanza 6. The entire poem seems to be stammering on this *que*-sound as though on the ineffable unknowing that transcends all knowing. Moreover, the frequent recurrence of the verb *quedar* (to remain) gives the whole performance an aura of quiet: the "peace" of the second stanza has been contagious and marked the whole poem. This is no longer the form of the *Canticle,* when the bride went searching for her Beloved. It may be that the poet now knows, after undergoing the terrible testing of Toledo, that he has been entirely carried by grace: even in the night all is light:

> this is the dark cloud
> which lit up the night ... [6]

Thus searching is really finding, unknowing is "supreme knowledge."[7] By himself the poet was powerless:

> The one who truly arrives there
> from himself falls away ... [8]

But the hearing of "great things"[9] relating to "the divine essence," has entirely been "the work of his mercy."[10]

Indeed, if the first five stanzas are descriptive of John of the Cross's experience, as, "so enraptured, / so absorbed and withdrawn,"[11] he was initiated to transcendent unknowing, the last three have fallen into the didactic genre. They no longer place the reader face to face with an experience that can only be stammered out. Rather, one is listening to an instructor who explains and compares.

Undoubtedly, the poem originated in a rewriting *a lo divino* of stanzas on a secular topic, like other previous compositions of John of the Cross. Yet this does not alter its meaning or its intent. Whether it came from John's Toledan captivity, or earlier, the passage from description to didactic instruction[12] highlights a dilemma that confronted the poet as soon as, having escaped his adversaries among the calced Carmelites, he picked up his activities among the discalced and with the sisters of Teresa of Jesus: how could he explain his mystical poems to those who wished to understand them yet recognized that they could not grasp their meaning? That the mystical moment of *Entréme* is followed by a didactic one detracts from the poetic purity of the whole. The solution that John of the Cross will soon adopt, or maybe simply stumble into, and that will be characteristic of his works in the eyes of posterity, will be different: he will write prose commentaries on his poems.

As is well known, John of the Cross began his treatise on the *Ascent of Mount Carmel,* which is a commentary on the first two stanzas of the poem of the *Dark Night,* in Andalusia, in the small house of the Calvario where he arrived at the end of 1578. As he was not too far from the Carmelite sisters of Beas de Segura, he visited them regularly and talked to them about contemplative life in the light of his poems, which thus came to function as his "text." At the same time, he began to elaborate orally on the *Spiritual Canticle.* The *Ascent of Mount Carmel* was eventually left unfinished;[13] the commentary on the *Canticle,* version (A), was terminated at Granada in 1584, at the time, or near the time, when the author started once more to comment on the *Dark Night* in another perspective.

These commentaries raise a special problem. The relation of each poem to its commentary is clear: it provides the basic text and the point of departure. The commentary at times—as is regularly the case in the *Ascent of Mount Carmel*—wanders a considerable distance from the text, which is then partially relegated to a role of "pretext." But what is the relation of the commentary to the poem? The poem is evidently not written for the commentary. Yet does not the commentary give the poem a new sense that it would not otherwise have? Is it possible, once the commentaries have been written, to read the poems as though the commentaries did not exist? Yet should one really believe that the theological commentator gave the only correct interpretation of the poet's insight? Some have studied the poetry with no or few references to the commentaries.[14] Others—and theologians have usually been among these—have spoken of the tractates as though these constituted the heart of John of the Cross's works, with an ecclesial dimension instead of the subjectivity of the poems.[15] The attitude that I feel bound to adopt is the following.

The poems generally stand by themselves, independently of the commentaries, which, in the case of the first *Canticle* and the *Dark Night*, were not foreseen when they saw the light. Yet self-evidently the additions to the *Canticle* that were made during the Andalusian phase of the poet's life, the first in 1582, the last between 1582 and 1584, were written with the awareness that they would be included in the commentary that was then under way. By the same token, the meaning of the latter may have impacted John's rereading of the poem. This is why version (A) of the *Canticle* should be identified as another poem than that of Toledo, the first *Canticle*.

In the case of the *Dark Night*, the poem exists by itself before the author forms the project of a commentary. From this point of view it is similar to the poems from Toledo. And the fact that it occasioned two commentaries that are rather different shows that it constitutes an integral whole, independent of the *Ascent of Mount Carmel* and of the treatise on the *Dark Night*, even if one may be led to read it in the light of these.

Let us now read, after *Entréme*, the poem of the *Night*. It follows the same general structure as the *Spiritual Canticle*, with the five-line stanza that Spanish stylistics calls a *lira*. But the poem, much shorter, has only five *liras*. Instead of a dialogue in three voices, it is a monologue in two moments. The poet remembers an event in his recent past. His escape from captivity has become the symbol of another adventure, of an escape out of self. No more sadness lurks under the words, no more anxiety serves as backdrop, even if it is with "anguish" that the author declares he fled; the tone is of joy. The adventure is "happy,"[16] the night that witnessed it is "happy." As in several passages of the *Canticle*, exclamations break the story with a recurring shout of joy: "Oh, happy adventure!" And stanza 5, at the center, is a sequence of exclamations, in which joy reaches its acme:

> O guiding night!
> O night more lovely than dawn!
> O night which united
> the Beloved with his beloved,
> the beloved transformed into her Beloved!

Joy is inseparable from the night. The night is featured in the poem in the guise of a friend, even the supreme friend: no longer like the creatures of the *Canticle*, which could no more than stammer, or the "nymphs of Judea," who, in their eagerness to celebrate the wedding, could awaken the Beloved by knocking at the threshold. On the contrary, night is now the agent of the union that is sung by the poet, the all-encompassing atmosphere of his adventure, the guide. This theme leads to the fifth stanza, which itself forms a hinge between the two halves of the poem. The first five stanzas celebrate the escape, the mystical movement toward the one whom she loves (for the poet puts himself in the feminine, facing the masculine of the Beloved). The night is evoked in many ways: by the night itself as it is directly named, by the "darkness," which appears both as a noun and as an adjective, by the secrecy of the staircase, which does not tell if the movement goes up or down the stairs, by the detail that no one noticed her, that no one saw her, by the "quiet" of the house. Along the same line, the poet specifies that he "did not look for anything," that there was no light, except within his heart, and that the place where the Beloved waited for her was in solitude: no one "appeared," not even, as one may note, the stag who, in the *Canticle*, was seen atop the mountain.[17]

The theme of the night is not negative. For the night itself is, in the second moment of the poem, luminous, on the model of the Paschal vigil as celebrated in the *Exsultet* of the deacon: *nox illuminatio mea in deliciis meis* (night is my light in my delights).[18] It is a "guide," surer than "the midday light." It is also accompanied by the flame of love (" . . . inflamed with desires in loves"),[19] by fire (" . . . that burned in my heart");[20] and where it leads the poet, the one whom she "knows well" is waiting for her.[21] Thus the night is entirely turned to a knowing, which is not, like sight by daylight, active, but rather passive; it leads, not really toward knowing, but toward being known. There is indeed unknowing; yet, within and beyond unknowing there is also being-known. This is the mystery of union, which is first summed up in the exclamations of stanza 5; it is the night of oneness, the night of love, in which union is transforming, since in their intimacy the "beloved" is "transformed into her Beloved."[22]

John of the Cross does not let us know if we have reached a summit, up the stairs, or an abyss, down the stairs. Uncertainty pertains to the night in which he wishes to plunge us along with himself. What is condensed in stanza 5 unfolds more slowly later. The last three stanzas sound quite differently from the first four. When it sang the mutual love, the fifth stanza changed the orientation of the poem. The house being now left behind in its nocturnal quiet, we have arrived at what is better than dawn. The Beloved is asleep in his beloved's arms; she caresses him; the cedars—that is, nature, the creatures—like eolian harps, softly vibrate under the breeze that flows from beyond the walls. Although he borrows an image from Garcilaso, John of the Cross may also be thinking of the high walls of the castle that dominate the city of Medina del Campo[23]: hence a scene of serenity, of the calm of two lovers beneath the castle walls, feeling the wind that makes the beloved shiver deliciously as she caresses her sleeping Lover and strokes his hair. Nothing else then counts; all her senses are suspended.

The last stanza brings back the theme of night, though at another level. Oblivion, abandonment, now dominate: self-oblivion, self-abandonment. Everything ceases to be, except the experience of love, for the beloved "remains." Forgetting herself, her "face" leaning over her Beloved,[24] she reaches the high point of her glorious adventure. And the final image, of concern "forgotten among the lilies," is not without relation to a symbolism that John of the Cross must have known. The lilies, which are presumably borrowed, along with the walls, from the *Song of Songs*,—the walls and the coolness of the breeze being also inspired by some lines in Garcilaso—are, in Christian iconography, symbols of purity, of joyful renunciation.[25] They signify oblivion and abandonment, the place where abandonment, transformed into self-offering, turned to promise, itself comes to bloom. The lilies on which the *Dark Night* ends recall pictures of the Annunciation, in which the dialogue between the angel and Mary, itself pointing to that between the Word and the Virgin, takes place near a vase with lilies. The paradox of mystical experience lies here. In most likelihood this was also, for John of the Cross, the paradox of the Christian Faith.

Was John of the Cross aware, as he was about to start his commentary, of the paradoxical aspect of the poem of the *Dark Night*? This seems to have been the case, given the unusual, not to say odd, structure of the two commentaries of it, the *Ascent of Mount Carmel* and the treatise of the *Dark Night*. Their redaction took place between 1578 and 1585, presumably in sequence, though one cannot rule out that they may have been written simultaneously.[26] In 1582–84 John of the Cross was also commenting on the *Spiritual Canticle.* He therefore worked at several levels, alternately, in keeping with the needs and requests of the sisters, chiefly those of Beas and of Granada, to whom he explained orally, in talks and homilies, the meaning of his poems and their connection with the inner life. The structure of the *Canticle* commentary is simple, even self-evident, as it follows the poem step by step. But the real structure of the others, patterned on John's own mystical experience and his theological understanding of it, remains far removed from the poem. For the *Canticle* John of the Cross proceeds verse after verse to the end. Although he commences the poem of the *Night* in the same way, no doubt with the intent of going through all the stanzas and verses in order, he leaves off long before the end. As regards the *Ascent,* the first stanza corresponds to Book One; yet as many as thirteen chapters cover the first verse, but only one chapter covers the second verse, and verses 3 to 5 come in the last chapter. Books Two and Three are presented as commentaries on the second stanza, but the verses are not examined one by one. The general theme of the stanza provides the point of departure for a development that apparently forgets the text. The remaining parts of the poem are not commented on at all, the author having interrupted his work, never to return to it.

As regards the *Dark Night,* Book One starts all over again with the first stanza, and again gives lopsided attention to the first verse. Being cited at the end of the prologue, and again at the end of chapter 7, this verse is the subject matter of the first ten chapters. The second verse, cited at the end of chapter 10, is commented on at the beginning of chapter 11, in which the third and fourth verses are also cited. The fifth verse appears toward the end of chapter 13, where it sums up the effects of the mystical night previously described.

Instead of continuing with the second stanza, as one would have expected it, Book Two, after three introductory chapters, picks up once more the first stanza, and gives it, counting the *Ascent,* a third commentary. Once again the first verse predominates, as it takes up the first ten chapters. The second verse is then cited and com-

mented on until the end of chapter 13. Then the last three verses
are quoted one after the other in a very brief space, at the end of
chapter 13 and in chapter 14. Their commentary is only one chapter
long. The commentary on the second stanza is more even: chapter
15 as introduction, chapter 16 for the first verse, chapters 17 to 21
for the second, then one chapter on each of the remaining verses.
The third stanza is introduced in chapter 25; but the work ends
unexpectedly after quoting the first verse, "In the happy night."

As one may see, John of the Cross, who binds himself to strict
rules of versification as accepted in his time, is free from all struc-
tural regularity in his commentaries, despite their didactic and at
times scholastic contents. The freedom of the poem lies in its
images, not in its form, that of the commentary resides in the form,
the content being dictated by the objective datum of the experience.
Yet if one may understand the disjuncted aspect of these two books
in their relation to their common text, one cannot help surmising
that John of the Cross did find himself in a bind that he could not
easily overcome. Really, the idea of a didactic discourse on a poetic
text could hardly fit the requirements of a master in mystical theol-
ogy (to speak like Teresa of Avila),[27] in his project of teaching the
Carmelite sisters who were called to the contemplative way. This
demanded a progressive, at times elementary, manner. One may
further wonder if the author's problem remained confined within
the order of form and style, or spread to a wider domain. As regards
form and style, John of the Cross, who was as free here as everywhere
else, easily hit on a solution: a disorderly order, an unstructured
structure, a holy chaos that organizes itself as it goes, in keeping
with the needs of every moment and question. If there was a deeper
problem, the solution was not so easy.

It is not necessary for our study
to proceed to a thorough analysis of the commentaries on the poem
of the *Night*. This has been done many a time.[28] Yet an inquiry
into selected themes of the *Ascent of Mount Carmel* and the *Dark
Night* may throw light on our research. The chief theme is of course
that of the night. This is a many-sided symbol: John of the Cross
identifies the dark night of his escape with the purification of the
soul, which itself has many aspects. There will be the successive

purifications of sense, active and passive, and the active and passive purifications of spirit; and they will all bear on the three levels of the intellect, the memory, and the will. Moreover, there will be a comparison, even an identification, of nocturnal darkness and crea- turely weakness, of the night and the nothingness (*nada*) that mark the only way to the whole (*todo*), as in the axioms on the *todo-nada* that frame the drawing of Mount Carmel and are repeated within the commentary.[29] The night will be the nudity of spirit of those who have embarked on the ascent of the mountain. It will be faith, the only "blindman's guide" toward the light. It will be the "knowl- edge" given by faith to the Church Militant, "where it is still night." It will even be, paradoxically, God, of whom John of the Cross has said that he "is also for the soul a part, or the third cause, of this night," the first two causes being the blindness of sense and the obscurity of faith.[30] Admittedly, the mystical doctor sees neither identity nor equivalence between these symbolic dimensions of night. Linguistically, the word is polysemic, with numerous conno- tations around a common core, the darkness.[31] Philosophically, the meaning of the term is not univocal, but analogical.[32] Theologically, according to a traditional image, God is "light," even "inaccessible light." In the Creed of Nicaea-Constantinople, God is *lumen*, and the divine Word, *lumen de lumine*. In relation to creatures, such as he is perceived, or rather unperceived, by them, God can only be darkness. The following text is of major importance for John of the Cross's doctrine of night as well as for an understanding of the problem that John had to face as he commented on his poetry:

> The third part, that period before dawn, approximates the light of day. The darkness is not like that of midnight, since in this third period of the night we approach the illumination of day. And this daylight we compare to God. Although it is true that God is for the soul, speaking naturally, as dark a night as faith is; yet since, these three parts of the night, which for the soul are naturally dark, having passed, God enlightens the soul super- naturally with the beam of his divine light, which is the principle of the perfect union which follows after the third night, this one may be said to be less dark.[33]

John of the Cross explains that if the night of faith is darker than that of sense, this is because it deprives the soul of its own rational light. As the night of spirit, it is more deeply obscure than that of sensibility. It holds in itself "contraries."[34] These are obstacles that one meets along the path of purification, contradictions that are more or less profound and more or less temporary. At another level contraries are not obstacles, but rather the very condition of the night. At this point the language of the mystical doctor is strictly exact: "For," says he, "we must prove now how this second part, faith, is night to the spirit just as the first is to the senses. Then we shall also discuss the contraries that it has. . . ."[35] 'It' is the second night, the night of faith. The contraries in question are not in the first place the "impediments" that will be studied from chapter 10 on, after the treatise on faith that occupies chapters 3 to 9 of the second part of the *Ascent*. They are rather contraries that are within faith, contrasting yet inseparable dimensions of this night. The demonstration that faith is a night is the topic of chapter 3. The contraries immediately follow: the night gives light; "the night, being dark, illumines"; the soul "must be in darkness to have light along this way."[36] This theme is continued in chapters 4 to 9, when the author shows how and in what way faith, which is at the same time light and darkness, acts at this time as the soul's guide. John of the Cross is thus aware of an apparent contradiction in this doctrine: faith-night is also faith-light; God is himself day and night.

Similar contradictions accompany the use of some other symbols. Among others, the symbol of the way is a case in point. This is inspired by the image of the "three ways," to which John of the Cross refers explicitly on occasion.[37] It provides the central image of the *Ascent of Mount Carmel*, which deals with going up the mountain. Its use may be a delicate homage to Teresa of Avila, whose *Way of Perfection*, begun in 1562 for the instruction of the sisters of the convent of St. Joseph in Avila, then left aside, was eventually finished in 1569–70. In fact John of the Cross also speaks of "the way of perfection": the image appears as early as the prologue to the *Ascent*, in the form of both the verb *encaminar* (to walk along the way) and the noun *camino* (way). Souls, John of the Cross writes, should "let themselves be placed freely in the pure and certain way of union."[38] This is "a sublime way of dark contemplation and aridity."[39] In a first moment, the description of the way coincides with that of the night of sense: "It is necessary that the way and ascent to God be a habitual effort to renounce and mortify the appetites."[40] In a second moment, the way becomes the night of spirit, a "narrow path,"[41] that corresponds to the "nudity and purity of the three faculties of the soul." It is the narrow way of the Gospel of Matthew, 7:14,[42] a path where one goes "denuded of all and with no desire for anything."[43] It consists, not in "a multiplicity of considerations, modes, manners, tastes, . . . but in the only thing necessary, which is to know how to deny oneself both externally and internally, by devoting oneself to suffering for Christ and annihilating self in all things."[44] Once again we are confronted with a paradox. For John of the Cross affirms, with Holy Scripture: "Christ is the way," but he adds immediately: "This way is a death to our natural selves."[45] Such a death affects both the spiritual and the sensory levels of the soul. But how can Christ, who is "the truth and the life" (John, 14, 6), be also a way of death and annihilation? There is a contradiction, at least in the language. John of the Cross is aware of it, since he tries to remove what may be repulsive in the paradox. One should understand, he explains, that death to nature follows "the example of Christ." For Christ also "during his life, died spiritually to the sensitive part, and at his death he died naturally."[46] As regards spiritual dying, "at the moment of his death he was certainly annihilated in his soul, without consolation or relief, since the Father left him that way in innermost aridity in the lower part [of the soul]."[47] Matthew 27:46 is then cited, with its reference to Psalm 21, "My God, my God, why have you forsaken me?" A mystery lurks here—"the mystery of the door and the way of Christ"—that takes the form in the spiritual person of a simultaneous experience of two contraries. Nothing, *nada*, "the highest degree of humility," is at the same time "the spiritual union between the soul and God, which is the greatest and highest state which may be reached in this life." In order to attain it, one must "purify oneself of contraries,"[48] that is, as the following chapters of the *Ascent* will show, of everything that is not the faith.

The way is night; it is death to self; it is Christ. There still is more, for one should finally come, toward the summit, to a renunciation to the way, at the spot where the way becomes no-way. Let us take a look at the famous sketch of Mount Carmel, the original of which, now lost, had come from John of the Cross's own pen. It was drawn for the first time toward the end of 1578, shortly before the mystical doctor began his systematic writing of the *Ascent of Mount Carmel*. From an aesthetic and psychological point of view, the central image has been compared both to an animated doll, such as Juan de Yepes may have seen in the fiestas of Medina del Campo, and with which he may have toyed in his childhood, and also to a foetus, whose life is entirely in its lungs, its arms stuck to its body, its head disproportionate, protected by its enfolding placenta.[49] I would add that, if it is a doll, it is wearing an enormous hat, such as might protect a pilgrim from sun, rain, and snow, and also that, whether doll or foetus, it emerges from what could be a hedge, or a corn field, or even a line of lances held straight as for a parade. These lances-corn-hedge are no other than the verses of the poem of the *todo-nada*, which will be featured again at the end of chapter 13 of the first part of the *Ascent*. It is as though the sharp edges of its dialectic could converge, once again, only upon something still unfinished, an I-know-not-what, a stammering, a moment that is expectation without ever becoming fulfillment:

> To reach satisfaction in all
> desire satisfaction in nothing.
> To reach possession of all
> desire possession of nothing.
> To arrive at being all
> desire to be nothing.
> To come to the knowledge of all
> desire knowledge of nothing.[50]

To Magdalen of the Holy Spirit, John of the Cross will write in the same sense in 1589: "To possess God in all, you should possess nothing in all. For how can the heart that belongs to one belong completely to the other?"[51]

"To come" stands in contrast with "not to desire." One could say that a first positive attitude corrects in advance a second negative attitude, though the two are inseparable, like the means that necessarily go with the end. This contrast is underlined by a second version of the poem, which proceeds by way of opposite negations:

> To come to what you do not enjoy
> you must go where you have no joy.
> To come to what you do not know
> you must go where you do not know.
> To come to what you do not possess
> you must go where you do not possess.
> To come to what you are not
> you must go where you are not.[52]

- Here, the end as well as the means, the summit as well as the path, are formulated in negative terms. Moreover, from untaste to unknowing, from unknowing to non-possession, from non-possession to non-being, there is an obvious progress, but in negativity. The ascent of the mountain is foreseen, but it entails the disappearance of the alpinist. In the night of faith one climbs up to non-being by a scale of untaste, unknowing, non-possession. But your non-being, what you are not, is God, the Being who is for you Non-Being. Thus, as the end is no end, the way is no way. This is the very formula that John of the Cross wrote on top of his sketch of *Mount Carmel*, in what would be inside the hat of his doll or the placenta of his foetus: "Here there is no longer any way"; and he wrote on: "Because for the just there is no law, he is a law unto himself."[53] The idea of a way that is no-way is thus grounded in the Pauline doctrine of justification and of liberty: at the top, where one is justified in the night of faith, one is by the same token freed. Hence the third stanza of the poem:

> When you turn to something
> you cease to cast yourself on all.
> For to go from all to all
> you must deny yourself all in all.
> And when you come to possess all
> you must possess it without wanting it.
> For if you want something in all
> you have not in God alone your treasure.[54]

The *todo-nada* (all-nothing) of the beginning, and what really constitutes a *nada-nada* (nothing-nothing) in the middle, introduce an *algo-todo* (something-all) in third place. The creature is negated first as end, by contrast with the all of God; it is then negated as way, by analogy with the Non-Being of God; and it is finally recognized in its creaturely being and set before God at its true place, which it obtains without possessing it. A fourth stanza, it would seem, is missing: this would celebrate the creature being possessed by God in faith and, beyond faith, in glory. But such a stanza could not be written at this level of the treatise of the *Ascent*. We are still on the path that is not one, where there is liberty; but we cannot yet describe the ineffable encounter that grounds this freedom.

In the structure of John of the Cross's works, the *Ascent of Mount Carmel* could not reach the spot where, on top of the mountain, the way peters out. John of the Cross comes near to it in the treatise of the *Dark Night*. The prologue of it, following on the language of the *Ascent*, speaks of "the narrow path of eternal life,"[55] of "this narrow path." The first part of it, which corresponds to the night of sense, features the image of a "way of the spirit,"[56] a "way of contemplation," which soon divides into a "way of meditation or discourse,"[57] and "another way," "a way that is so different," which coincides with the threshold of passive contemplation. This is "the path and way of the spirit."[58] Already, however, this first book of the *Dark Night* foresees something more. The pilgrim will have to venture further, to start on "the narrow path which is the night of spirit."[59] At the end of the night of sense, when meditation has become impossible and the soul struggles on blindly, as best it can, in a no man's land without particular mode or shape, it finds itself (Psalm 63:2) "in a desert, waterless, dry, and pathless." But this "pathless land"[60] opens up "the experience and vision of the power of God." It consists in the inability to grasp God with ideas and to walk by means of discursive, imaginative meditation.

In the night of spirit, as he reflects on the first stanza of the *Dark Night*, John of the Cross keeps the image of the way. Yet numerous expressions indicate that it has been transformed into its negation. One must now walk along "new roads" to reach "new territories."[61] The soul finds itself "in a place far removed from every creature";[62] in delights, yet also in "a remarkably deep and vast wilderness, . . . an immense, unbounded desert." There it discovers the "way" leading to "the perfection of union with God."[63] And since these are not "humanly knowable," one should "advance humanly by not knowing, and divinely by ignorance." So uncharted is such a way that, according to Psalm 77:20, it lies "in the sea," where "its paths and its tracks are not known."[64] The pilgrimage along a way where "to descend is to ascend and to ascend is to descend,"[65] as is "the route leading to the union of love,"[66] "the road of solitude,"[67] takes the traveler to a way that is no-way, on top of Mount Carmel.

The way that is night, that is death to self, that is Christ, that is no-way, brings the circuit back to the paradox, already encountered, of an inner contradiction. The chosen image breaks and peters out trying to express the reality it unveils.

A parallel and complementary symbol is that of unknowing. This theme is linked to the image of the way, since, speaking of the necessary rejection of interior locutions, whether these proceed from self or from God, John of the Cross insists that "one should be extremely careful always to reject this knowledge, and should desire to journey to God by unknowing."[68] Although it does not stand at the center, this is a major idea in the writings of the Mystical Doctor. It recurs in soft tones throughout the *Ascent of Mount Carmel* and the *Dark Night*. It provides the thread of *Entréme*, the poem we have already studied. With his delicate poetic sensitivity, John of the Cross could not help asking and affirming the need for "no-taste" (*el no sabor*)[69] as an integral dimension of the journey to and in mystical contemplation. As a theologian he did not hesitate to see unknowing (*el no saber*)[70] as a condition for union with God. These two ideas are evidently related, and not only by the wordplay they allow in the Spanish language. Unknowing is to the acquisition of ideas and the knowledge of particulars what no-taste is to what the soul would easily develop toward the impressions of grace in its spiritual sensitivity.[71] As desire and taste for spiritual feelings should be relinquished, so should the particular knowledge of things be refused for the sake of the only knowledge of God, as God shows, or rather does not show, himself.

All that takes the form of nocturnal language under the pen of John of the Cross already constitutes an assertion or at least a suggestion, of the mystical unknowing. The formulas abound. At first sight they do not seem varied: the soul finds itself "without knowing how, . . . without knowing or understanding . . . without knowing where."[72] In fact, a successive reading of the two commentaries of the poem of the *Night* conveys the curious feeling that the author is functioning at two parallel yet contradictory levels. On the one hand, he repeats, often—and more and more as his analysis of the conditions required for contemplation advances—imperative formulas: "it should be known,"[73] . . . "it should be understood." Such expressions may at times seem superfluous, as though they simply stood for "that is to say." But John of the Cross, in his didactic writings, is concerned that the Carmelites understand and remember his teaching. The constant repetition of *es a saber* well underlines how necessary it is to know the conditions apart from which one cannot make progress in the way of union. On the other hand, this knowledge that the author communicates amounts to realizing, to knowing, that one should not know: "The soul remains as though ignorant of all things, since it knows only God without knowing how";[74] "One must pass on to unknowing."[75] Similar expressions abound: one should be "blind,"[76] "like the blind man," in "darkness and a void of understanding," in "the darkness of the intellect before God," "in oblivion and outside time." The soul will travel "new and unknown roads and abandon the familiar ones."[77] It is "asleep and in silence regarding earthly and heavenly things."[78] And John of the Cross hears the bride of the *Song of Songs*, who is present also in the horizon of the *Ascent of Mount Carmel*, "when she states that she went down to him, number unknowing among the effects that this sleep and oblivion produced in her, saying: *Nescivi* (I know not)."[79]

In reality there is not one unknowing; there are several. First of all a certain unknowing is required in the section of the way to the top that still has some markers: it should bear on the natural and acquired knowledge of things. Consciousness of particular objects, which is of course necessary in the empirical life of every day, must give room to unknowing as soon as attention bears, no longer on objects in their concrete particularity, in their contingent and limited being, in their practical value at the service of secular and personal purposes, even in their moral value as judged by the laws of Church and society, but on the Being who does not fall within the world of things and the field of measurements, and who escapes both scientific testing and empirical observation. John of the Cross has this unknowing in mind when he writes: "I affirm that the soul . . . must darken and blind itself in that part of its nature which bears relation to creatures and temporal things, which is the sensory and lower part."[80]

There is also, still in the order of the foreseeable, yet at a more advanced spot along the mystical itinerary, a deliberate ignoring of spiritual favors actually received from God at the two levels of feeling and of knowledge. John of the Cross's doctrine at this point amounts to his recurrent teaching on "locutions" or propositions spoken to us from a supernatural source.[81] Whether these are "successive," "formal," or "substantial," they must not be clung to; and, to make sure one does not cling to them, ignorance is the best part of wisdom. As successive, such words are, as it were, heard within oneself; as formal, they are found fully constituted in one's mind with no sense of having contributed to their formation or of having heard them as one hears the outside sound of words; as substantial, they effect what they mean, thus transforming the soul that finds itself suddenly changed. All of them should be systematically ignored. Their effect does not depend on their recipient. Whether welcome or rejected, they reach their goal infallibly when God so decides. God does through them what he wants when he so wants, without any interference by the soul. In order to avoid attachment to spiritual values and the temptation not to go by naked faith, the only safe way is that of unknowing. John of the Cross therefore extends to supernatural locutions or words the principle that he has stated concerning feelings, objects, phenomena, and all events with a supernatural origin: one must never seek them. This is his constant doctrine regarding extraordinary graces. "Saying that all must be rejected, one has said enough to avoid error";[82] "I say only that a person should be on guard against these revelations in order to walk in purity and without error in the night of faith toward union."[83] The application of this principle to supernatural words is no less radical: "I only repeat that my main teaching is to pay no heed whatsoever to them."[84] Substantial words alone count; yet here also the soul has to remain in unknowing; it need not pay attention, since in relation to them "the soul has nothing to do, desire, not desire, reject, or fear."[85]

Between formal and substantial words one passes from one unknowing to another. The first bears on distinct and particular points of knowledge, which have to be eliminated from consciousness. The soul has the capacity to entertain them or not, according to its attention and assent to particular objects. The second belongs to another order: it is received with total passivity. It constitutes in fact a third form of unknowing, which is not selected by choice but is elicited interiorly by divine action. It is not due to circumstances surrounding the way, but to the inner structure of mystical experience.

One finds a fourth type of unknowing in the works of John of the Cross. This type is especially underlined at the summit, where the way becomes no-way, though it already marks the previous phases of ascent. It simply derives from the obvious fact that, by the very nature of reality, God is, strictly speaking, unknowable to the creaturely mind. Of the night John has affirmed: "A person in darkness does not receive adequate enlightenment save by another darkness."[86] God is darkness to the intellect. Night, darkness, unknowing are closely related if not exactly interchangeable terms. They mutually connote one another. Known only to faith, God remains unknown to the natural intellect. Thus faith will be, as our following chapter will explain it at length, a night, "an obscure and dark cloud to the soul." Faith is dark because it is light, an "excessive light," that infinitely escapes the cognitive capacity of the natural man: "God himself is as dark a night to the soul as is faith."[87] By this very fact, however, he "supernaturally illumines the soul with a ray of his divine light." In other words light and dark coincide.

John of the Cross nears asymptotically the idea that unknowing, as caused in the intellect by faith's excessive light, constitutes the true cognition. As he writes in his treatise of the *Dark Night*, contemplation is "an obscure wisdom."[88] In *Entréme* he admits its unknowability as regards the place, the cognitive process ("And my spirit was given, / not understanding, an understanding"), the capacity to speak ("that I was left stammering").[89] He comes close to looking on this unknowing as a knowing:

> Of peace and of piety
> it was the perfect science,

in profound solitude
understood, straight way . . .

and his science grows so much . . .

this is why the one who knew it . . .

This knowing which is unknowing . . .

It is of such high excellence,
this supreme knowing . . .

Yet as he tries to suggest the object of this science, John of the Cross at first can only fall back into negation, in keeping with the refrain, "all knowing transcending":

and his knowledge so increases
that he is left unknowing,
all knowing transcending.

In a second moment, identified in the last stanza, the poet borrows images from the language of sense organs:

And if you wish to hear it,
this supreme knowledge consists
in a lofty feeling
of the divine essence;
it is the work of his mercy
to make one stay not understanding
all knowing transcending.

Having already been abandoned in the twofold night of sense, left behind by the twofold night of spirit, sense is open to a transvaluation of its processes: hearing and feeling become symbolic of a knowledge above all knowledge, of a knowing that remains unknowing. Such symbols abound in the poetry and the commentaries of the *Canticle* and the *Flame of love.*

It is quite remarkable that John of the Cross does not go beyond this asymptotic line, which nears, without ever coinciding with, the identity of the two contraries that are ignorance and knowledge. There is a knowing that is unknowing, a feeling, a touch, a hearing, a taste "of what [the soul] neither sees nor touches nor is capable of seeing or touching in this life, which is God, who is incomprehensible and transcendent."[90] God dwells beyond whatever natural and supernatural knowing may be obtained of him. Likewise, the summit of the mystical ascent does not pertain to the realm of knowledge but to that of love. As regards cognition, the journey passes from unknowing to ignorance: one must go toward the divine perfections "humanly without knowing, divinely in ignorance."[91]

Yet let us not misread the language. John of the Cross speaks of knowledge, science, truth known, of "knowing the all," as in the *todo-nada* verses, of hidden and secret wisdom, as in his commentary on the *Canticle*.[92] Atop the mountain, however, the experience of God is beyond knowledge; it is a union with, rather than a vision of, God, a wisdom, yet secret, unknown. There is indeed knowing that is unknowing; there is no "learned ignorance." The two terms, knowing and unknowing, are not interchangeable in the equation that has been established and interpreted by John of the Cross in the light of his experience. Knowing is the subject, not the predicate. In other words the subject is God, inaccessible knowledge, incomprehensible science, unknowable knowing, hidden wisdom; but this subject gives itself a predicate that is, precisely, the unknowing, the ignorance that belongs to creaturely being. Not on the basis of human ignorance does the Christian mystic reach the experience of God through spiritual sight, hearing, tasting, smelling, touching. Rather is it on the basis of divine knowing beyond all human capacity that God gives himself to be known without knowledge, in love.

CHAPTER 5

THE CONTRARIES

---

ohn of the Cross has more
and more forcefully underlined that union with God at the end of
the mystical ascent is consummated in loving unknowing or, equiva-
lently, in unknowing love. This poses a problem that should be
carefully assessed. On the one hand, how can one affirm—that is,
implicitly at least, know—what cannot be known? There is at this
point a problem of thought and language that should find its solution
in the structure of linguistic symbolism. Yet it also leads to a more
basic question regarding the nature of spiritual experience and of
union with God: for this union to be possible in the perspective
that has been constantly emphasized by John of the Cross, the
nature of faith must be such that it enables one to posit jointly
affirmation and negation, knowing and unknowing. For, as the mys-
tical doctor often states it, all that happens in the experience that
is recorded in his poetry and explained in his commentaries takes
place within faith. The nights are expected events along the pilgrim-
age of faith. The ascent of the mountain has no other motif and no
other guide than faith. The spiritual espousals, described from stanza
11 of the *Canticle* onwards, first as engagement and promise and
then as marriage and gift, belong to the same horizon. As the experi-
ence of God's self-revelation, faith is unknowing as well as knowing.
But is it a kernel of knowledge in a shell of unknowing, or a kernel
of unknowing hidden in the pulp of more superficial knowledge?

A study of John of the Cross's theology of faith is urgent, even
though it has already been done by others along different lines.[1] Yet
a number of preliminary remarks, which will make up the bulk of
the present chapter, will prepare us to read the master texts of John

of the Cross on the matter of faith.

Before approaching these texts, one could attempt to recover the historical antecedents that may have inspired John of the Cross in his analysis of the nights and of unknowing. Such a line of research, which will not be pursued here, would turn to the "luminous cloud," the "total unknowing," the "neither this nor that," the "true ignorance," of Denys, whose influence was universal, if somewhat vague, in the spirituality of the Western Middle Ages, and of whom John of the Cross must have known some writings, especially the *Mystical Theology*.[2] Gregory the Great (c. 540–604) also used the image of the darkness in his *Moralia in Job*, though in another semantic field: it primarily designated the dark zone of sin.[3] This is not the most frequent meaning of the term in the works of John of the Cross; yet it also is found in them. Gregory introduced also into the literature of Western Christian mysticism the theme of love as knowledge: "By love we know"; "love itself is knowledge."[4] Among the medieval authors, one should examine the influence of William of St. Thierry (c. 1080–1149) who, following Gregory, spoke of the "love-knowledge," by which the soul "understands without understanding," and who used the expression, "doct ignorance."[5] Already Bernard of Clairvaux (1090–1153) alluded to the "silence," the "slumber," in which the soul "sees invisible things, hears ineffable words."[6] One should speak of the Victorines,[7] and especially of Bonaventure at the seventh chapter of his *Journey of the Soul into God*. With the help of long quotations from Denys, the Seraphic Doctor shows the soul, at the summit of the mystical ascent, transcending the realm of knowledge: "If you seek how this happens, ask grace, not knowledge, desire, not understanding, . . . darkness, not clarity."[8] Still in the Franciscan tradition, one should read several pages of the *Third Alphabet*, a work that was familiar to Teresa of Avila, in which Francisco de Osuna (d. 1541/42) showed the soul needing to be "blind, deaf, and dumb" (Third Letter) and even "voided of all that is created" (Fourth Letter) in order to practice recollection *(recogimiento)*.[9] Although the symbol of the night is not used here, this comes close to the doctrine of John of the Cross.

One would presumably think also of the *Cloud of Unknowing*, an anonymous writing from the fourteenth century in England, conceivably composed in a Cistercian circle: the cloud is divided into a cloud of forgetting, between self and the world, and a cloud of unknowing, between self and God.[10] In England, too, Walter Hilton (d. 1396) recommends entering into darkness in order to discover, beyond the dark, the light of the true day.[11] Yet John of the Cross could not have known the English authors, who, like himself, wrote in their vernacular to meet the needs of their contemporaries, and whose works were not yet translated, whether in Latin or in Spanish. Moreover, their conception of the night seems to diverge notably from his.

With the mystics of the Rhineland and the Netherlands, however, a certain filiation is likely, the heart of their doctrine being already known in Spain through the Latin translations made by Surius (1522–78).[12] The image of the night is featured in John Ruysbroeck as well as in the homilies of Tauler. It is also used by Harphius (d. 1477), whose *Theologia mystica* underwent numerous printings in 1538 and after.

Although it would be most important to ascertain what John of the Cross may have known, through his studies and his readings, of the long spiritual and theological tradition that spoke of the hidden God *(Deus absconditus)* and of mystical unknowing, the sources, be they literary, theological, or spiritual, would not explain John of the Cross's own movement when, making himself the theologian of his experience, he started the commentaries on his poems. At the most they would throw light on some details here and there. Yet one of these may have great importance. This touches on the question of what relationship binds, or does not bind, John of the Cross and Nicholas of Cusa (1401–64).[13] Nicholas had presented the doct ignorance, not exactly as a symbolic description of the summits of mystical experience, but rather as a technique of ascent. One should carefully note the ambiguity of the expression: his *docta ignorantia* is at the same time, given the double meaning of the Latin expression, a "learned ignorance," whose teacher is the Holy Spirit, and a "learnt ignorance," also taught by the Spirit.

In the first meaning, ignorance knows from love what intellectual knowledge cannot grasp. In the second, ignorance knows nothing; it is simply recognized and known. Yet something suggests a link, be it a link of opposition, between the largely schoolish and didactic mysticism of the cardinal of St-Peter-in-Chains and the theological expression of the Spanish mystic's experience: Nicholas's *docta ignorantia* is tied to his conception of the "coincidence of opposites."

Beyond the coincidence of opposites God may be perceived, "seen," by the mystic. In the ordinary world of thought, ruled by the principle of noncontradiction, God remains invisible. The coincidence of opposites, as it were, suspends the principle of noncontradiction, and marks out a realm where thought, which functions under the principle of noncontradiction, cannot reach. Thus the coincidence of opposites acts as an impassable wall before the human intellect. Yet through the gate, which is carefully watched by the archangel standing at the entrance to Paradise, one can perceive God beyond the intellect, in what can no longer be rational thinking.[14] God lives in eternity, beyond the distinction between past and present. He is Oneness. In him, word, hearing, taste, tact, reason, knowledge, intelligence, are identical. In God, to know and to be known are one and the same thing. To perceive this, according to Nicholas of Cusa, requires giving up the human mode of cognition, eschewing knowledge. Union to God is effected beyond all human knowing, in an experience that is, properly speaking, inconceivable.

Was there, in the illuminism of the sixteenth century, among the *alhumbrados* who were hunted by the Spanish Inquisition in its decrees of 1525, 1574, 1578, and who threw suspicion on all mysticism in the eyes of some inquisitors, a use of the notion of the coincidence of opposites that, by applying it to the domain of practice and of morality, changed its meaning? It would seem that some of the *alhumbrados* claimed that they could reach a state beyond sinfulness, in which, as Eulogio de la Virgen del Carmen phrases it, "All comes from God, and this is why there is no longer any responsibility in temptation."[15] That, at a high level of the mystical ascent, "all comes from God," need not entail the consequence that such a confirmation in grace renders sinless for the mystic what is sinful for ordinary Christians.[16] That such a conclusion had actually been reached and practiced by some groups of *alhumbrados*, could have come by way of an aberrant application of the principle of the coincidence of opposites: in a convergence of good and evil, evil, remaining such but being absorbed in grace, would now be of no consequence and could be practiced without sin.

If there exists a domain in which opposites coincide, where contradictions are resorbed in some higher synthesis, one is far from the doctrine of John of the Cross. For him there is no higher unity transcending the opposition of *todo* and *nada*. Each excludes the other. In an infinitely more radical way than for all ancient and modern gnosticisms, one must, in order to reach all, seek nothing. But to seek nothing is not to look for something that would be, precisely, no-thing; it means, literally, to seek nothing, that is, not to seek. Between all and nothing there cannot be a "complementarity of mutual affirmation."[17] There is mutual exclusion, or rather, since nothing is not a real entity, but only the concept of non-entity, there is no relation between all and nothing. In reality, all is enough. The merely imaginative negation of it is called nothing. When John of the Cross speaks of the nothing that opposes the all, he does not have in mind something that is, but that which is not, nothingness, nil. The contraries of the all, the nature of which will have to be determined, have their domain in the night, from which they are never extracted to be absorbed or transcended in a higher experience or a transcendent synthesis. They keep their proper being, conditioned as they are by the structure of being and of human life on the one hand, by the infinity of the divine Being and Life on the other. In the exact measure in which they oppose the all, however, they annihilate themselves.

John of the Cross warns his reader several times against the notion that the contraries one meets on the slopes of Mount Carmel might be reconcilable, complementary, or even simply compatible. He has recourse for this to a philosophical principle that he formulates in simple terms: "Two contraries, as philosophy teaches, cannot enter into one subject."[18] John rarely refers to philosophy, partly because he has no interest in it, partly because the sisters for whom he writes have only a remote acquaintance, or none at all, with the theses that are familiar in the schools. It is therefore at first sight intriguing that the philosophical principle of the incompatibility of contraries should recur under his pen at key points in his works.

Before looking at these passages, let us examine the principle itself: "Two contraries cannot enter into one subject." At face value this looks like a variation on the principle of non-contradiction, which may be formulated thus: no being can be itself and its contrary. Yet, whereas the principle of non-contradiction pertains to the philosophy of being and finds its domain in the area of metaphysics and ontology, the formula of John of the Cross touches on the practical aspect of existence that could be expressed in popular language: one cannot run after two hares at once! As applied to the requirements of the inner life, this becomes: the soul cannot be filled with concern for God and with its contrary. John of the Cross had presumably learned this principle during his studies in Salamanca. It appears in a prominent place in the literature of the schools, in Bonaventure as well as in Thomas Aquinas.[19] The latter's *Commentary on the Sentences* gives it the following form: "Contraries can never be united in such a way that they would be in the same place in the same manner, and this is not how the creature is united to God."[20] As one may see, application of the philosophical principle to the relations between God and his creature was already standard in the scholastic tradition.

Yet there was no unanimity among the schoolmen on the nature of relationships between contraries. These relationships are obviously relations of oppositions. Contraries contradict each other in regard to a given point of view. Thus, black and white are contraries in the field of color, not in other fields (not, for instance, in race). Bonaventure expresses this in the remark that contraries necessarily fall in the same genus.[21] Thomas has a more nuanced formula on this very point. Contraries, for him, are not only different species within one genus: objects may be diversified and opposed by virtue, not only of their species, but also of their genus. Yet, "although many contraries differ in their species by virtue of the diversity of reality, they nonetheless pertain to the same cognitive principle, for each is known through the other."[22] A species may contradict another; a genus may be the contrary of another. Yet in all relations of contradiction each may be known from the nature of the other. "Who knows one of the contraries knows the other."[23] Thus, contraries always have something in common, if not in the area of their concrete being in its species or genus, at least in the field of cognition and the cognitive process. The language of John of the Cross would therefore seem to be more at home in a Thomist than in a Bonaventurian theology. Yet Thomas Aquinas remains more exact than the Mystical Doctor. The axiom, "Two contraries cannot enter into one subject," needs to be completed with the precision provided by Thomas: "Nothing hinders contraries to be in one thing, though not in the same manner."[24]

Whatever formula better corresponds to Thomism, neither for Thomas nor for Bonaventure is God the contradiction of his creatures. In reality God has no contrary, whether in being or out of being. God is absolutely beyond all series and cannot be defined by opposition to anything or anyone. Moreover, if it is indeed correct that who knows one contrary thereby knows its opposite, no object can be found in empirical or scientific experience, knowledge of which would include that of an opposite that would be identical with God. For Thomas Aquinas, who differs in this from the Augustinian tradition still embodied in the Franciscan school, there exists no cognitive principle the application of which to whatever object would necessarily bring about a knowledge of God. Encountering God is of another order than encounters with creatures. Vesperal knowledge does not stand on a par with matutinal knowledge.[25] Through the former, the one who truly knows a creature can rise to a certain knowledge of the Creator: this opens the analogical and anagogical path of meditation, which has been a fruitful source for all spiritualities of ascent to God up the scale of creation. Through the latter the one who knows God in Himself knows by the same token, with no other cognitive act, all that is somehow in God, and thereby the creature in what is most central in it, at the point where it originates in the movement by which God thinks and wills it. Along such lines John of the Cross read the first chapter of the Gospel of John: "All that was made was life in Him,"[26] that is, in God.

This brief look at the scholastic conception of contraries throws light on John of the Cross's formulations. For the Mystical Doctor remains well within the Thomist line of thought. The relation to God that develops in the ascent of Mount Carmel goes through phases of intense interior strife. These are occasioned by the incompatibility of two contraries: attachment to creatures and love for God. *Ascent* (Book 1:4, 2) contains a central text where the sentence, "Two contraries cannot coexist in the same subject," justifies the demands of the "dark night of mortification of appetites and denial of pleasure in all things."[27] The problem here is to explain the reason for, with the nature and the process of, the active night of sense. Before God, all affections for creatures are sheer darkness. This is the message of Scripture under the image of the light opposed to darkness in John 1:5. It is supported by philosophy, with the principle of the mutual exclusion of contraries. Hence John of the Cross concludes directly with the statement: "Darkness, such as attachment to creatures, and the light which God is, are contraries and bear no likeness or similarity between them."[28]

Affections for creatures are thus posited as opposed to God as light. The following explanations list and develop diverse aspects of the opposition of these contraries. On one side the "baseness of the creature" derives from its being "nothing," "sheer darkness," "less than nothing," "nothing and less than nothing."[29] The creature is "what is not." The "beauty of creatures," their "grace and their gifts," are "utter lack of grace"; their "goodness" is "mischievousness"; their "wisdom" is "complete and supreme ignorance."[30] There is also a "sovereignty and freedom of the world" that is "utter slavery, anguish, and captivity." All "delights and satisfactions of the will," the "wealth and glory of creation," are "utter poverty and misery."[31] On the other side John of the Cross evokes "the sublimity of the Creator."[32] To nothingness he opposes the fulness of Being "that which is," the "infinite beauty of God." His "grace," His "infinite goodness," His "infinite wisdom," the "freedom and sovereignty of the Spirit of God," "all the delights that God is, . . . the wealth that God is."[33] Thus, compared with God creatures are nothing and less than nothing. Undoubtedly, the point is not that one should denigrate the ontological reality and worth of created being. John of the Cross is not concerned with philosophical judgments and evaluations. It is not in itself that the created world has no value, but only when, by the affection that men have for it, it takes in their heart the place that belongs to the Creator.

This comparison is not presented by John of the Cross as descriptive of the obstacles opposed to union with God by earthly affections, though these are precisely the reason why the night of sense is necessary. The contrast is not between two kinds of feelings, going respectively to the creatures and to God. In the teaching of the *Ascent*, feelings that are beautiful, pure, good, lofty, do not count; the soul does not rise to God through its good intentions and its spiritual satisfactions. The contrast lies between affection for creatures and God. Yet if it is indeed true, in the Thomism from which John of the Cross borrows the framework of his theological writings, that the ultimate end of humankind and of all its affections is no other than God, it remains that a mere affection, even for creatures, is by no means the contrary of God. God cannot have contraries in the created world. For God is of another order, neither correlative nor comparable with that of creation. One may then ask: Is there in John of the Cross a pious exaggeration behind the inexactitude of his language? Is there, which would be more serious, a mistake? No doubt, the Mystical Doctor could argue from the many ways in which both scholastic thought and the spiritual literature inspired by it were self-correcting. Theology had forged the instrument of analogical language: through analogy of attribution first, and next through analogy of proper proportionality, this enables us to speak of the divine mystery in a way that is not false.[34] Spiritual theology also had measured the scope of the language of progress along the three ways of affirmation, negation, and eminence.[35] Yet John of the Cross scarcely alludes to these techniques. As is clear in the prologue to his commentary on the *Canticle*, he adopts a much more radical position, which simply acknowledges the impossibility of speech: "It would be ignorance to think that sayings of love understood mystically, as are those of the present stanzas, can be fairly explained by words of any kind."[36] Even the Holy Spirit "cannot express the abundance of his meaning [in Scripture] in common and vulgar terms." One has to speak of the mysteries, as the Spirit does, "in strange figures and similitudes." The dilemma, to have to speak, and to be unable to do so, is resolved, in keeping with John of the Cross's interpretation of Scripture, by finding refuge in strange discourse: this is still speech, but far from the beaten paths and the usual meanings of terms.

John of the Cross is aware of the general handicap that besets theological and mystical language. He even knows how to overcome it for his readers, provided they understand something, by experience, of the "strange" language he will use. He will offer "figures, comparisons, and similitudes." Yet only as these are "read with the simplicity of the spirit of love and understanding that is embodied in them," will their meaning be grasped.

Applying this general notion to the question of contraries, one is caught on the horns of a dilemma, which already appears as a "strange similitude": God is presented as a contrary, even though he has no contrary. Let us read chapter 6 of the *Ascent of Mount Carmel*. John remarks at first that affection for creatures causes two sorts of harm, negative and positive, to the soul. The negative harm is explained in light of the principle of the mutual exclusion of contraries: "The more reality this appetite has in the soul, the less open is the soul to God, for two contraries cannot coexist in the same subject, as the philosophers say, and as we also mentioned in chapter 4. Since attachment to God and attachment to creatures are contraries, they cannot coexist in the same will."[37]

John of the Cross here speaks of the contradiction between two loves, as though these were two species within one genus, two species of the genus, love. In fact Thomas Aquinas and scholasticism in general had endorsed the principle that "the mean and the extremes are in the same genus."[38] Yet the text of John of the Cross is self-correcting in that the contradiction of opposite affections hides a deeper contradiction of another order, between creature and Creator, "sensory and spiritual, visible and invisible, temporal and eternal, heavenly food that is pure and spiritual, and food that is entirely sensory, the nakedness of Christ and attachment to something."[39] Creator and creature do not share one genus, in keeping with the scholastic axiom: "God is not in any genus."[40] Two levels are therefore mingled in the text of the *Ascent*: the emotional and psychological contradiction between two loves, and the ontological chasm between Creator and creature. The Creator is spiritual, invisible, eternal, paradoxically manifested here below in the nakedness of Christ, tasted by the creature, no less paradoxically, as purely spiritual food. The creature pertains to the order of the sensory, the visible, the temporal, and is engaged in eating the merely sensory food of the senses. Although it is of an entirely different order, the psychological contradiction of two sorts of food highlights the ontological abyss between God and creation. On the one side a hunger, a desire, is felt by the creature for all creatures. On the other there is a "fulness fostered by the Spirit of God,"[41] which John also calls an "uncreated fulness." At a first level, hunger is clearly not identical with fulness, "since hunger and fulness are contraries" and "cannot coexist in the same person." The fulness that is effected in the soul by the Spirit of God is itself of the created order, and thus may be opposed to hunger. In addition there must be a second level, that of the "uncreated fulness," that can be located nowhere but in God. Now, if an uncreated fulness is truly opposed to hunger and desire, this cannot be in God, in whom there is neither hunger nor desire. In order to escape the dilemma that has thus been posited, there must be for the creature, under given conditions, a created participation in uncreated fulness.

At this point John of the Cross does not formulate this implication. Yet he ends on a conclusion no less radical and strange. In order to purify the soul of its appetites and its contradictions, God, he asserts, has to perform a greater work than when he created it out of nothing.[42] For affections and appetites resist "God more than nothingness does, since nothingness does not resist." This ties up with the previous point: the creature is "nothing and less than nothing." It resists God when it takes itself for something. By itself, it does not even belong to the order of being.

The theme of the mutual exclusion of contraries also belongs to the tractate on the *Dark Night*, where it serves to illustrate the painful dimension of the night of spirit. The problem is not to establish the need for the purification to be undergone during the soul's pilgrimage toward union with God; it is to point out the nature of this purification. The pain of this phase of the ascent to God derives from the fact that, if indeed two contraries cannot coexist forever in the soul, they nonetheless coexist for a certain amount of time, until one of them triumphs over the other. There can be no peaceful coexistence between them. Their open or silent struggle causes the pains felt during this night of spirit: "Since this divine infused contemplation has many extremely good properties, and the still unpurged soul that receives it has many extreme miseries, and because two contraries cannot coexist in one subject, the soul must necessarily undergo affliction and suffering. Because of the purgation of its imperfections caused by this contemplation, the soul becomes a battlefield in which these two contraries combat each other."[43]

The meaning is clear: coexistence of the soul's misery with infused contemplation is radically unstable. The latter has to drive out the former. Such a purification, however, is a struggle. It is painful for the soul as it finds itself drawn in opposite directions by hostile forces. The principle of the mutual exclusion of contraries takes on a function that may be called agonistic: it explains the sufferings of the night of spirit as resulting by the struggle of two contraries.

As a result a complementary question comes to mind. Do the "miseries" and the "good properties" correspond to two human attitudes that are essentially contradictory, as though one could not love a creature in any way while loving God? Or do these two loves behave as contraries, at this moment, by virtue of the nature of the contemplation to which the soul has been introduced?

In the following chapter, where he could just as well keep the theme of contraries, John of the Cross replaces it with that of "extremes." The theme remains that of the night of spirit: "The third kind of pain and affliction that the soul suffers here is caused by two other extremes, divine and human, which are joined here."[44] The next few lines identify these extremes with care: "The divine extreme is the purgative contemplation, and the human is the soul, the receiver of this contemplation." The divine extreme purifies the soul, "stripping it of the habitual affections and properties of the old man to which it is strongly united, attached, and conformed." The soul plunges into thick darkness, where it "feels that it is melting away and being undone by a cruel spiritual death." Thus Jonas suffered in the belly of the sea monster. For "it is fitting that the soul be in this sepulchre of dark death in order to attain the spiritual resurrection for which it hopes." In the night of spirit the very presence of God is felt and known in suffering.

This experience tallies with the explanation given in the *Ascent of Mount Carmel*. Extremes can be united only if they are alike: "That the two extremes, the soul and the divine Wisdom, may be united, they will have to come to accord by means of a certain likeness."[45] The soul suffers from the lack of resemblance in the extremes she feels in itself: the divine Wisdom or Word interiorly present, and itself in its creaturely nature. Extremes that are not alike act as contraries. There must take place either a transformation of the one in the likeness of the other, or the elimination of one of them. The human, provisionally considered contrary to God, will have to be transformed in the likeness of the divine Word; its evil or simply inferior affections will have to be expelled or annihilated.

We read in the *Dark Night*: " . . . in the spirit the possession of one contrary removes of itself the actual possession and sentiment of the other contrary."[46]

As one may see, the image of the extremes comes close, in John of the Cross's language, to that of the contraries. Yet they differ in such a way that an answer may be given to the above question. As extremes, the human and the divine exclude each other, not by antagonism, but by dissemblance. This exclusion will disappear as soon as a sufficient likeness will have been established between them. And as it is not the divine that can change, the human will have to receive a likeness of God.

Let us now remember the romance on the Incarnation: the bride, made in the image of the Son, differs from him in her flesh. Whence the words of the Father:

> In perfect love
> This law holds:
> That the lover become
> Like the one he loves;
> For the greater their likeness
> The greater their delight.
> Surely your bride's delight
> Would greatly increase
> Were she to see you like her,
> In her own flesh.[47]

In John's vision the entire process of the Incarnation amounts to polishing the likeness of the Word that has been placed in the human by its creation "in the image." The purifications of the mystical night are the reverse of this movement. They constitute a phase, at the deepest human level, and, this time, from the human side, of the search for a closer resemblance between these two extremes, the creature and the divine Word.

Further on in the treatise on the *Dark Night* the opposition of contraries illustrates the idea that differences may be incompatible: "The reason is that the affections, sentiments, and apprehensions of the perfect spirit, because they are divine, are of another sort and are so eminent and so different from the natural that their actual and habitual possession demands the habitual and actual annihilation and expulsion of natural affections and apprehensions, like two contraries which cannot coexist in one subject."[48]

Beyond this confrontation, "after the expulsion of all the actual and habitual obstacles which it formerly had, as we have said," the soul will be "ready to experience the sublime and marvelous touches of divine love," and will "behold itself transformed in these divine touches."[49] Here lies for the faithful the possibility of closer likeness to divine Wisdom. A way opens for the natural spirit to become perfect spirit. One has now to discover the passage to the way.

As he begins his commentary on the second stanza of the *Dark Night*, John of the Cross recalls the nature of the night. The soul "in its song continues to recount some of the properties of the darkness of this night." In this darkness it "subtly freed itself and escaped from its contraries, which always hindered its passage, for in the darkness of night it changed garb and disguised itself with three colored garments, which we shall discuss later; and by a very secret ladder, of which no one in the house knew, which, as we shall also explain at the proper place, is the living faith, covered and hidden by which it went out."[50]

Faith is the secret ladder by which to escape the conflict of contraries. It hides in itself the secret of liberation. Through it the way of freedom is open. It leads beyond the battlefield of the sundry contraries that one meets on the slopes of Mount Carmel. This brings John of the Cross, the doctor of the night, to become, above all in the second book of the *Dark Night*, the doctor of faith. His long analyses of the obstacles of all kinds, often called contraries,[51] that he has identified as defects of beginners and imperfections of proficients, converge upon this point. Before examining, in our next chapter, the experience of faith in the context of contemplation as understood by John of the Cross, we need to see how the commentaries on the *Canticle* and the *Flame of Love* present the expulsion of contraries from the soul.

In these two works the related images of contraries and of extremes are used, as in the *Dark Night*, to describe the struggle within the soul, and the sufferings that flow from them.

In stanza 8 of the *Canticle*, the present life, the life of this world, is contrasted with life in God. The soul realizes "that it has its natural life in God, through the being that it has in Him, and likewise its spiritual life through the love with which it loves."[52] It complains about lingering in this corporal life. It would prefer to be "truly living where it has its life through essence and through love." This is again, in the special perspective of the *Canticle,* the theme of night, since the soul, who is seeking for its beloved among creatures, cannot find him there. He seems to be hiding. All the bodily life veils his presence. In these conditions

> the insistence that the soul lays upon this is great, for it declares that it is suffering in two contrary ways—namely, in its natural life in the body and in its spiritual life in God, which in themselves are contrary; and since it lives in both, it has perforce to suffer great torment, for natural life is to it as death, since it deprives it of the spiritual life wherein it has employed all its being, life, and operations through love and affection.

This is of course the same doctrine as above. Two contraries draw the soul apart before she is admitted to the spiritual espousals. These contraries are not the soul and God, but rather the natural and the spiritual lives, life in nature, with its eating, drinking, sleeping, dispersion in everyday's thousand chores, and life in the spirit, focused on the one thing necessary. Compared to the latter, the former is death. Daily thinning out of attention in activities, even good ones, implies, at this level of the soul's ascent, its dying to centering on God's inner presence. The needs of natural, social, and moral life vie with the orientation of the whole self, through love, to the one thing necessary. Being, life, actions occupy the soul with its faculties and functions. Whatever it may do by itself to obtain union with God through its good intentions in all that it is and does, the soul unavoidably meets with failure, whence its torment.

If we turn to the parallel passage of *Canticle* (B), the author seems to be aware of an underlying paradox. If natural life and spiritual life are, as has been explained, contraries, God and nature are not. The theological objection remains to formulating this experience in terms of conflict: whatever one may feel in oneself and express in symbols and metaphors, God and created nature are not contraries, since God, who is outside and beyond all genus, cannot have a contrary. Although it follows the same line as version (A), version (B) of the *Canticle* makes it clearer in what sense one may speak of contradiction here. Life in nature and life in spirit "are contraries insofar as the one wars against the other."[53] The soul suffers from this, "since the one painful life thwarts the other delightful one." In the one the soul has "all its being and life by nature"; in the other "all its operations and affections through love."

The *Living Flame* also opposes these two contraries, though it intermingles the vocabulary of contradictions with that of extremes. Though distinct, the two images clarify and reinforce each other: " . . . for—oh, wondrous thing!—there arise within it contraries against contraries, some of which, as the philosophers say, bring the others to light; and they make war in the soul, striving to expel each other in order that they may reign within it. For, as this flame is of the brightest light, and assails the soul, its light shines in the darkness of the soul, which is also extreme."[54] In the context this has to do with the action of the Holy Spirit, who prepares the soul for the union of the espousals and the marriage. Version (B), which at this point is somewhat different in form, is also more paradoxical, as it introduces God himself in the dialectic it describes:

> For (O wonderful thing!) contraries rise up at this time against contraries—those of the soul against those of God which assail it. And as the philosophers say: One contrary when close to the other makes it more manifest. They war within the soul, striving to expel each other in order to reign. That is: The virtues and properties of God, extremely perfect, war against the habits and properties of the soul, extremely imperfect; and the soul suffers these two contraries within itself.[55]

In both texts the theme of extremes is then pursued further in a sort of commentary on John 1:5: "The darkness does not understand the light."

In the course of this chapter we have discovered a certain number of contraries with which John of the Cross illustrates the struggle of the soul with itself. In another parlance they are the components of the darkness that is opposed

to light in the soul. The light comes from God, the darkness belongs
to the human, even if one should acknowledge that, as created
realities, its ingredients ultimately proceed from God. Let us place
these main contraries in parallel columns:

Light of God[56]	affection for creatures
height of the Creator[57]	lowness of the creature
what is[58]	what is not
beauty of God	beauty of creatures
grace of God	graces and gifts of creatures
goodness of God	goodness (evil)
wisdom of God[59]	wisdom (pure and supreme ignorance)
liberty and dominion[60]	dominion and liberty (supreme servitude)
delight which God is[61]	delights and savors of the will
wealth which God is[62]	wealth and glory of the creature (supreme poverty and misery)
capacity of God[63]	desire for things
affection for God	affection for creatures
Creator	creature
spiritual	sensory
invisible	visible
eternal	temporal
heavenly food	sensory food
nakedness of Christ	satisfaction
fulness cause by the Spirit of God[64]	hunger
uncreated fulness	hunger
divine contemplation[65]	imperfections of the soul
divine extreme[66]	human extreme
affections of the perfect spirit[67]	affections of the natural spirit
spiritual life[68]	natural life
spiritual life	death
delight-ful life[69]	toilsome life
contraries of God[70]	contraries of the soul

One glance sufficiently shows that John of the Cross has done little more than identify *todo* and *nada*. He has listed many aspects of the All in opposition to corresponding aspects of "nothing." In so doing he has passed from abstraction and generalities to the concrete and to particularities. He has raised the question for his reader: what is the nothing that I must renounce today if I desire to be united to the All? To directors of conscience he has proposed a principle: in each case seek which aspect of the All will be attractive enough to wean a person away from the opposite aspect of nothing. Yet he has also unveiled the inherent dilemma of all ascent of Mount Carmel. His list of human contraries includes many realities without which one cannot live here below: grace and gifts, human goodness, liberty. The temporal and the visible cannot be abolished in this life, for we live in time despite the contingency of time, and in space despite the limited and changing, yet always visible, horizons of space. Must we truly reject all creaturely beauty?[71] Must we abandon all affection for creatures? Even bodily food, in its necessity for earthly existence, cannot be given up. Hunger and desire, in their very inferiority facing all uncreated fulness, keep a positive sense ordered to this fulness.

In order to bring the mystical logic of John of the Cross in full light, one needs a principle that will both unite and separate the All and the nothing.

CHAPTER 6

FAITH

aith is rarely mentioned in
the poetry of John of the Cross: once in the romance on the Incarnation; twice in the poem "For all the beauty." This is all the more
to be noticed as hope is often cited and love appears constantly.
The word *hope* is itself featured three times, and the verb *to hope*
also three times, in "I live, but not in myself"; once, and the verb
once, in "After a transport of love"; twice, and the verb once, in
the paraphrase of Psalm 137. As to *love* it would be superfluous to
count how often it is mentioned, whether as noun, as verb, as
adjective, or as past participle: most the poems are filled with references to the Beloved.

If we analyze the reality rather than the terms, however, the scene
changes. The entire itinerary of the *Ascent of Mount Carmel* takes
place in faith. Faith is the topic of the poem, the *Dark Night*, with
its two commentaries and their analysis of the first theological
virtue. Yet seldom is faith the subject matter or theme of the poems.
It provides their environment and framework rather than their focus;
it is the field of action, not the action. The poem of the Fountain,
"For I know well," is an exception. The first eight stanzas speak of
a knowledge—"I know"—that, since it refers to the mysteries of
the Trinity and the Incarnation, can only come from faith. Moreover,
it leads to a vision of the fountain in the Eucharist, obviously a
matter of faith.[1] One should probably also cite the stanzas "I entered
where I knew not," in which faith is lived in its dimension of
unknowing above all-knowing.

When it is explicitly mentioned, *faith* does not always keep the
same function. When the status of angels and that of men are con-

trasted in the romance on the Incarnation, angels appear already as possessors though human beings are only travelers (*viatores*). As creatures of down below, these live in the hope of faith:

> those of below in the hope
> of the faith He infused in them.[2]

Is the hope of faith a faith that is also hope, or a hope that, though formally distinct from faith, is yet given, infused, along with it? Whatever the answer, the rest of the poem opens up a perspective on the future, thus stressing the second of the theological virtues, hope, rather than the first, faith. On the contrary the poem "For all the beauty" speaks directly of faith itself. Faith is the key that reveals both the spiritual taste (st. 2) and the vision of beauty (st. 5):

> And its faith ascends so high
> That it tastes I-know-not-what
> That is found per adventure.[3]

> Yet such being His beauty
> That it is seen only by faith,
> One tastes it in I-know-not-what
> That is found per adventure.[4]

In this way faith acts as a key, opening up the soul to sensations of another order than the senses. In taste and vision it points to an I-know-not-what that we shall have to identify. In this case, then, faith must underlie many passages of the poems of John of the Cross where it is not explicitly mentioned. Spiritual tastes abound in the *Spiritual Canticle,* along with a new vision of nature and new perspectives on the horizon of human life as lived in searching for the Beloved. This I-know-not-what even occupies a prominent place in stanza 7 of the *Canticle.*

As it is obviously removed from the allegorical genre, the poetry of John of the Cross contains no image that would typically correspond to the theological virtue of faith. When it is not called by its name, faith belongs to the symbolic order. It primarily relates to the symbol of the night, which of course constitutes the warp and woof of the *Dark Night* and provides the central problematic of its two commentaries. As the second night of the soul, or the second moment of this night (John uses the two images indifferently), set between an unknowing of all creatures and the unknowable reality of the divine Being, faith is darkness to the intellect. The reality it connects with is beyond natural knowledge. Yet faith is not only darkness; it is also the place where the contraries that are the All (*todo*) and the nothing (*nada*) meet and oppose each other. Their confrontation sparks a light—an obscure light—thanks to which faith can act as true guide of the soul, in fact as its only guide, until the Beloved is met with during the third night, or the third moment of the night, just before dawn. In the *Dark Night* faith leads the soul in its escape:

> With no other light or guide
> Than the one that burned in my heart.[5]

Now this guide, which is clearly identified with faith in the *Ascent of Mount Carmel*, is equivalent to love at the end of the commentary on the *Dark Night*. On the one hand, John of the Cross states, as he will later explain it at length: "The soul consequently affirms that it departed 'in darkness and secure.' For anyone fortunate enough to possess the ability to journey in the obscurity of faith, as a blind man with his guide, and depart from all natural phantasms and intellectual reasonings, walks securely."[6] On the other hand, John also writes, before suddenly abandoning his commentary on the *Dark Night*: " . . . love alone, which at this period burns by soliciting the heart for the Beloved, is what guides and moves it and makes it soar to God in an unknown way along the road of solitude."[7]

Already one could ask, when reading the romance on the Incarnation, is faith really distinct from hope? A complementary question may be formulated at this point: is the faith of John of the Cross really distinct from love? This would be the case if the Mystical Doctor simply followed scholastic theology in its teaching on the theological virtues. But, analyzing the Christian contemplative experience, John cares little for speculation, except where this can provide illustrations for concrete aspects of the experience. Indeed, John of the Cross well knows the scholastic theology of faith, and above all that of Thomas Aquinas. Yet the construction of the *Summa theologica* is quite different from his own.[8]

In the *Ascent of Mount Carmel*, the contraries of faith are not, as in the *Summa*, sins in the strict sense: they are impediments from the natural order, which hinder faith in its role as "guide for the blind." All the lights of natural reason, all spiritual satisfactions, all acquired particular points of knowledge, whether they relate to material creation or to the realities of the interior and spiritual life, are contraries; they belong on the side of nothing over against the All. One must renounce them if faith is to act as guide, in darkness, to the All.[9]

Commenting on his poems, John of the Cross did attempt to incorporate the scholastic theology of faith in his own mystical theology. This is not without ambiguity, as one may gather from the texts of the *Ascent* that refer to faith as night and guide of the soul. Several passages of the commentary on the *Spiritual Canticle* will help us to envisage what faith is for John of the Cross.

The approach to faith adopted by John of the Cross in the *Ascent of Mount Carmel* starts from what "the theologians say": faith is "a certain and obscure habit of the soul."[10] This is equivalently the doctrine of Thomas Aquinas: "Faith is a habitus of the soul, through which eternal life begins in us, which makes the intellect assent to things that are not evident."[11] Thus there would be in faith, at the same time, obscurity and certainty. On the one hand, the object that is believed is not evident in the eyes of the human intellect. On the other, the intellect gives it nonetheless an unreserved assent, which St. Thomas explains as the result of an intervention of the will, itself inspired and strengthened by grace.[12] As a "habitus" faith is a capacity to act, a capacity to believe.[13]

The letter of John of the Cross's first explanations of faith thus embodies the Thomist principles. The obscurity of faith derives from the nature of revealed truths. These are "above all natural light and exceed all human intellect without any proportion."[14] But what follows no longer belongs to Thomism: faith not only believes, it also impedes understanding: "As a result, the excessive light of faith bestowed on man is darkness for him, because a brighter light will eclipse and suppress a dimmer one. . . . Similarly the light of faith in its abundance suppresses and overwhelms that of the intellect. For the intellect, by its own power, comprehends only natural knowledge, though it has the potency to be raised to a supernatural act whenever our Lord wishes."

This text makes two points. In the first place, the human intellect is an obediential capacity under the divine action that raises it, by pure grace, to a higher level than that of mere natural knowledge. In other words God acts on the intellect without destroying it, by filling in it a capacity that remains, at the natural level, a mere virtuality, with no right to, or anticipation of, the graces that God will give. In the second place, such an elevation of faith oppresses the soul in its natural resources, filling it with such a bright light that the intellect finds itself blinded. Thus faith is not only a cognitive habitus related to knowledge of the revealed or supernatural order. It also is an experience of blindness. Yet, paradoxically, this very blindness constitutes a new sort of light. Faith is a night, but the night is itself a precondition of dawn. It separates two kinds of lights, that of natural cognition and that of union to God in the spiritual espousals and marriage.

Echoing here scholastic theology, John of the Cross locates faith among the theological virtues, along with hope and love or charity, as in the *Ascent of Mount Carmel*, when he connects these three virtues with the soul's faculties, in keeping with a scholastic idea deriving from St. Augustine.[15] Here too one may sense a latent conflict between speculation and experience. Thomism, which set faith in the intellect with the intervention of the will, located the virtues of hope and of love in the will, thus departing from the Augustinian scheme according to which memory is the first faculty of the soul. John of the Cross returns to Augustine; he sees hope as the theological virtue of memory.[16] In the more allegorical language of the *Dark Night*, faith is a white garment, a kind of T-shirt; it serves as foundation for the green vest of hope, which is itself covered by a purple coat or mantle, charity.[17] In John of the Cross's perspective, it is irrelevant to wonder if the will intervenes during the act of faith in order, through a will to believe, to enable the intellect to assent with certainty to doctrines that are not evident. For faith, just like hope and love, is in the human soul by pure grace, with no precondition on the part of the psyche other than its obediential capacity. Moreover, the act of the intellect in faith is not an assent; it is not a positive act related to divine revelation.

On the contrary it is a voiding, an emptying, a negative act that is possible only by grace. "Faith darkens and empties the intellect of all its natural understanding and thereby prepares it for union with the divine wisdom."[18] Likewise, memory is void by hope; and "charity also empties and annihilates the affections and appetites of the will of whatever is not God, and centers them on Him alone. Thus charity prepares the will and unites it with God through love."

Now, seeking why faith, as seen by John of the Cross, is in the first place negative, and properly called a darkness or night for the soul and the intellect, one soon discovers that the scholastic answer to the question of the object of faith has been considerably modified. For Thomas Aquinas the object of faith is twofold: it includes both God in his self-revelation, and the articles of the creed, formulated by the Church and proposed to the faithful, *ex auditu*, in the oral proclamation of the gospel.[19] Does such a double object break the unity of faith? Indeed no, since the ultimate object, which is God, remains in the line of the proximate object, the article of faith, which precisely points in its direction. The formula, or, in the scholastic expression, the "enuntiable," presented by the Church in the form of the articles of the creed, is meant to lead to God, the "primary Truth," who alone is the "formal object of faith."[20]

John of the Cross keeps St. Paul's principle that faith is by hearing: "*Fides ex auditu*. This amounts to saying that faith is not a knowledge derived from the senses, but an assent of the soul to what enters through hearing."[21] The expression is ambiguous: what comes in by hearing is clearly something felt, mediated by sense. Yet it is correct, if faith is not a process of acquisition, but only of reception. In the context what comes from hearing is the Church's teaching, which "informs us of matters we have never seen or known either in themselves or in their likenesses, since there are none." Before such a knowing, which escapes both sense and rational evidence, one should "bow and blind our natural light." The objects of teaching, which are the formulations of the gospel, come from sense (hearing), but their truth corresponds to no evidence of sense or reason.

John of the Cross identifies these articles with the "truths of Scripture." They include "the works of the incarnation and the truths of faith."²² In the chapter of the *Ascent* where "the second kind of revelation," which is "the disclosure of secrets and hidden mysteries"²³ is studied, John notes that this disclosure happens in two ways, in keeping with the old distinction between theology and economy: "The first concerns God himself, which includes the revelation of the mystery of the most holy Trinity and Unity of God. The second concerns God in his works; this comprises the remaining articles of our Catholic faith and the propositions of truths that can be explicitly formulated about these works."

As so often happens in John of the Cross's prose, the expression is awkward, yet the sense comes out clearly: the object of faith includes the prophetic revelations of the Old Testament, bearing on what has been revealed about God and the divine promises, "the universe in general," or events concerning "kingdoms, provinces, states, families, and individuals." God, the author adds, "even in our time . . . grants revelations of this second category to whom He wills." He may inform certain persons, in a prophetic way, of what concerns their own future, or the world situation, or confirm to them the truths of faith already revealed to the Church.

The same principle applies here as to spiritual visions: one should not "store up or treasure" them.²⁴ Since "there are no more articles to be revealed to the Church about the substance of our faith,"²⁵ nothing among such particulars should retain our attention. One must "preserve the purity of faith." If God reveals to us again the truths that have already been revealed to the Church, we should believe them, "not because they are revealed again, but because they were already sufficiently revealed to the Church." Or better, "closing the mind to them, the soul should rest simply on the doctrine of the Church and its faith."

The Christian beliefs have been given once for all. Nothing needs to be added. One should adhere to them as is fitting, in keeping with what they are in reality. To the person who focuses attention only on their formulation, they remain like the names of colors to a blindman: "Only their names would be grasped, since the names are perceptible through hearing; but never their form or image, because these colors were never seen by him."²⁶ Furthermore, revealed truths cannot be rationally analyzed without damage to the purity of faith through the illusion of intellectual comprehension: "Other knowledge is acquired through the light of the intellect, but not the knowledge that faith gives. Faith nullifies the light of the intellect, and if this light is not darkened, the knowledge of faith is lost."[27]

That faith should impede the process of natural cognition, even regarding the articles of faith and what is known through them: this paradox is undoubtedly not Thomist. For then grace does not prolong nature, perfecting it in its own line in such a way that the exercise of natural reason may be at the service of faith, according to the principles of the *Summa theologica*.[28] On the contrary John of the Cross negates all contributions of natural reason to the comprehension of "what faith says." To remain pure faith must even demand the destruction of reason.[29] John of the Cross is thus profoundly aware of the radical difference that separates and even opposes the movement of faith and that of natural cognition, even when the latter bears on the articles of the creed. The movement of faith does not reinforce the natural knowledge of what the creed says. It rather voids the mind of it: "The soul must void itself of all that may fall in its capacity, so that, although it may know more supernatural things, it must always remain as if deprived of them and in darkness, like the blindman, holding on to dark faith, taking it as guide and as light, and attaching itself to nothing of what it understands, tastes, feels, and imagines."[30] The principle already formulated in regard to natural knowledge obtained in extraordinary ways (such as visions, successive or formal locutions, infused ideas) is still valid for the natural cognitive process. Faith is above all that can be "understood, tasted, felt, and imagined." If we do not effectively denude our intellectual powers, we "will not reach what is greater—what faith teaches." In this text "what faith teaches" no longer designates the articles of the creed, but what the articles point to beyond all human intellection.

The status of the formulas of faith is clarified in the commentary on stanza 11 of the *Spiritual Canticle:*

> O spring like crystal,
> If in these your silvered reflections,
> You would form suddenly
> The desired eyes,
> Which I bear outlined in my heart!

This is commented in these words:

> The propositions and articles which faith sets before us she
> [the bride] calls a silvered surface. . . . Faith is compared to silver
> with respect to the propositions which it teaches us, and the
> truths and substance which they contain in themselves are
> compared to gold; for that same substance which we now be-
> lieve, clothed and covered with the silver of faith, we shall
> behold and enjoy in the life to come, fully revealed, and with
> the gold of faith laid bare.[31]

As a point of fact, the poem does not allude to gold. The commen-
tary adds the gold in order to underline the difference between the
articles as taught and believed, and what it calls their substance,
and even, a few steps higher in the ascent of Mount Carmel, their
"understood substance." The propositions of faith, silver plating on
the divine reality, are "obscure and wrapped," the truths they teach
are "covered up and unformed,"[32] "formlessly and darkly veiled"
in the articles of faith. Later, "in the clear vision of God, then the
substance of faith will remain, stripped of this veil of silver, and in
color as gold."[33] The truths of God will then be discovered "clearly
and formally."[34] Indeed, the true God is already manifested to us
"covered with the silver of faith." And this silver that hides the
reality sharpens our desire for fuller knowledge. The soul therefore
exclaims:

> Oh, "If on that thy silvered surface;" by which she means the
> articles aforementioned, wherewith thou hast covered the gold
> of the divine rays, which are the "desired eyes" whereof she
> next speaks, saying:
>   You should form suddenly
>   The desired eyes![35]

From silver to gold there is the same infinite distance as between
night and dawn, blindness and sight, a mere sketch and the final
painting. Thus we may understand the expression, "what faith
teaches." It refers at times to articles and propositions, to nocturnal,
imperfect cognition, at times to the substantial reality, the divine
ray, the eternal glory perceived in the vision.

The identity of "what faith teaches" is confirmed by the commentary of stanza 13 of the *Canticle*. Explaining "resounding rivers, / the whisper of amorous breezes", which the poem associates to the Beloved, John of the Cross alludes to the notion, which has been traditional since Origen's commentary on the *Song of Songs*,[36] of the spiritual senses. Yet rather than engage in the sort of speculation that would seek to identify each sense and its object, he confines himself to the symbolic order, in view of the question: in regard to the divine communications in the spiritual espousals, what is the meaning of such images as taste, sight, hearing, smell? John remarks that in Scripture the most spiritual and highest divine communications are symbolized by hearing, the other senses being more evocative of the sweetness, the fullness, the richness of the divine communications. The symbol of God's "voice" entails, on the side of the reception of what is heard, the symbol of hearing. The voice of God is received in "the inmost substance of the soul" in the shape of a "most subtle and delicate knowledge,"[37] an "understood substance, stripped of accidents and imaginary forms." The "passive intellect" receives it, without the active intervention of the mind that would take place in the normal cognitive process of this-worldly things, "because it receives it passively, doing naught on its own behalf." So spiritual a communication, in which the soul does not act but is acted upon, is indicated by the symbol of hearing. Generally, in Scripture divine communication through hearing signifies "a manifestation of these naked truths in the understanding, or a revelation of the secrets of God, which are purely spiritual visions or revelations."[38] St. Paul did not write, in 2 Corinthians 12:4: "*Vidit arcana verba*, still less, *Gustavit arcana verba*, but, *Audivit arcana verba, quae non licet homini loqui*. Which is as though he had said: I heard secret words which it is not lawful for a man to utter."

Thus, the moment of faith is twofold. Besides hearing the Church's proclamation there is an interior hearing, the purely passive reception of the substance of what God says: "For even as faith, as St. Paul says likewise, comes by bodily hearing, even so that which faith teaches us, which is the understood substance, comes by spiritual hearing." As though John wanted to suggest that the image of spiritual senses should not be taken literally, hearing is then equated with sight: "Wherein it is clearly declared that to hear Him with the ear of the soul is to see Him with the eye of passive understanding. . . . Wherefore this hearing of the soul is seeing with the understanding."

In reality the language that John of the Cross has borrowed from Aristotelian epistemology (passive and active intellect) conveys here a doctrine that is rather different from the hylomorphism of its origin. For Aristotle, followed by Thomas Aquinas, all that is known by experience is received in the shape of an "impress species," which is a copy of the object of knowledge; received by the sense organs, this image is worked on by the active intellect, which abstracts therefrom the elements of universality that will make its comprehension possible. Once transformed by the active intellect into an abstract "express species," this is presented to the passive intellect that, with its help, understands the object it represents. Such would be the unconscious process of all cognition. The only exception would be, according to Aquinas, an infused knowledge that God would place in the intellect in a universal, already intelligible, form.[39]

The perspective of the Mystical Doctor is different. The knowledge of the formula of faith goes through the common process of the knowledge of words (successive, in the language of *Ascent*, 2:28), in which the two intellects take part as in Aristotle's schema. But knowledge of the substance of what faith teaches—the true sense of the formulas—is purely passive, entirely received. God alone acts in it. The intellect, which at this point is called passive, is not what philosophical analysis has isolated from the total cognitive process. It is, on the contrary, the whole soul, which has become, under the impact of the divine gift, totally receptive; the substance of the soul has structured itself as night in order to receive the light. Passivity, the second function of the intellect according to Thomas Aquinas, has been extended to the whole soul.

Just as the hylomorphism of knowledge has been transformed to account for the experience of faith as pure gift, the Pauline principle, "from hearing," has also been reinterpreted. It is now understood in two complementary ways. As regards the content of the gospel, one has to hear the external words spoken in teaching and preaching; but as regards what they mean, one must listen interiorly to "the subtle and delicate communication of the Spirit."[40] "What faith teaches," "what faith says" in the formulations of preaching and in credal statements, can be understood only in the inner experience that coincides with the spiritual espousals, when the night begins to give way to dawn. Up to this moment, before the "substance" of faith is "understood," faith remains dark; it is blind. For "what faith teaches" is no other than God himself, who infinitely transcends all understanding by created intellects:

> St. Paul implied this in his assertion: *Accedentem ad Deum oportet credere quod est* (He who would approach union with God should believe that He is) [Heb. 11:6]. This is like saying: To attain union with God, a person should advance neither by understanding nor by the support of his own experience or by feeling or imagination, but by belief in God's being. For God's being cannot be grasped by the intellect, appetite, imagination, or any other sense, nor can it be known in this life. The most that can be known and tasted of God in this life is infinitely distant from God and the pure possession of Him.[41]

The mark of faith, in its substance, is to establish contact between the faithful and the divine Being. The curious expression, "belief in God's being"[42] (or, more literally, "to believe His being") appears at a point where, from the angle of the profession of faith, one could have expected, "to believe that He is." It has no other purpose than to indicate this transcendental experiential dimension of faith. In the night, as one waits for dawn, one should entrust oneself to the Being of God beyond all formulations and all objects belonging to this world, beyond all proclamations and articles.

There already is, in the present life, at the moment of the spiritual espousals and marriage, an authentic experience of the substance of the faith. Reaching beyond the formulas does not depend on the intellect. It is not an understanding, but, in keeping with the espousals metaphor, an experience of love. Love, however, is not conceived as in classical Thomism. It does not consist in a motion of the will that so strengthens the intellect as to make it capable of assenting to the statements of faith with certainty in spite of their lack of evidence.[43] For John of the Cross, the intervention of love in faith parallels the purely passive reception by the intellect, blinded by the divine light, of the substance hidden under the formulations. The outline of the desired eyes is twofold; or there are two superimposed outlines. The one is made of blind knowledge, the other of love:

> But above this outline of faith there is another outline in the soul of the lover, which is of love, and this is according to the will; wherein the image of the Beloved is outlined in such a manner, and so completely and vividly pictured, when there is union of love, that it is true to say that the Beloved lives in the lover and the lover in the Beloved; and such manner of likeness does love make in the transformation of the two that are in love that it may be said that each is the other and that both are one.[44]

Faith is therefore, ultimately, more love than knowing. It is a direct, "substantial" experience, that, both in the ordinary language of common sense and in that, more technical, of speculative theology, pertains to the register of charity rather than to that of assent. One should therefore avoid reading John of the Cross's passages concerning faith as though they were scholastic discourses.[45] In them, faith is quite other than in the tractate of theologians. It includes hope and love. The whole person lives it and is transformed by it. Thus John of the Cross writes, at the beginning of the *Ascent of Mount Carmel:* the soul "soon enters the second night by living in faith alone, not a faith that is exclusive of charity, but a faith that excludes other intellectual knowledge, as we shall explain later. For faith does not fall into the province of sense."[46] It is not that charity would accompany faith, as it were, outside of it, as though the theological virtues had to act together by conjunction of the diverse faculties of the soul. Undoubtedly, John of the Cross distinguishes functionally between intellect, memory, and will, in which he locates respectively faith, hope, and love. But such a distinction applies only to the acts that originate in man. An act that proceeds from God to be passively received in man, who thereby becomes faithful, affects and commits the whole soul. At this level faith and love are two names for one reality, which is lived totally as both obscure knowledge and union of love. John of the Cross explains it in this way: "The state of perfection, which consists in perfect love of God and contempt of self, cannot exist without knowledge of God and of self."[47] Here, love is knowledge. Yet the perspective is reversed at once: knowledge is love: "Contemplation is a science of love, which, as we have said, is an infused loving knowledge of God, that both illumines and enamors the soul, until it leads it step by step to God, its Creator, since love alone is that which unites and conjoins the soul with God."[48] This is equivalently what has been said elsewhere of faith, as "the proximate and proportional means of union to God."[49]

Faith emerges from all this as a totality in which analysis may of course distinguish between faith in the strict sense, hope, and charity; yet experience cannot see these virtues as three successive, separable states of the soul. Whereas speculative theology places each of the theological virtues within one of the faculties of the soul, experience shows them so closely tied together that they cannot be truly distinct. Faith is love and hope, and conversely. What is said of one applies to the others because they are neither two nor three, but one: one substantial attitude of voiding before God who comes to fill the soul by uniting it to himself.

Indeed, John of the Cross can speak of a union "in the faculties" by the three theological virtues.[50] Now, however, union with God follows the emptying of the faculties: in faith the intellect does not understand; in hope the memory is empty; in love the will desires nothing. For if God can by himself fill and satisfy the faculties of the soul, he cannot be connumerated with things of this world. God is not another thing that may be known, expected, desired, by nature: "Consequently these three virtues place a soul in darkness and emptiness in respect to all things."[51] The *Ascent of Mount Carmel* is structured in keeping with this principle.[52]

Elsewhere, John of the Cross uses another image: he speaks of the substance of the soul rather than of its faculties. One may even feel that he prefers a substantial language to express the deepest reality and to describe the summits of mystical experience. Already we have referred to the "understood substance" of faith. The "substantial locutions" of the *Ascent* belong to what John of the Cross identifies as the heart of mystical experience: besides "successive locutions," heard by the soul's ear, "formal locutions," infused by supernatural gift, there are "substantial locutions," spoken by God, through which the soul finds itself interiorly transformed without having had to act. These are "important and valuable because of

the life, virtue, and incomparable blessings they impart to the soul.
A locution of this sort does more good for a person than a whole
lifetime of deeds."[53] All other supernatural communications must
be refused and relinquished; but substantial words cannot be re-
jected. They impose their effect. They are active, performative words.
Through them God does what he proclaims. They are called substan-
tial because they transform the substance of the soul.

The description of union to God in the *Ascent of Mount Carmel*
does affirm that God may at times unite himself to the faculties
of the soul separately; yet he also unites himself to them as a whole,
taken together, in a "total" union, which itself can be provisional
or permanent.[54] At its deepest this last form of mystical union is
a "total and permanent union in the substance of the soul as regards
the obscure habitus of union; for, as regards the act [of union], we
shall show later, with divine help, that there cannot be a permanent
union in the faculties in this life, but only a provisional union."[55]
Such a union in the substance, by divine gift, will be a "union of
likeness."[56]

It is precisely to the substance of
the soul that God communicates himself in the spiritual marriage,
and already, though less continuously, in the espousals. This is
described in stanza 32 of the *Canticle*, when the bride, addressing
her Beloved, beseeches:

> Hide yourself, dearest,
> Turn your face to the mountains,
> And do not wish to speak;
> But look at her companions
> As she goes through strange islands.

As the commentary explains it, "The face of God is his divinity,
and the mountains are the faculties of the soul—memory, under-
standing, and will."[57] The bride asks that her faculties be filled by
God, so that she may receive from him "divine intelligence ...,
divine love ..., divine possession of glory." Yet the soul's faculties
will not thereby become mediators of union; rather, they will find
themselves filled with an overflow that will pour into them when

the substance of the soul is filled with God. The face of God is "essential communication of his Divinity, without any kind of intermediary in the soul, through certain contact thereof with the Divinity. This is a thing far removed from all sense and accidents, inasmuch as it is a touch of pure substances—that is, of the soul and the Divinity."

The divine communications no longer come from the outside; they are "so substantial and so intimate" that they cannot be understood by creatures. "For substance cannot be communicated in the senses, and thus a thing that can be apprehended by sense is not essentially God."[58]

This sort of expression recurs in the *Living Flame,* when John of the Cross admires the infinite tenderness of God's omnipotence. How delicate is the Almighty! "Oh, delicate touch, Thou Word, Son of God, who, through the delicateness of thy divine being, dost subtly penetrate the substance of my soul."[59]

God should not tell it to the world, since the world cannot understand it! Yet John of the Cross also says: "Thou shalt touch them the more delicately because Thou art hidden in the substance of their souls, which have been beautified and made delicate."[60] This deeply interior touch of deification is all the more interior "according as thy divine being wherewith Thou touchest the soul is far removed from all ways and manners, and free from all outward husk of form and figure!"[61] God's tenderness is proportional to his power. The amplitude of his touch is measured by his interiority to the soul. No longer at the surface, or in transient acts of the faculties, or in steady habits that help to act with ease, does God make himself felt in the deep and sweet touches of spiritual marriage. To speak truly, God no longer makes himself felt, for what now takes place does not pertain to the domain of feeling, be this physical sensation, psychic impression, or affective sentiment; it belongs to the realm of being and substance. Whence the language of John of the Cross: "believe his Being," "touch of naked substances," "essential communication," "divine touches in the substance of the soul in the loving substance of God."[62]

What happens at the level of substance may also be described in terms of knowing-unknowing as well as in terms of love. John of the Cross's presentation and explanation of spiritual experience effect what St. Bonaventure would have called a "reduction" of the

spiritual faculties to the substance of the soul.[63] To know by way
of wisdom rather than of science implies going back to the highest
causes of what one tries to know. The faculties of memory, intellect,
and love are properly understood only when identified with the very
substance of the soul in its capacity to act. Hope, faith, and charity
are the substance of the soul in its union to God as ground, truth,
and purpose of creaturely being. The most intimate divine touches
therefore reach, not indeed the faculties as distinct potencies at-
tracted by particular objects and separate actions, but rather the
substance of the soul at its deepest, the faculties being then plunged
in darkness. This will be followed by a transformation of created
being, and hence, as we shall see, by a recovery of the faculties and
of sense at a higher plane of being.

The substantial language amounts, in respect to being, to what
the symbol of the night represents in respect to the knowing which
is an unknowing, or the symbol of the "way which is no way" in
the *Ascent of Mount Carmel,* or, in a more philosophical vein, to
the "modeless mode": "As regards the road to union, entering on
the road means leaving one's own road, or better, moving on to the
goal; and turning from one's own mode implies entry into what
has no mode, that is, God. . . . Having the courage to pass beyond
the exterior and interior limits of one's nature, one enters within
supernatural bounds, that have no mode, yet in substance possess
all modes."[64]

We are now in a position to under-
stand the doctrine that John of the Cross sums up in the saying
that faith is "the proximate means of ascent to union with God."[65]
This theme runs like a refrain through the *Ascent of Mount Carmel,*
to which it provides an indispensable key. It is equally central to the
other commentaries. Yet its interpretation requires careful attention.

Let us remember the warning that is inserted in the prologue to
the *Ascent:* this work has not been composed for the sake of every-
one, but only for "some persons of our holy Order of the primitive
observance of Mount Carmel, both friars and nuns, whom God
favors by putting them on the path leading up this mount, since
they are the ones who asked me to write this work. Because they
are already detached to a great extent from the temporal things of

this world, they will more easily grasp this doctrine on the nakedness of spirit."[66]

When John of the Cross speaks of faith, he has in mind faith as it is lived by those who have begun to ascend Mount Carmel. As is shown by the dedication of the commentary on the *Living Flame* to dona Ana de Peñalosa, these are not confined to monasteries. They may be called by their vocation to live in the world. Yet for the ones as for the others, faith is not only an acceptance of the formulations of the gospel in the Scriptures, the traditional creeds, and the Church's proclamation. Such a recognition has of course served as point of departure for all believers, who make their intellect captive to the divine revelation known by hearing. At this stage of the beginners' journey, faith is properly called a virtue: it is already a power (the meaning of *virtus* in Latin) that enables them to act in a new mode, unknown to unbelievers. It is then naturally associated with other virtues. As in all the Catholic theology of his time, John of the Cross takes it for granted that there are three theological virtues and four cardinal moral virtues. The former provide the framework for the *Ascent of Mount Carmel*. Yet the Mystical Doctor is not concerned about this faith of beginners, which, because its immediate object is known by hearing, still depends in part on a purely natural cognitive process.

Besides, John of the Cross never considers faith in its "unformed" state as determined by the scholastic authors. Faith without love, which can be no more than belief, plays no role in his thought. He warns us of this himself: the faith that constitutes the second night of the soul "does not exclude charity."[67] The backdrop to this statement comes from scholastic theology, according to which faith, if it is to contribute to salvation, must be informed by charity. The hylomorphic theories of Aristotle, as these were understood and applied by medieval theologians, have left their mark on this approach. But John of the Cross cares little for Aristotle and philosophy. What matters to him is simply that faith must be living in the soul, and that such a life never thrives apart from love.

Moreover, the faith of which John of the Cross speaks has dimensions that cannot pertain to the mere belief in revealed truths, even informed by charity. "This abyss of faith"[68] in which everything is absorbed as in a night, evokes much more than a conviction of certainty before revealed truths. The faith of John of the Cross is such that it inspires seemingly contradictory analogies. The source of a "wondrous light,"[69] it is also "dark and pure."[70] Whether it is called light or night, it contains in itself a direction, a movement, for it is a way: "The way of approach to you, O God, is a holy way, namely, purity of faith."[71]

Faith has thus become a power of interior transformation. At times John of the Cross classifies it among the virtues. He then attempts to show, as in the second part of the *Ascent of Mount Carmel,* how it transforms the intellect by blinding it, by steeping it in a night that leads to this other night that God is for the human creature. At times faith appears as a universal and total principle of transformation of the faithful. Then, it is "that admirable means of advancing to God, our goal,"[72] "the proximate means for the high union with God through love,"[73] "the means which touches Him and bears with him a proximate likeness,"[74] "the proximate and proportionate means to union with God,"[75] "the legitimate and proximate means of union with God,"[76] "the proper and adequate means by which the soul unites itself to God."[77] Such affirmations are confirmed by the opposite reflection, concerning what cannot unite to God. Spiritual visions "which remain impressed within the soul"[78] should simply be ignored and relinquished. Because "they deal with creatures that bear no proportion or essential conformity to God," they "cannot serve the intellect as a proximate means of union with God."

This raises the question of the analogy of being. Is there any kind of resemblance and proportion in their being between the Creator and his creatures? John of the Cross was writing after the Fourth Council of the Lateran (1215), which had summed up the previous theological tradition in a remarkable formula: "Between the Creator and the creature one cannot find a resemblance without finding a greater dissemblance."[79] This amounts to saying that all signs of a resemblance between God and creatures are set within a greater dissemblance, and therefore that all likeness between God and the soul implies as its context a more global unlikeness. When he considers God as night for the soul, the Mystical Doctor affirms above all that a dissimilarity separates them ineluctably. Experience reveals God as the Unknown who, blinding the soul as he comes to it, plunges it into the night. Yet as he also speaks of union with God, John needs to show that a union of radically dissimilar realities is nonetheless possible. In so doing he explicitly refers to the problem of analogy: "Let it be recalled, then, that according to a philosophical axiom all means must be proportionate to their end. That is, they must manifest a certain accord with and likeness to the end—of such a degree that they would be sufficient for the attainment of the desired goal."[80] Some examples follow: a lane has to touch the city where it leads; fire has to touch the log, heat being the means of union that will enable the log to burn. Likewise, "if the intellect is to reach union with God in this life, insofar as is possible, it must take that means which touches Him and bears a proximate likeness with Him."

John of the Cross in fact has mixed together two kinds of analogies. His first instance belongs to the order of analogy "from one to one" (*unius ad unum*): the path touches the city. The second is of the order of analogy of attribution "from two to a third" (*duorum ad tertium*): the two entities of log and fire are joined through a third, heat, that already has direct contact with the fire. As one may see, this second analogy presupposes the first. John of the Cross concludes from this that union to God must have the characteristics of both. Both analogies are covered by the expression, "proximate means."

Applying this principle to the created universe as a whole, the Doctor of Carmel has no difficulty showing that the creature, be it "superior or inferior,"[81] has neither direct contact with God nor likeness to the divine Being. Yet the reason for this does not follow from the illustrations provided. It stems from a third sort of analogy, in which one may recognize the exact translation of the formula of the fourth Lateran Council. To the question of an analogy between the Creator and the creature a twofold answer is now proffered. Yes: "All creatures carry with them a certain relationship to God and a trace of Him (greater or less according to the perfection of their being)." But, no: "God has no relation or essential likeness to them; rather, the difference that lies between his divine Being and their being is infinite." The concept of analogy that is involved here is called "of proper proportionality." This analogy goes "from two to two" (*duorum ad duo*). It construes a proportion that, even if it implies a certain likeness in keeping with the level of created being that is considered, contributes nothing to bridging the abyss between creatures and the Creator.

One reaches therefore a negative conclusion: there is neither contact nor essential likeness between God and creaturely being. Nothing that can be fancied by imagination or conceived by reason can provide a "proximate means of union with God."[82] Furthermore, "everything that the intellect can understand, the will experience, and the imagination picture, is most unlike and disproportioned to God, as we have said."[83] Nothing of all that can "serve as a proximate means for the high union with God through love." A proximate means must exhibit sufficient likeness to God. And this would imply, in John of the Cross's perspective, that it is in direct contact with the divine Being. Whence the conclusion: "Manifestly, then, none of these ideas can serve the intellect as a proximate means leading to God. In order to draw nearer the divine ray the intellect must advance by unknowing rather than by the desire to know, and by blinking itself and remaining in darkness rather than by opening its eyes."

This elimination of all creatures as proximate means of union with God, on the ground that none of them shows sufficient likeness to the divine Being or enjoys direct contact with it, opens the gate to the only means of union, faith, which "alone is the proximate and proportional means for the soul to unite itself to God."[84] John of the Cross attempts to show how faith is such a proportionate means: "For the likeness between faith and God is so close that no other difference exists than between God as believed and God as seen. Just as God is infinite, faith proposes Him to us as infinite; as there are three Persons in one God, it presents Him to us in this way; and as God is dark to our intellect, so does faith dazzle and blind us."

Such a likeness or proportion results from the effect wrought by faith in the soul: the infinite and Triune God is known, yet in unknowing and in darkness. This third point allows us to think that John of the Cross at this point is not alluding to the articles of faith and their groping formulations of the mystery of the divine essence and the Trinity. By themselves the creeds do not dazzle the intellect to which they rather bring, along with a vocabulary, a limited external light. Yet no sooner does the soul endeavor to understand, to taste, and to love God, does it find itself plunging into the night. Faith is the proportional means of union to God, in that it makes us know God as he is: it "believes his Being." Faith is also a proximate means, that is, in direct contact with God; and thereby it is unknowing, night, and darkness to the soul. How faith touches God and makes the believer touch God, John of the Cross does not really explain. Could he explain it, he would have passed beyond the night of faith: God would then be seen and no longer believed.

The antecedents of John of the Cross's doctrine on faith are to be found among the ancient and medieval mystics rather than in the theologians. Faith-darkness, faith-love, love-intellection are well attested, if not frequent, themes of the mystical doctrine of the Middle Ages. Denys and Bonaventure for the night, Gregory the Great and William of St. Thierry for the knowing of love, may be sources of the Mystical Doctor's thought rather than Thomas Aquinas, even though the Angelic Doctor also insists, in his tractate on the "divine names," on our fundamental unknowing of God.[85]

Yet if the sixteenth century did itself witness another theology of faith that came close to that of John of the Cross, one has to look for it, paradoxically perhaps, in the works of Martin Luther.[86] The diverging careers of the two great reformers should not lead us astray. For Luther, who presumably was indebted for it to the Rhineland mysticism with which he was acquainted through his editions of what he called the *Theologia germanica*,[87] faith demands a total renunciation both to rational knowing (whence the pejorative expression of "harlot reason") and to the natural will (whence the "unfree will," which brought Luther in conflict with Erasmus). Here also the relationship of faith to creaturely being is negative. Faith is an outside garment. God gives it by a sovereign and absolute act. It is like the substantial words of John of the Cross, which effect what they mean. Not only is faith an assent to credal formulas; it is first of all an inner life that transforms the sinner by making him pass from his own sin to the alien justice of Christ and that entails love and hope as its necessary fruits. It brings about a total reversal of worldly values and an intimate union with Christ. God known in faith is, for the German theologian as for the Spanish mystic, hidden.

He is the *Deus absconditus*, the hidden God of apophatic theologies and of the mysticisms of unknowing. For the one as for the other, the path is that of faith alone; it is, in contrast with the human need for security, a "wayless way."

Admittedly there are differences. And above all Luther is concerned about the beginners who constitute the great mass of the people of God, whereas John of the Cross writes for contemplatives, whose transformation by faith is already advanced. Yet if the Mystical Doctor can guide people in the ascent of Mount Carmel, this is because the ways of access to the foot of the mountain are those that Martin Luther mapped out. As a scholar who is well acquainted with the thought of Luther puts it, the German reformer "does not perhaps sufficiently explain what sanctification is. But all his efforts tended to fight all that threatens sanctification."[88] His most acute insights support the teaching of John of the Cross in the *Ascent of Mount Carmel*.

This excessively cursory comparison of the two great reformers posits a critical question in regard to the theology of John of the Cross. For Luther "faith alone" runs parallel to "Christ alone," in whom faith finds all at once its source, its justification, and its object. Luther's focus on Christ seems, at least on the surface, better marked than that of John of the Cross, whose references are more openly Trinitarian. Yet could it have been by accident or absentmindedness that the Doctor of Carmel chose to call himself, "of the Cross?" For the answer to this question, we will have to consider how the Mystical Doctor identifies the Beloved.

CHAPTER 7

THE SECOND *CANTICLE*

Starting back from the *Canticle* of thirty-one stanzas composed in Toledo, such as it was outlined in chapter 3, we already know the fundamental structure of the poem of thirty-nine stanzas. The basic theme of the poem being the search for her Beloved by a human lover, the pursuit of this theme reveals a framework that was formulated as follows:[1]

Search (I)	st. 1–4
Preliminary answer (1)	st. 5
Search-desire (II)	st. 6–11
First full answer (2)	st. 12
Encounter (I), responding to search (I)	st. 13–16
Encounter (II), responding to search-desire (II)	st. 17–27
Second full answer (3)	st. 28–30
Conclusion	st. 31

As we have seen, this conclusion—the lover's dream—placed her at a threshold which, in her dream, she thought was already beyond her. This was the entrance to the ultimate encounter with the Beloved.

We actually know very little of the reasons why John of the Cross added eight stanzas to his poem. Most certainly the addition was made in two parts: first, stanzas 32–43, then, some time later, 35–39. More information is available on the last part, thanks to the clear testimony of a Carmelite sister at Beas, Francisca de la Madre de Dios.

After his escape from the friary in Toledo where he had been captive, John rested for several weeks at the home of don Pedro Gonzalez de Mendoza. After taking part in the general chapter of the men's Reformed Carmel that took place in Almodóvar in October 1578 he was appointed to a small community of friars in the southern province of Jaén, in Andalusia, at a spot called the *Calvario.* John spent seven and a half months there. As this was only a few kilometers distant from the Carmelite sisters of Beas de Segura, he traveled there once a week as their regular confessor. One of the sisters was Francisca de la Madre de Dios, to whom John of the Cross later gave his *Sayings of Light and Love.* In his ensuing assignments, in Baeza and in Granada, John kept contact with the convent of Beas. Toward the end of 1581 he saw the great Teresa for the last time, in Avila, whence he returned to Granada by way of Beas. From the end of January 1582 John resided in Granada as prior of the reformed community. It must have been in 1583 or 1584, when he was finishing his commentary (A) on the *Spiritual Canticle,* that he wrote stanzas 35–39 during a visit to the Carmelites of Beas de Segura. In a conversation he asked Sister Francisca how she made her mental prayer. Francisca answered that her prayer consisted "in looking at the beauty of God and rejoicing that he has it."[2] Francisca's account of the episode continues: "The saint found such joy in this that for several days he said most elevated things, that we admired, about God's beauty; and so, carried away by this love, he wrote five stanzas, beginning with 'Let us rejoice, Beloved / And let us go to see in your beauty . . . '."

An indirect suggestion sufficed to turn all the thoughts of John of the Cross toward the beauty of God, a topic that was not featured in the *Canticle* of Toledo, and to compose the five stanzas. One should presumably retain from Francisca's story that all of these verses, and not only stanza 35, are focused on the divine beauty.

As to stanzas 32–34, they already were in existence at that point. They must have come to light, either in 1581 or 1582, when John was prior in Baeza, where he had charge of the students of the Order, or in 1583–84 in Granada, shortly before the inspiration of the last five stanzas. As is suggested by the internal evidence, these were not born of a spontaneous poetic explosion, sparked, like the verses on divine beauty, by a fortunate accident. Rather, they resulted from deliberate composition.

The testimony of a Carmelite priest, Jerome de San José, has drawn attention to the fact that only in stanza 32 is the Beloved called by the term of endearment, *Carillo* (literally, "little dear"). According to Jerome this would have been suggested to the poet by a popular song that he heard sung by a child while he was still in captivity in Toledo.[3] He would have heard three verses of a humoristic love-song:

> I am dying of love,
> Little Dear, what shall I do?
> —Well then, die, ohé!

However, this story is highly suspect. In the first place, stanza 32 was not written in captivity. In the second, it would have been most unlikely that John could have heard a child singing in the street, the tiny vent of his captivity cell not overlooking the street.[4]

Despite the lack of direct testimony, I would be inclined to think that Francisca de la Madre de Dios was herself no stranger to the inspiration of stanzas 32–34. For notes 26 and 27 of the *Sayings of Light and Love*—addressed to her—may provide a clue to the sequence of the stanzas. First, the end of note 26 contains an invitation to hide: "Go forth and exult in your glory! Hide yourself in it and rejoice, and you will obtain the supplications of your heart."[5] Next, note 27 evokes the peace of solitude: "The very pure spirit does not meddle with exterior attachments or human respects, but it communes inwardly with God, alone and in solitude as to all forms, and with delightful tranquillity, for the knowledge of God is received in divine silence." Now, these are exactly the themes of stanzas 32 and 34 of the *Canticle*. Stanza 32 begins with an invitation to hide: "Hide yourself, Little Dear"; and stanza 34 underlines, in each of its verses, the solitude of the dove:

> In solitude she lived,
> In solitude she has now built her nest,
> In solitude he guides her
> All alone, her Dear One,
> Also in solitude of love wounded.

One may object that the "Hide yourself" of stanza 32 is addressed to the Beloved, whereas that of the *Sayings of Light and Love* is an invitation to the soul. Yet the author seems to answer, in his commentary on the poem: "As though she were to say: 'Dear Spouse of mine, withdraw thee into the inmost part of my soul, communicating thyself to it after a secret fashion, and manifesting to it thy hidden wonders, which are far removed from all mortal eyes.'"[6] In other words the solitude to which she invites the Beloved is her own. Here, the commentary is closer to the poem than for the preceding sections, since its redaction is under way when the poet adds the present verses. Moreover, as is sufficiently indicated by the "declaration" on stanza 34, solitude, freedom, and love are all realities that are implied one in the other and reciprocal attitudes shared by the Beloved and the lover. The exchange of beauty, which will follow stanza 35, is not far distant. The conversation with Sister Francisca will take place in a spiritual context already prepared by stanzas 32 and 34 and by the spiritual intimacy of the *Sayings of Light and Love*.

As to stanza 33, with its "White little dove" that does not echo anything in the *Sayings*, it comes at the right spot, as we will see further down, between the call to the Beloved to hide, and the Beloved's description of the solitude of the loving soul.

Stanzas 32–34 exhibit characteristics of a purposeful adjunction. This is clear from the first verses. After the dream of stanza 31, where, in the guise of nymphs, the soul evoked the daughters of Judea, asking them not to wake her up by making noise in the garden for she was asleep in her Beloved's arms, the soul now turns to her Beloved. Her first words, "Hide yourself," reverse the perspective of the first stanza of the poem: "Where are you hiding . . . ?" In other words we are at a new departure; we begin a new reading. What was a hiding place at the start of the poem and was not desired because the lover thought it separated her from her Beloved, is now desired precisely as hiding place. For she knows that she can be united with the Beloved only in hiding and in secret. Such a reversed situation in relation to the beginning of the poem can only result from waking up to reality. The soul emerges from her mystical slumber, awakens to a new level of being, and understands the secret conditions of union with the Beloved. The following verses sharpen the change of perspective by re-using words that have already been pronounced, visions that have already been seen, but also by placing them at this new level where the lover henceforth lives:

Turn with your face to the mountains:

These are the "mountains" of stanza 3, in which the soul used to wander in search of her Beloved.

And desire not to say it:

so that the Beloved may behave like the creatures of stanza 6: they could not tell the lover what she wished to know; yet for them it was incapacity to speak, while for him it is a necessary attitude to protect the secrecy of their encounter.

But look at the companions:

the Beloved is invited to look at the creatures that the lover addressed in stanza 4 and that could not then answer her; but under the gaze and before the face of the Beloved the creatures acquire a new meaning: they are now the companions

Of her who goes through strange islands:

we are once again at the "strange islands" of stanza 12, where the lover found her Beloved at last in the very nature of this world, his creation, which so shared in his love that she could then exclaim:

> My Beloved, the mountains,
> solitary wooded valleys,
> strange islands . . .

In this way the bride reminds him of their union. The creatures-companions no longer belong to the order of nature-reflection, as in stanza 4, but to that of nature-silence, for the Bridegroom alone should now speak.

In turn the Bridegroom looks again at the vistas opened by the

spiritual marriage and evoked by the bride at her waking. He recalls
that the bride, like the dove—as he called her in stanza 12 ("Come
back, dove . . . ")—has responded to his call. She has returned. Her
return is delicately described in stanza 33:

> The small white dove
> To the ark with the twig has returned;
> And already the turtledove
> Her desired mate
> By the green banks has found.

Here the diminutives *palomica* (little dove) and *tortolica* (small
turtledove) are terms of endearment that echo the diminutive *Carillo*
(little dear) employed by the bride. One may see them as signs of
an intimacy that is growing in tenderness. And thus the added
stanzas lead us to a deeper level of the spiritual marriage between
the soul and the Beloved. These are now in secret solitude, but a
shared solitude, as appears in stanza 34, where solitude is evoked
in each verse, echoing again at another level the "sonorous solitude"
of stanza 14.

The Beloved is himself "by love wounded." Formerly a "wounded
stag" (st. 12) who sought fresh air high up in the mountain, he now
simply becomes the soul's companion, who will live with her in
solitude in her own nest. Between the two of them a wondrous
exchange takes place: the Bridegroom is led to take the bride's place;
he lives, in his own way, in reverse, the quest that she formerly
lived as she sought after him. Thus he goes seeking her in the
mountains . . . , in the stillness . . . , among her companions in the
strange islands . . . ; he becomes the small dove's companion on the
green river banks . . . , making her solitude his own . . . , and, like
her, he has been wounded by love.[7]

The intuition of divine beauty,
sparked by Sister Francisca's confidence, fell in the right context.
The solitude exchange continued, yet transformed into an exchange
of beauty, as appears both from the poem and from the commentary.

Hitherto, the beauty (*hermosura*) evoked in the *Canticle* has been
twofold. There has been the beauty of stanza 5: it reached creatures

from the eyes of the Beloved who, passing by, had looked at them, thus giving them the quality of nature-reflection after being a nature-trace in the first stanzas of the poem. There also has been the beauty of stanza 24, associated to "gracefulness"; it likewise derived from the eyes of the Beloved caressing his lover: she has thus received the quality, through the Bridegroom's gift, of nature-icon. It is always the Beloved who, as he passes by, spreads beauty on all that he touches with his glance. Beauty is not inborn in creaturely being; it is a gracious gift. More precisely, it is what remains of a passing glance from the "desired eyes," whose imprint the lover already carries in her heart. Yet this imprint does not suffice to create beauty: this has to come from the eyes themselves, from the loving eyes, of the Beloved.

The verses of stanza 35 are marked by a restrained overflow that the commentary will let out:

> Let us rejoice, Beloved,
> And let us go to see in your beauty . . .

The beauty in question is no longer that of creatures, but that of the Beloved himself. By the same token it belongs to the lover. From this shared beauty, which is common to both since the Beloved has given it totally to her, the transformation of the past into the future continues. The "high caverns of stone" where they will go together (stanza 36) recapitulate the "caverns of lions" of stanza 15 as well as the "cellar" of 17. Instead of heraldic coats of arms around the nuptial bed, transcosmic depths, the attributes of the divine Word, form a halo around the universe. "Over there" (*allí*) they both will enter, in a place of unveiling similar to the thrice-repeated "over there" of stanza 18, the "interior cellar" where, in a bold image, he had given her the breast. Now, however, the Beloved is more than a life-giving breast; he is life itself, bestowing on her what he already gave her "the other day," that is, according to the commentary, on the day of her baptism or even, in the remoter past, on the day of her creation in Adam in the "grace and innocence" of original justice.[8] This gift of "cleanness and purity" must coincide with a state of "transformation" and "perfection." This perfect being is imaged by the creatures of stanza 38, as previously by those of stanza 13: imaging does more than show, since the image is identical with what it represents, in the flame of the Holy Spirit. Yet one should not forget that stanzas 35–38 are set in the future tense. They express the bride's hopes and they formulate an invitation to the Beloved to perfect his gift. The experience that is anticipated in hope is not yet directly lived. It will be the experience of eternity beyond death.

In his commentary on beauty John of the Cross lets himself be carried away by pure, unrestrained lyricism. The text, which has often been quoted, needs to be read with great care. It sums up, as one may say, the deepest meaning of the *Spiritual Canticle.* The beauty of the Beloved becomes that of the bride, and vice versa:

> Which signifies: Let us so act that, by means of this exercise of love aforementioned, we may come to see ourselves in thy beauty: that is, that we may be alike in beauty, and that thy beauty may be such that, when one of us looks at the other, each may be like to thee in thy beauty, and may see himself in thy beauty, which will be the transforming of me in thy beauty; and thus I shall see thee in thy beauty and Thou wilt see me in thy beauty; and Thou wilt see thyself in me in thy beauty, and I shall see myself in Thee in thy beauty; and thus I may be like to Thee in thy beauty, and Thou mayest be like to me in thy beauty, and my beauty may be thy beauty, and thy beauty my beauty; and I shall be Thou in thy beauty and Thou wilt be I in thy beauty, because thy beauty itself will be my beauty.[9]

This unforgettable text traces a progress from the exchange of love between the human creature and the Creator in spiritual marriage to the mutual experience of divine beauty. This experience is itself gradual, going from a similarity in beauty to the point where, in exchange of looks, each seems to be the other; and further to the point where each really sees the other in divine beauty; and finally to the point where each will see himself in the other, still in the divine beauty that belongs to the Bridegroom. The beauty of the one will indeed be also the other's, so that, all in all, each will be the other too.

More clearly than in the poem, the commentary shows that this is much more than an evocation of eternal life. Already in spiritual marriage this exchange in divine beauty starts, and it will never be over. Such is the meaning of the verse, "Let us enter farther into the thicket": "This thicket of wisdom and knowledge of God is so profound and vast that, for all that the soul may know, she can ever enter farther still, so vast it is. . . . "[10]

Theologically, according to the commentary, the process of the adoption of the children of God goes that far. In the already symbolic language of a certain scholasticism, which was known to John of the Cross, this gave access to "morning knowledge" (knowledge of creatures in the divine Word), which entailed a higher degree of "evening knowledge" (knowledge of the Word in creatures)[11]: this twofold aspect of divine Wisdom, to which the soul is initiated, starts her on a new reading and a new experience of the created world. Hence the theme of stanza 38, whose listing,

> The breathing of the air,
> The song of the sweet nightingale,
> The grove and its beauty,
> In the serene night,
> With a flame that consumes and gives no pain,

prolongs that of stanzas 13 and 14 ("My Beloved, the mountains . . . "). At the acme of mystical experience, the world of nature is reintegrated into divine beauty. The wayless way of the mountaintop leads to a discovery of realities that were passed along the lanes of former times, but now at their authentic level of being. They are at the same time in the Word and toward the Word: the soul is initiated into two aspects of the divine Wisdom.

To what point does the mystical doctor take the identification of creaturely being with eternal beauty? In keeping with his usual reading of John: 1:3-4, *Quod factum est in Ipso vita erat*, he believes indeed, "All that was made was life in Him," namely, in the Father.[12] Therein lies the source of the beauty of all creatures, and it is itself the beauty of the Creator. Yet let us also remember a reference, in the commentary on stanza 16, to a verse of the *Song of Songs*, 5, 6: "My lover put his hand through the opening; my heart trembled within me. . . . " In the biblical text, the woman is sleeping in the nude. Her lover tries to enter by passing his hand through a hole in the door, in order to lift the latch from inside. The woman, suddenly awake, hesitates for a moment: Should she put on a night-gown before opening? In verse 5 she rises as she is, in stark naked-ness, and opens to the Beloved. John of the Cross in fact does not comment on verse 5, but he introduces the theme of the nude in his interpretation of verse 4.

John of the Cross departs from most exegetes, and especially from Luis de León,[13] who had been anxious, for scholarly reasons, to stay close to the Hebrew text, and whose work he seems to have been acquainted with, in that he picks up a suggestion from the Latin vulgate. When it specified *et venter meus intremuit ad tactum ejus* (and my belly shivered at his touch), the Vulgate changed the perspec-tive provided by the Greek translation of the Septuagint ("my belly shivers for him"). This shift enabled John of the Cross to identify the opening, not with a hole in the door through which one may pass the hand from outside, but with a slit in the bride's dress. A play of words that was possible in Spanish (*manera*, meaning, in the language of the period, either a manner or a slit in a woman's robe) made his bold translation possible. The caress of the girl's belly by her Beloved, which she remembers at this point as only a slight touch, since He had only passed his hand through an opening of her gown, is deliberately chosen as a symbol of the divine touch. One may see in this a restoration of the nude—that will be so avoided in the Catholic piety and ethics of the next centuries, yet concerning which the Middle Ages had felt no complex[14]—as sym-bolic of the divine. John of the Cross selected a moment in the human game of love to make it an image of mystical love. A long tradition was in fact behind this: it had been transmitted by the medieval commentaries on the *Song of Songs*, even though John's interpretation of verse 4 seems peculiar to him. The slit in the fiancée's garment becomes the "manner" in which the divine touch is perceived; the beauty of the belly, which is imagined before being seen, has become the very beauty of God.

We have arrived at the threshold of blessed eternity. The dream of stanza 31, in which the lover mistakenly thought she had passed the threshold, brought the first *Canticle* to an end. It now finds its true focus in an experience that is no longer dreamed, but is lived. This marks the end of the second version of the poem. The last stanza (39) puts the final period to it, far from all on-lookers, in the absence of Aminadab, in the stillness of the lifting of the siege, and in the quiet descent of the horse at sight of the waters.

The association of horse with water may seem surprising. Neither the one nor the other is featured in the *Song of Songs* even though the horse of the *Canticle* may contain an allusion to the "chariots of Aminadab" of the Latin Vulgate (6, 11). Yet rather than a possible connection between the image of horsemen and the name of Aminadab, an episode in the biblical story of Gideon may be relevant: Gideon's volunteer army being too bulky, Gideon decides to keep only those soldiers who will drink from the stream without kneeling, lapping up water in the palm of their hands (Judges 7:4–8). The image of thirst-slaking waters serving as a test for sorting out men is not unconnected with the selection effected by the mystical ascent, which is also, as we have seen, a descent. In addition John of the Cross had inherited from his youth a strange relationship to water. While still very young, in the vicinity of Fontiveros, he had fallen into a pond when playing with friends. An adult who was passing by picked him out, but not before the child thought he saw a beautiful lady stretch her hand to him, and, feeling that his own hand was too dirty, he declined to take hers. . . . [15] Some years later, in 1551, as his family were moving, presumably on foot, from Arévalo to Medina del Campo, John was frightened by a big fish in a lake, and he made the sign of the cross before the fish disappeared. Several years later, in Medina, when the youth was a student at the School of Doctrine, he was pushed by another boy and fell into a well. And finally, in the night of his flight from the Toledo jail, he risked his life when he let himself fall in the dark from the end of the sheet he was using as a rope, down to the narrow walkway up above the river Tagus, the waters of which he could hear far below.

Water attracts; it frightens; yet it also is the water of life. It quiets down and it carries those who trust to the point where the horsemen—the offensive arm in the armies of the time—at the sight of the waters stop and descend. It may not be irrelevant to note that in 1584, at a time that could not have been far distant from the writing of these verses, John of the Cross, then prior in Granada, had an aqueduct constructed for which he may have designed the blueprint.[16]

From the Toledo *Canticle* to the last stanzas of the first *Canticle* of Andalusia one may detect a continuity of images. The same ones, generally, recur, borrowed from several earlier stanzas. Yet one may also feel the air of Andalusia, where "the juice of pomegranates" is more natural than in the colder atmosphere of the poet's native Castilla. As to "the song of the sweet nightingale,"[17] in which the Spanish name of the bird is not the common *ruiseñor*, but the classical form, *filomela* (philomel), it suggests, to those who are acquainted with the classical myth, the transformation of evil into good by divine grace. Philomel, the inadvertently bigamous and incestuous wife of King Tereus, is metamorphosed into a nightingale when the king is about to slay her, along with her sister Procne (herself changed into a swallow). The song of the sweet philomel therefore stands for the total transformation, the passage from evil to good at the deepest level of created being, which takes place at the climax of mystical experience. Juan de Yepes, who had been a pupil of Jesuit teachers in Medina del Campo, was acquainted with the mythological legends of the ancients as these were brought back to fashionable taste by the Renaissance. Undoubtedly, here is the source of the image used by John of the Cross, rather than in the romantic verse of Garcilaso de la Vega: "Philomel sighs in a sweet song."[18]

Can one speak of a new structure for the poem as a whole? John of the Cross did not merely add a few verses to his poem as a sort of complement. Nor did he deliberately rewrite the entire *Canticle*. More simply, the occasion turned up, along with the inspiration, further to explore and to formulate a high point of mystical contemplation to which he presumably had not attained at the time of his captivity. The new stanzas have therefore, in fact, created a new poem by providing the *Canticle* with a more advanced ending. Without replacing the conclusion of stanza 31, this ending brings the description further. In other words the relation of the second *Canticle* to the first is supplementary rather than complementary or substitutive.

The topical structure of the poem has now taken the following shape:

st. 1–4	Quest (I)
st. 5	Preliminary answer (1)
st. 6–12	Quest-desire (II)

st. 12	First full answer (2)
st. 13–16	First encounter (in creatures) (A)
st. 17–26	Second encounter (in himself) (B)
st. 27–30	Second full answer (3), made
	by the chorus (st. 27)
	then by the Bridegroom (st. 28–30)
st. 31–32	Sleep and awakening of the bride
st. 33–34	Third encounter (C)
st. 35–38	New quest (invitation to a last encounter) (D)
st. 39	Final rest

Moreover, if one pays attention to who is speaking, one may soon detect an additional, parallel structure. After an introduction that takes up the first four stanzas, the poem is divided into two sections, each of which is introduced by the chorus. After the first proclamation by the chorus (st. 5), the bride and the Bridegroom address each other: first the bride speaks, then the Bridegroom, and once more the bride. After a second intervention of the chorus (st. 27), another exchange takes place between the two of them, beginning with the Bridegroom. Thus the poem presents itself with a dramatic texture superimposed on the topical one:

Bride	st. 1–4		
Chorus (I)	st. 5	Chorus (II)	st. 27
Bride	st. 6–12	Bridegroom	st. 28–30
Bridegroom	st. 12	Bride	st. 31–32
Bride	st. 13–26	Bridegroom	st. 33–34
		Bride	st. 35–38
		Chorus (III)	st. 39

This double dialogue constitutes the *Spiritual Canticle* as drama. Already the first stanzas mark the poem with its fundamental orientation to the future, under the symbol of a quest for the Beloved. Then, between the bride and the Bridegroom there rises, in the face-to-face of their words, the lovers' reciprocal desire. Twice is the chorus heard, repeating and summarizing what has taken place or has been said. This echo by a third party, which however speaks in solidarity with the bride, sparks the desire of the bride and the Bridegroom for each other. The first words of the Bridegroom, in stanza 12, go fast: one thick stanza attracts the longer, slower speech of the bride. The first part of this is entirely turned to the future, the satisfaction of desire, and union with the Beloved. By contrast, the second section starts with a longer discourse by the Bridegroom, as though, after the bride's passionate declaration, he could commit himself further: he recalls the part before inviting the universe to remain in silence. After the bride's call to the "nymphs of Judea" (st. 31) and to her Beloved (st. 32), the latter continues his memory-tale, in an interpretation of the past that gives it its authentic meaning (st. 33–34). Only after these last words of the Bridegroom does the bride speak, in the future tense, in a piece that is definitively oriented to the ultimate union with her Beloved.

The lover speaks, in the main, in the future; the Beloved in the past. For the poem identifies him with what lies ahead; he is the one to whom the lover goes in her long quest. Meanwhile, he waits, attracting to himself and adorning the soul for their lasting encounter.

Is this, at that time, in the author's mind, the final form of the *Canticle*? This question will have to be answered in relation to text (B) of the poem. Yet one point seems already definite. Whereas the first *Canticle* had come to light without any reference to a commentary, the second took shape while John of the Cross was engaged in commenting on both the *Dark Night* and the *Canticle*. Stanzas 32–39 were therefore composed, if not in order to provide material for the commentary, at least with the awareness that there would be a commentary on them. This simple fact leads to the conclusion that their commentary should be much closer to the text and intent of the poetry than is the case with the first thirty-one stanzas of the *Canticle*. One should therefore accept the commentator's verdict: stanzas 33–34 record words spoken by the Beloved, even though the reader might have thought more spontaneously that the chorus was speaking, since the text refers to both the lover and her Dear One in the third person.

John of the Cross had in fact to face a problem of proportion: how could he give proper space to three factors? There was first the original mystical experience, which he had lived before, during, and after his captivity; there was also the poetic expression of this experience, which was, at the same time or alternately, inspired and carefully wrought. There was finally the theological interpretation, which itself had to cope with the two levels of the text and of the experience. Methodological reflections inserted in the prologues to the main commentaries suggest how John of the Cross handled the ensuing problem.[19]

The most developed prologues are those to the *Ascent*, to the *Canticle*, and to the *Living Flame*. They deal substantially with the same points, which may be reduced to five: (1) the question of the addressee, or: for whom is John writing? (2) the subject and its difficulties, or: how to speak of the inexpressible? (3) the instrument, or: what symbols to choose in order to formulate the ineffable? (4) the reading, or: how to read and interpret such symbols? (5) the context, or: how does the text relate to the Scriptures and to the Church?

The immediate addressee varies, yet only within the narrow field of "some of the persons of our holy Order of the Primitive Observance of Mount Carmel, both friars and nuns."[20] The *Ascent* is composed for those Carmelites who, having been called to the summit of the mountain, have started on the ascent; the *Dark Night* is destined to those who, like the soul who speaks in the poem, have "reached the state of perfection–that is, union with God—and passed through severe trials and conflicts by means of the spiritual exercise that leads one along the narrow way to eternal life";[21] the *Canticle* is also addressed "to those that, by the favour of God, have left behind the beginners' state," and, like Mother Anne de Jesus, at whose request the commentary was written, have been led "farther into the bosom of His divine love";[22] the *Living Flame*, dedicated to dona Ana de Mercado y Peñalosa, assumes that the reader, like the writer, has already walked for some time along the way of spiritual transformation, becoming like wood transformed by fire.[23] This dedication also implies that, if John is chiefly concerned with the men and women of the reformed Carmel, he does not exclude lay Christians from the contemplative life. Yet he entertains no illusion as to his public. He knows well enough, as he clearly explains, that souls fall into several categories according to their response to the attraction of the mystical way.

Some of them, who have received from God "talent and grace for advancing, and should they desire to make the effort they would arrive at this high state, yet continue in their lowly method of communion with God because they do not want or know how to advance, or because they receive no direction on breaking away from the methods of beginners."[24] They keep fighting against the way in which God wants to guide them, and they try to uplift themselves with their own resources rather than follow the grace they receive "on the pure and reliable road leading to union." Others are slowed down by directors of conscience and spiritual advisors who confuse the "sublime path of dark contemplation and aridity" with some state or other of the psychological or moral order. Others still imagine themselves far advanced in contemplation when they are way behind, while there are those who, being far advanced, do not even suspect it. The ones stay back because they want to do it all; others slow down, lingering among graces and favors that they ought to ignore. Where the mystical poet has told of his personal experience, the theological commentator will work at a spiritual pedagogy, teaching the ways of mystical life to both learners of the love of God and directors of conscience.

The topic, as the author often insists, is the way of contemplation or "mystical theology," in which the Christian mysteries are not, as in scholastic theology, merely known in the head, but are also in "the science of love, wherein these verities are not only known but also experienced."[25] Such a topic, as the prologue to the *Ascent* warns us, will naturally seem "dark" to many readers, since it deals with "the dark night through which a soul advances toward God."[26] In other words we will not find in it "moral and delightful things addressed to the kind of spiritual people who like to approach God along sweet and satisfying paths," but rather "a substantial and solid doctrine for all those who desire to reach this nakedness of spirit." Yet let us make no mistake. To speak of poetry in the sense of John of the Cross does not imply moralities, sweetness, savor, or quaintness.[27] His poetry images the true life, to which he wishes to initiate his readers.

The topic of the *Canticle* and the *Living Flame* lies, in the main, beyond the nights that are outlined in the *Ascent* and the *Dark Night*, in which their nature is explained. John of the Cross does not propose any neat theory on the degrees of spiritual life.[28] He does not even propose a theory at all. He describes and interprets an experience, according to which the spiritual life, whether envisioned as an ascent toward the top of Mount Carmel or conceived as a descent to the deepest levels of the self, implies an unbroken continuity. Through the active and passive nights of sense and of spirit as described in the *Ascent* and the *Dark Night,* one reaches to the spiritual espousal, and hence to the spiritual marriage of the soul with God, her Beloved: such is the topic of the *Spiritual Canticle.* As to the *Living Flame,* it places us near to the summit, where, to the soul who truly loves, God grants the grace to "live and dwell in the Father, the Son, and the Holy Spirit in the life of God."[29]

What formulations can encapsulate such an experience? John of the Cross is deeply aware of the radical inadequacy of human discourse. This conviction leads him to recognize the necessity of the indirect language of symbols. In the area covered by the *Ascent of Mount Carmel,* "the darknesses and trials, spiritual and temporal, that fortunate souls ordinarily encounter on their way to the high state of perfection are so numerous and profound that human science cannot understand them adequately; nor does experience of them equip one to explain them. He who suffers them will know what this experience is like, but he will find himself unable to describe it."[30] As to the *Canticle,* "It would be ignorance to think that sayings of love understood mystically, such as those of the present stanzas, can be fairly explained by words of any kind."[31] Likewise, the *Living Flame* relates to "things so interior and spiritual that words commonly fail to describe them, since spirit transcends sense and it is with difficulty that anything can be said of the substance thereof. For it is hard to speak of that which passes in the depths of spirit if one does not have deep spirituality."[32] John of the Cross has decided to try and speak of it, as he confides to Ana de Peñalosa, because "the Lord appears to have opened knowledge somewhat to me and given me some fervour." He will do it, however, "knowing for certain that by my own power I can say naught that is of any value, especially in things of such sublimity and substance."

How then can one speak of what cannot be said clearly? As he felt constrained by the needs of the Carmelite nuns and friars and, more generally, of all those Christians who walk along the mystic way, John of the Cross could not stay silent. In the prologue to the *Ascent,* he states his intention "not to rely on experience or knowledge,"[33] which can both be misleading, but rather to find his help "in Sacred Scripture, at least in the most important matters, or those which are difficult to understand." With the prologue to the

Canticle he seems more aware that, by so doing, he borrows from Scripture, not indeed texts, proofs, or "authorities" in the scholastic sense of the term, but "figures, comparisons, and similitudes."[34] Such symbols, however, should not be read at face value or haphazardly: "These similitudes, if they be not read with the simplicity of the spirit of love and understanding embodied in them, appear to be nonsense rather than the expression of reason, as may be seen in the divine *Songs of Solomon* and in other books of the divine Scriptures, where, since the Holy Spirit cannot express the abundance of his meaning in common and vulgar terms, He utters mysteries in strange figures and similitudes."

Symbols are always richer than their interpretation, as one may gather, John of the Cross remarks, from reading biblical commentaries. As to his own stanzas, "composed in abounding mystical intelligence, they cannot be fairly expounded, nor shall I attempt so to expound them, but only to throw upon them some light of a general kind." Furthermore, it is by no means necessary to attempt an exhaustive explanation, since "mystical wisdom (which comes through love, whereof the present stanzas treat) needs not to be comprehended distinctly in order to produce love and affection in the soul; it is like to faith, whereby we love God without comprehending Him."[35]

The process is not quite the same as in the prologue to the *Ascent of Mount Carmel.* In the latter John of the Cross wanted to use Scripture while also learning from experience and science. In the former he does not wish to "rely on experience," whether his own or others', though hoping to learn from both, "unless it be confirmed and expounded by authorities from the divine Scripture, at least in those things which appear to be the most difficult of comprehension."[36] In other words he plans to stay nearer to Scripture in the *Canticle,* in which difficult points are more numerous than in the *Ascent.* In any case the commentary will be a kind of dialogue between experience and Scripture, though an unequal dialogue, since experience will borrow from Scripture the symbols of its expression. Adherence to Holy Writ is still more firmly formulated in the prologue to the *Living Flame of Love:* " . . . anchoring myself in the divine Scripture, . . . I shall make bold to say that which I know."[37] Yet John warns that "all which is said herein is as far removed from all that there is to say as is a picture from life." Life, precisely, lies in that the soul speaks "when it is at last transformed and perfected interiorly in the fire of love; not only is it united with this fire but it has now become one living flame with it."[38] The scriptural symbols to be used reveal their meaning only to faith. And this must be a faith that is also love, a faith that apprehends, not through the intellect, but through what it tastes and what it loves.

This borrowing from Scripture of his main poetic symbols and of manifold illustrations and images with which the Mystical Doctor interspersed his commentaries raises the question, which is briefly touched upon in the prologues, of the respective places of Holy Writ and of Holy Church in his works. Is John of the Cross truly, as he suggests, a deeply biblical-minded author? Indeed he is, yet on condition that Scripture be read as a book dealing primarily with the relations between God and the soul who loves God in faith.[39] In other words the *Song of Songs*—understood, in keeping with a Christian spiritual tradition that itself had inherited and transformed a rabbinic tradition, as the mutual singing of the soul enamored of God and of God enamored of the soul–provides the key to the Scriptures. It is the inner norm of Scripture, functioning, in the modern phrase, like a "canon within the canon."

Yet John of the Cross does not only appeal to Scripture as to an abundant source of symbols that perfectly mesh with the Christian experience of the mystical love of God. He is also aware of the possibility of mistakes in interpreting Scripture. This he duly notes in his prologue to the *Ascent of Mount Carmel:* "If I should misunderstand or be mistaken on some point, whether I deduce it from Scripture or not, my intention will not be to deviate from the true meaning of Sacred Scripture or from the doctrine of our Holy Mother the Catholic Church. If this should happen, I submit entirely to the Church, or even to anyone who judges more competently about the matter than I."[40] Similar declarations accompany John's other major works. If nothing of the kind is said at the start of the *Dark Night,* this is because the content of this writing immediately follows that of the *Ascent.* In the *Canticle* the author forewarns that he intends to subject all he says "to better judgement, and to submit entirely to that of Holy Mother Church."[41] In the *Living Flame of Love,* he likewise confesses: "Wherefore my part herein will be limited to the defects and errors that this book may contain, for which reason I submit it all to the better judgement and understanding of our

Mother the Catholic Roman Church, under whose guidance no one goes astray."[42]

Should we conclude from this that the commentaries to which John of the Cross devoted so much time and effort during so many years have no intrinsic value in his eyes, that he would be prepared to change anything in them at the Inquisition's request, and that they would only represent what was necessary or diplomatic to turn over to the public domain in order to be free to explain his poems privately to small groups of initiates? Such an interpretation would forget that his commentaries came to light, by and large, a sizable time after the poems, that it would have been simpler to remain silent and at least not to write them at all, if indeed John feared being accused of illuminism before the tribunal of the Inquisition. Could one, going further, seriously present John of the Cross as "rebel" to the Church, even though, by diplomacy or temperament, a "docile rebel"?[43] This would amount to engage in fiction and to invent a novel with no foundation whatsoever in the life and writings of the reformer of Carmel. "Holy Mother Church," of which he speaks, is indeed the sacramental and spiritual community that has given him the Scriptures and, through its mystical tradition, has also handed him the key to Scripture. In light of the prologues, one should therefore slightly modify the diagram that we have proposed for the factors with which John of the Cross had to count in his work. Besides experience, the poetic expression of this experience, and the theological interpretation of both, there also were Holy Scripture, in close touch with the poetic expression, and the Church, which was itself involved, through its doctrine and tradition, in the theological interpretation. Yet these five components of John's theological horizon harmonized together without any other tension than that of his own imagination, as, explaining his experience to himself and to others, he practiced types of exegesis with which the modern world has lost acquaintance,[44] and allegorizations of his poetry of which he certainly could not have thought as he wrote it. At any rate it was with total serenity that, in the Church and inspired by Scripture, he wrote his commentaries on the poetry that had been born of his experience.

CHAPTER 8

THE BELOVED

The question of the identity of the Beloved is raised by a passage of the romance on the Incarnation, which may be compared with the language of John of the Cross in his commentaries. The first section of the romance sets in poetic form the Trinitarian doctrine that has served as dogmatic framework for the poet's experience. On the pattern of the beginning of the fourth Gospel, the Mystical Doctor evokes the Word of God. Then, since the Word is also called Son, he speaks of the Father: the Father and the Son stand in a relationship of lover and beloved, and they mutually indwell each other. Mention of the Three follows:

> Three Persons, and one Beloved
> Among all Three there was,
> And one love in them all
> And one Lover it made them,
> And the Lover is the Beloved
> In whom each one lived.[1]

By thus equating the Lover and the Beloved, John of the Cross, whether consciously or not, departed from the Trinitarian theologies based on the analysis of love, as that of St. Augustine in Book 8 of his treatise *On the Trinity*,[2] or that of Richard of St. Victor (1104–73) in his book bearing the same title.[3] For the bishop of Hippo, *amans, quod amatur, amor*, (the one who loves, what is loved, the love between them) is a methodological starting point. It provides a basic analogy that, through progressive transformations, becomes, in Book

11, the psychological analogy of memory, intellect, and love. According to the monk of St. Victor, who devotes a good part of his volume to analyzing Trinitarian love, the Father is the Lover, who loves the Son, his Beloved, along with the Holy Spirit, their Co-beloved. The presence of the Co-beloved ensures that the love of the first two Persons is infinitely open and altruistic rather than, as it would be without this breaking of the exclusive circle of Lover and Beloved, infinitely closed and selfish.

Now, John of the Cross's romance follows neither of these models. The only Beloved, who exists as Three Persons, is identical, not with any one Person in particular, but with the divine Being of the Three. This is explicitly affirmed a few verses further:

> For this reason it was infinite
> The love that united them,
> For Three have one single Love
> That was called their essence . . .

Love is no other than the divine essence. John of the Cross is no doubt inspired, at this point, both by the opening of the Johannine Gospel as by the First Epistle: "God is love" (1 John:4, 8). Yet this very fact takes him far from the theology of Thomas Aquinas, who understood love in God both as a free act of the divine will and as a proper name of the Holy Spirit,[4] this name being grounded in that the Third Person proceeds, as Thomas and Augustine taught, by way of love.[5] For John of the Cross, love is first of all neither a relation between Persons nor a Person; it is the very essence of the Godhead, the *ousia* of the Three Persons. In essence God is lover, beloved, and love, in such a way that love is not distinct from beloved, lover from love, love from beloved.

Admittedly, the poet obscures the picture by falling back, with the first verses of the second section of the romance, on a more classical vocabulary:

> In that immense love
> Proceeding from the Two,
> Words of great joy
> The Father spoke to the Son . . .[6]

In the Western theology that the Mystical Doctor follows, the love proceeding from the Father and the Son cannot be but the Holy Spirit. The Spirit is therefore presented here as the One in whom the Father, loving the Son, speaks to Him. This entitles the Spirit to be seen as Personal Love on the backdrop of essential love. Yet it is not possible to decide whether John of the Cross takes this to be only an appropriation to the Third Person of the essential love common to the Three, or would say, with Aquinas, that, "notionally" speaking, "to love is no other than to 'spirate' love."[7] Thomas concludes, and one may presume that John would agree: "It is said that the Father and the Son love both each other and ourselves with the Holy Spirit, or with proceeding Love." Thus the Father addresses the Son in John's romance:

> To him who loves you, Son,
> Myself I will give,
> And the love I have for you
> The same I will have for him,
> For his having loved
> One I have so much loved.

Indeed, one does not ask a poet, in the fire of inspiration or in the throes of perfecting the form of his poem, to foresee all the theological implications of his words. A poem is not a scholastic tractate. It is therefore not in view of a systematic comparison that I have brought up the Trinitarian theologies of Augustine, Richard of St. Victor, and Thomas Aquinas. My purpose is only to illustrate that John of the Cross's thoughts on the Trinity, which are as rich as they are nuanced, allow him to posit successively that love is the very essence of God, that the Spirit is the Love that proceeds from the first two Persons and in which the Father speaks to the Son, and finally that this same Love indwells the hearts of the faithful who love the Son.

In this case, however, the question is pointedly raised: Who is the Beloved sung in the poems, to whom John of the Cross prays, and of whom he speaks in his commentaries? Would it be the divine essence? or the Word? or the Spirit? or yet the Father, the source of every good gift?

> Three Persons, and one Beloved
> Among all Three there was . . .

As we read the poems of John of the Cross we may notice that they use relatively few titles to designate the Beloved. In the *Spiritual Canticle*, Beloved (*Amado*) appears in stanzas 1, 4, 8, 12, 17, 26, 27, 35; two other terms with related meanings are found in stanza 32: Dearie (*Carillo*), and in stanza 37: Darling (*Querido*). One should add the expression "My Life" (*Vida mia*) in stanza 37, where it does not refer to the poet's earthly life, but to the true source of all life, the Beloved. In the poem of the *Night*, only one title is used, in stanza 5: Beloved; in the *Living Flame*, also one title, in stanza 3: Darling.

The poems that remained without commentary do not feature terms of endearment. In the paraphrase of Psalm 137 one finds the common designation, Christ (*Cristo*). In the stanzas "I live, but not in myself . . . " the expression My God (*Dios mio*) is found in stanzas 2, 7, 8, and Lord (*Señor*) in 6. Elsewhere the poet does not use titles for the Beloved. Enlarging the category, however, one may mention the "little shepherd" (*pastorcico*) of the poem that begins with the word, and, in the romance on the incarnation, the classical terms of Trinitarian theology: Word, God, Son, Father, Holy Spirit, to which one should add, in sections 4 and 5, Bridegroom (*Esposo*) and Lord. Finally, the word *Godhead* (*Divinidad*), recurs twice in the fifth stanza of "For all the beauty . . . "

In summary this somewhat limited vocabulary has a double focus: the traditional theology relative to the mystery of the Holy Trinity and the language of love, which itself seems, in the light of the commentaries, to hinge on the expression of nuptial love.

The panorama broadens, but also becomes much more complex, as we read the commentaries. One ought to distinguish between terms that introduce a biblical quotation and those that belong integrally to the writer's own discourse, whether this explains or illustrates some point in the poetry or some aspect of spirituality, or is addressed in prayer to the Beloved. The first have little relevance to our discussion; they take the form of "Christ teaches," "Our Lord says," "Our Savior says," "the divine Wisdom writes."

Similar, though tending to become more personal, is the frequent expression of the commentary on the *Canticle*: "As the Bridegroom says in the *Songs* . . . "

Other titles pertain to the explanation and interpretation of the poems. The massive fact here is the absolute dominance of the word

God. This term recurs constantly in all the commentaries. From the start the reader is plunged into a theocentric universe that is not unlike that of Thomas Aquinas. Yet the accent is not placed on theological speculation. In addition the word *God* acquires special connotations that are proper to John of the Cross's usage: it designates the source and the ultimate purpose of the union to which the soul aspires, the origin and the final object of her desire. Undoubtedly, the more frequent meaning of it refers to what is common to the three Persons. It is an essential term, focused on the essence of the Godhead, what the Greek Fathers called the *ousia.* It is tantamount to the word *Godhead* that appears several times, and to another term that is found only once in all the works of John of the Cross: *Deity.* In turn each of these two nouns resonates with its own connotations. Godhead, or Divinity, is used three times, twice in the *Dark Night,* once in the *Living Flame,* in the phrase: " . . . the touch of the Godhead"; other instances of the word relate it to a feeling or impression of perceiving, either the "glory" and "light" of the Godhead, or the Godhead itself in its immensity.[8] In other words the vocabulary of John of the Cross applies the word *Godhead* to communications that come from God to us, and hence to our perception of the divine attributes in their aspect of glory and light, or to our reception of a touch from God. As to the term *Deity,* it appears only at the point where, at the end of the *Living Flame of Love,* John comes to the end of his career as an author. This is the moment of the highest experience of the Spirit. John admits that he cannot, and in fact, does not even wish to, speak of it adequately. What he would say would unavoidably remain far removed from the reality: "For it is a breathing of God himself, wherein, in that awakening of lofty knowledge of the Deity, the Holy Spirit breathes into the soul in proportion to the knowledge wherein He most profoundly absorbs it in the Holy Spirit, inspiring it with most delicate love for Himself according to what it has seen."[9]

If the formulation does seem awkward, the sense appears clearly: a double, simultaneous aspiration or breathing, by the Spirit and in the Spirit, entails for the soul both depth of knowledge and delicacy of love. The word *deity* stands for the abyss of God, as the soul finally gauges it through the supreme work of the Spirit at the summit of the mystic ascent. The word itself presumably derives from the vocabulary of Denys, which John of the Cross occasionally uses, although he also avoids it generally because of its obscurity and its speculative character. Yet the word is appropriate at this point, which evokes the totally ineffable moment of union with God through the Holy Spirit. It in fact does more than underline the "apophatism" of mystical union; it also opens an avenue onto the identity of the Spirit, as the Third Person, with the divine essence. Thus John of the Cross's writing ends face to face with the joint origination, in the divine essence or Deity, of the eternal aspiration of the Spirit and of His temporal aspiration of the creature.

Several other terms also stress the experiential dimension of the language of John of the Cross in relation to God. As an experience of the three Persons, the mystical insight is ultimately an unveiling of the divine uniqueness in its depth and its unity. The end of it is "the divine conjunction and union of the soul with the divine substance,"[10] a union "mouth to mouth: the pure and naked essence of God (the mouth of God in love) with the pure and naked essence of the soul (the mouth of the soul in the love of God)."[11] John also speaks, though only once, of "the Supreme Principle," clearly identified, not with the Father, but with the Godhead that "touches" the soul.[12] In the same vein, God is "the most high God,"[13] "His Majesty,"[14] "the Creator,"[15] "the King of Heaven,"[16] and finally, "the Holy Trinity."[17] Such expressions, even the last one, aim to evoke the oneness of the divine essence rather than, though of course without excluding, the threeness of Persons. The name *God* is by far the most frequent in the works of the Mystical Doctor, where it recurs in fact constantly. Would this be a mark of the Thomism that John had studied at the University of Salamanca? Thomas Aquinas, influenced by Books 1 to 7 of St. Augustine's *On the Trinity*, examined at length the divine nature or essence before exploring, within this one essence, the distinction of Persons.[18] Yet *God*, with its twofold dimension of richness (it says "all") and poverty (it says all "vaguely"), recurs too often under the pen of John of the Cross for it to be no more than an echo of scholastic theology. To tell the truth, there is not, for him, a distinct experience of the divine nature apart from the experience of one of the divine Persons. The soul's encounter with each Person, in keeping with the proper distinctness and authenticity of this Person, unveils the infinitely simple and infinitely varied depth and wealth of the divine essence, which is not only commonly shared by the Three, but also is identically each one.[19]

                  As is normal in Trinitarian theology, the name of the Father is not used very often. One pronounces it only with discretion and awe. For the Father is the totally ineffable Person, never directly perceived, but only through the face of the Word and in the action of the Spirit, the Person whose originless originality leaves visible traces nowhere, whose figure is discerned only by the experience, which is characteristic of advanced mystical states, of finding oneself assumed in, and associated to, the generation of the Word and the spiration of the Spirit. It is in the romance on the Incarnation that references to the Father are the most numerous. This should be no cause for surprise, since the romance tells the tale of the relations between the Father and the Son, which act as backdrop for the story of the Incarnation. In this poem, *God* designates at times the Father, at times the Godhead. The Father faces his Word, who is called his Son; they are together like Lover and Beloved. With a most accurate theological discernment, the Doctor of Carmel depicts the First Person as Principle and God, in whom the divine Word dwells and lives. In regard to the Word, God is Father, sharing his glory with the Son. Possession of the same being, union in the same love, the identification of this love as the very essence of the three Persons lead to the procession of "this immense Love"—the Holy Spirit—in which the Father and the Son are in dialogue. With delicacy and accuracy, the Son is shown as responding to the Father and calling Him thus only after being himself called Son, by the First Person. The mark of the Father is to find all joy in this Son:

> I am pleased with you alone,
> O life of my life!
> You are the light of my light,
> You are my wisdom,
> The image of my substance,
> In whom I am well pleased.[20]

The Father is also the Creator. And the created world is only the content of one word from Him. This word itself is no more than an aside in the divine exchange with the Son:

> Let it be done then (said the Father),
> For your love has deserved it;
> And by these words
> The world was made . . . [21]

The romance suggests that, if the Father is not named at all in the greater poems and is named but little in the commentaries, his image remains permanently sketched behind all that is said of the Son. Whenever John speaks of the Son of God, his language evokes the paradoxical image of the invisible Father.[22] Moreover, throughout the *Ascent,* in which terms of endearment are scarce, the image of the Father predominates indeed: as the ultimate source and the final end of all life, the Father pulls the soul toward the pathless way that reaches to the top of Mount Carmel. Besides, if the recurrence of the word *God* at all in the pages of John's writings finally refers to the abysmal depth of the divine essence in which the three Persons are one without distinction, the first personal connotation of the word applies to the Father. In the personal sense, God is the Father, in keeping with the common Greek theology, preserved through the Middle Ages by the mystical tradition. Yet if God as divine Essence predominates in the generality of John of the Cross's works, the Father is primarily intended by the term *God* in certain key passages. Thus in the *Ascent,* when John explains that God has one Word only, which is his Son;[23] or also in the *Canticle,* where "God looked at all things in this image of his Son alone."[24] Notwithstanding, these two meanings of the word *God*—as essence and as first Person—are not alien to each other. To speak of God as the Father is to say that in Him the divine essence is uncommunicable to creatures. The Father is as ultimately unknowable as the divine essence. He makes himself known only through the Son and in the Spirit.

This highlights the paradox of the Trinitarian trajectory in John of the Cross's works. Among his major writings, the *Ascent-Dark Night* constitutes the book of the Father: it is uncompleted because uncompletable. The *Spiritual Canticle* is the song of the Son and its interpretation. The *Living Flame* is the fire of the Spirit. The paradox resides in that, if the Father, from whom "comes every good and every perfect gift" (James 1:16), necessarily stands at the point of departure of every movement toward himself, He also is waiting at the end; the Son leads, in the Spirit, to Him. The elementary work of initiation, which the *Ascent of Mount Carmel* amounts to, draws its worth only from the conclusion toward which it leads but which it cannot itself reach. John so knows this that he evokes the Father at the end of his commentaries on the *Canticle* and the *Flame* (at least in version [B] of the latter). To the Lord Jesus, he writes at the close of the *Canticle*, "belong honour and glory together with the Father and the Holy Spirit *in saecula saeculorum. Amen.*"[25] And again, at the end of the *Living Flame*: "For, the spiration being full of blessing and glory, in it the Holy Spirit has filled the soul with goodness and glory, wherein He has inspired it with love for himself, which transcends all description and all sense, in the deep things of God, to whom be honour and glory. Amen."[26] God, here, is the ineffable Father.

Reading the *Ascent of Mount Carmel* with an eye for the names of the Son will reveal, in the first chapters, a most remarkable fact. Whereas in the book as a whole the Son of God is commonly called with such classical appellations as Christ, Son of God, Our Lord, Our Savior, he is designated in the second chapter as the soul's Bride. A hasty perusal, intent on anticipating parallels with the *Spiritual Canticle*, might skip over this detail: the Word is the Bride, in the feminine gender. Admittedly, this happens only once, though one would have to read as far as chapter 14 to find Christ called with the more familiar masculine term, the soul's Bridegroom, her Beloved.[27] There can hardly be at the beginning of the *Ascent* a moment of inattention or a slip of the tongue on the part of the author. Indeed, feminine appellations for the Word, Son of God, Bride of the soul, were not unknown to medieval piety.[28] It can be explained here by the biblical text on which John of the Cross is commenting. This is not, as in the *Canticle* and in other passages of the *Ascent*, the *Song of Songs*; it is the episode of the three bridal nights in the book of *Tobias*. The angel has invited young Tobias not to have intercourse with his bride Rachel during the first three nights of their marriage on account of a special danger from a demon. The three nights are respectively equated by the commentator to the purification of the soul, to faith, and to God himself:

> When this third night (God's communication to the spirit, which usually occurs in extreme darkness of soul) has passed, a union with the Bride, which is the Wisdom of God, then follows. The angel also told Tobias that, after the third night had come to an end, he would be joined to his bride in the fear of the Lord. Now, when the fear of the Lord is perfect, love is also perfect, and love is perfect when the transformation of the soul in God is achieved.[29]

The image of the Bride, which is strongly suggested by the text of *Tobias*, is equally rooted in the traditional notion of wisdom. The Wisdom of the book of *Proverbs*, which associates it, as John of the Cross does, with the fear of God, speaks to humans; like the Word in St. John's Gospel, she is with God; she builds her house and wants to bring to it all who wish to eat and drink with her.[30] The text of *Proverbs* is commented at length in the *Ascent*.[31] John of the Cross does not cite the corresponding passage of Ecclesiasticus 24, which identifies Wisdom and Torah (the Law), yet he soon mentions the "desire for the perfect fulfillment of His Law and the carrying of His cross."[32] Wisdom, which is the Word of God, is the Bride of the soul. The biblical Wisdom teaches; she is a mistress of life and of knowledge. Precisely, the first book of the *Ascent of Mount Carmel* deals with elementary spiritual teaching. One must learn the alphabet that is indispensable to the ascension of the mountain. One must listen to the Bride, for she does know. This alphabet or elementary doctrine is no other than the formulation of the rules of *todo-nada* in chapter 13 with the poem already analyzed, "To reach satisfaction in all. . . ."[33] One must renounce all that is not God.

The title, Wisdom of God, is a very special qualifier of the divine Word in the remaining parts of the *Ascent*. John of the Cross does not forget, even if he no longer stresses, the function of Wisdom as the Bride of the soul. Yet, beginning with chapter 14, he reverses the image suggested by the book of *Tobias*. The *Spiritual Canticle*, on which he is working at the same time, impresses on him, with the help of the *Song of Songs,* that the Word should be Bridegroom rather than Bride. In this chapter, which immediately follows the poem of *todo-nada,* Christ is called Bridegroom and Beloved for the first time in this commentary. The context calls for passing "through this dark night of sense to union with the Beloved,"[34] which is not possible unless there be "another, more intense enkindling of another, greater love (which is that of her Bridegroom)." Once it has been truly united with the Wisdom of God, its Bride, by way of an intimate conviction of the doctrine and reality of the *todo-nada,* the soul, as partaker of the divine Wisdom, becomes Bride also. From this moment on, the Word, changing roles, no longer seeks but lets himself be sought; there is no need for him to act as a school mistress; he can become the Bridegroom. Yet teaching is never totally done; the soul should always learn further. Accordingly the Word remains, through the *Ascent,* "Wisdom of God,"[35] "divine Wisdom," "the simple and pure Wisdom, which is the Son of God,"[36] "all God's Wisdom generally, which is the Son of God."[37] The term *Wisdom* is all the better a key to the *Ascent* as the word *Bridegroom* remains rarely used: after the principle has been established, in chapter 14 of Book 1, that the Word is indeed the Bridegroom of the soul, this title recurs only once, in a passage that refers to the Bridegroom of the *Song of Songs* as well as to the *Mansions* of Teresa of Avila, a book in which she explains spiritual marriage.[38]

The word *Beloved* is also seldom used,[39] though both terms become more frequent, yet not numerous, in the *Dark Night,* whose tone is germane to that of the *Ascent of Mount Carmel* since it functions as a continuation of the latter. As early as the "declaration" of its second part, the *Night* mentions the soul's Bridegroom,[40] who, in the course of the commentary, will in fact be called "her divine Beloved, . . . the Beloved . . . "[41] and, at the end, "the Bridegroom," "the Beloved."[42] The entire tractate is enshrined between these nuptial titles, the Bridegroom remaining also "the divine Wisdom to which she [the soul] was united,"[43] this divine Wisdom,"[44] as well as, "the said Wisdom,"[45] "the same Wisdom of God."[46] Union to this divine Wisdom brings the soul to taste in herself "a loving wisdom."[47]

Besides such nuptial and sapiential titles, the *Ascent* and the *Dark Night* are strewn with names referring to the two poles of all classical christologies: the power and greatness of the Word of God, and the humility of Jesus of Nazareth. On the one hand, Christ is, as we have seen, Son of God, "my beloved Son," and also "His Majesty,"[48] an expression that had the favor of Teresa and that John of the Cross applied also to God,[49] "Lord, not of the earth only, but of heaven also."[50] On the other, he is the Christ, Jesus-Christ,[51] who was determined to do the Father's will, who carried "the pure spiritual cross and poverty of spirit,"[52] who is "the gate,"[53] in whom there dwells "the mystery of the gate and the way." The two dimensions, divine and human, of the Word made flesh, the Wisdom of God, join together in such expressions as, "the sacred Body of Our Lord Jesus Christ,"[54] "faith in Our Lord Jesus Christ," "love for Christ the Bridegroom,"[55] "the quiet peace and delight of the hidden Bridegroom." This last formula, which is found near a quotation from the *Song of Songs*, brings us close to the symbolic language of the *Spiritual Canticle*. Christ is indeed the soul's Bridegroom, her Beloved, as well as the Father's Beloved Son. The dialectic of the *Song of Songs* has now definitively replaced the perspective of the book of Tobias.

The commentary on the *Spiritual Canticle* is entirely dominated by the two images of the Bridegroom and the Beloved, which occur throughout the work in parallel with the name of God, which is itself as frequent here as in the other books of John of the Cross. The theology is emphatically theocentric, as in the *Ascent of Mount Carmel*, and the christology is a christology of love. The theme of the romance on the Incarnation comes back, yet this time in the perspective of the soul in love: Christ shows himself to her as the Lover, the Beloved, the Bridegroom. John of the Cross as an author was then pursuing the two parallel approaches of the *Ascent* and of the *Canticle*, as he composed these two books during the same period. The first approach analyzes the conditions of the search for God, which are themselves implied by the very reality that God is. The second tells the tale of the quest and of the privileged moments of encounter to which it leads. There of course are common points between these two commentaries. Among others, the names Jesus and Jesus-Christ are relatively rare. John apparently prefers to use Christ and such titles as Our Lord, Our Savior, the Son of God. Yet the appellation Jesus Christ appears once in the *Ascent,* in a context that refers to love. How should one behave in the active night of sense? As John insists, one should renounce all purely human pleasures and satisfactions; the soul must "renounce and remain empty [of them] for the love of Jesus Christ, who in this life found no other gratification or desire than in fulfilling his Father's will, which He called his meat and his food."[56]

Likewise, apart from a lone reference to "the Lord Jesus praying to the Father" in the Garden of Olives,[57] the *Canticle* contains the name of Jesus only once, in its conclusion: "Whereto [i.e., to interior recollection] may the Lord Jesus, the Bridegroom, be pleased to bring all such as invoke His most holy name, to whom belong honour and glory together with the Father and the Holy Spirit *in saecula saeculorum.* Amen."[58]

What inference, if any, may be drawn from this evident reluctance to use the name of Jesus? Should we believe that the whole purpose of the *Spiritual Canticle* is to bring the reader to the point where this most personal of the names of the Beloved can be received in a pure heart?[59] This would imply, mistakenly, that the name is not previously known. Devotion to the name of Jesus was already featured in the sermons of St. Bernard on the *Song of Songs.* It spread fairly widely in the fourteenth and fifteenth centuries,[60] thanks to the preaching of the Dominican, St. Vincent Ferrer (c. 1350–1419), who was also a Spaniard, and of the Italian Franciscan, St. Bernardin of Siena (1380–1444). It was also known among the Rhineland mystics, as for instance in the works of Johannes Tauler (1300–61) in Strasbourg: John of the Cross was acquainted with their Latin translation by the Carthusian Surius. Did such a devotion have an impact on the Doctor of Carmel? To affirm such an influence would amount to seeing the revelation of the name of Jesus as one of the summits of mystical experience according to John of the Cross. It would imply reserving this revelation to the time of spiritual marriage. But this would generally contradict the purpose of the devotion to the name of Jesus. This is usually not presented as the acme of a long period of interior ascent, but rather as the beginning of a growing familiarity with the spiritual wealth hidden under, yet conveyed by, the Name. This is true of both the Western devotion to the name of Jesus and the Eastern practice of the "prayer of Jesus."[61] There is no reason to think that John of the Cross was at odds with the orientation of the medieval devotion; yet he was not simply following it. He was doing something else.

It seems characteristic of the Mystical Doctor's writings that the name of Jesus is tied to an experience of the divine love. If John of the Cross does not often appeal to the name in his commentaries and never in his poetry, his letters are nonetheless strewn with it, usually in a formula like: "May Jesus be in your soul, my daughter in Christ."[62] With some of his correspondents, with whom he is less familiar or whom he perhaps does not know so well, John makes himself more formal, replacing "in your soul," with, "in Your Reverence."[63] Several times he writes: "May Jesus Mary be in your soul."[64] The association of the two names of Jesus and Mary was itself known in the medieval devotion to the name of Jesus. Yet, "Jesus Mary" being the subject of a verb in the singular,[65] one gets the impression that this is only one name, as though one read: "Jesus, son of Mary." In any case this is never an empty formula of formal courtesy. John really sends his wish to his correspondents, who for the most part are his "daughters in Christ," the Carmelite sisters and a few other women for whom he acts as spiritual director, that they would experience the love of God. The name of Jesus acts as a symbol of the presence and the intimate knowledge of the Savior. To have Jesus in one's soul is equivalently to know and taste one's most sweet Spouse. As John asks the Carmelites of Beas de Segura on 18 November 1586, after what must have been a complaint that he does not write to them often enough, can they truly believe that, when he fails to write, he has lost interest in "how with great ease [they] can become saints and walk in the joy of the beloved Bridegroom with great delight and sure protection?"[66] The name of Jesus in the soul precisely signifies the fruitful, fruitive presence of divine love in oneself. One can then see why it should not be proclaimed to all and sundry, who might not understand it.

Admittedly, the terms of endearment, Bridegroom, Beloved, abound where the name of Jesus remains unpronounced. In fact the rhythm of recurrence of those two terms frames the commentary on the *Canticle*. From its first lines the soul's Beloved is clearly identified with "the Word, Son of God, her Bridegroom";[67] the soul invokes him: "Word, my Bridegroom." In relation to the Father, he is "his Wisdom, . . . his only Son";[68] in relation to humankind he is the "Creator"; in relation to the Virgin Mary, he is "her beloved

Son." With the Father and the Spirit the Word "is hidden essentially in the inmost center of the soul." She herself desires nothing other than "the possession of the Spouse in this life by grace" with the "presence and clear vision of his essence . . . in glory."[69] Only when he has no rival in the soul, which is then "entirely with him," can she call him her Beloved. Just as the beginning of the *Canticle* formulates the soul's desire to be entirely his, the predicate *Beloved*, an exclusive term, anticipates the total fulfillment of the desire that has been expressed. *Bridegroom*, also an exclusive term, is nonetheless used in a broad sense, which applies equally to the anticipation, before the espousals, and to the espousals and the marriage. It is already in use when the Word is Bridegroom only in the desire of the soul in quest of him. Until stanza 11, however, the word *Beloved* is predominant among numerous complementary appellations.

Beginning with stanza 11, where one comes to the "crystal fountain," (and John, in keeping with the sound of the words rather than with etymology or meaning, connects crystal with Christ), the term *Bridegroom* appears more often. We have reached the threshold of the spiritual espousal. Up to the end of the first *Canticle* (st. 31), Bridegroom and Beloved recur abundantly, along with some other appellations: the Lord Jesus,[70] who is Word, Bridegroom, and Beloved, is also the Wisdom of God, His Majesty, the King of heaven, the Son of God, the Guest (*Aposentador*).

The additions of the second *Canticle* start, in stanzas 32–33, with a new concentration on the nuptial terms Beloved and Bridegroom to which one should add, as in the verses that are commented upon, Little Dear and Darling. Once again, the next stanzas, 34–39, use the classical titles, Wisdom of God, Word, Word Bridegroom, Son, natural Son, divine Word. Being parallel to the nuptial terms, these titles multiply the aspects and list the rich qualities of the Beloved, thus leading to the fullness of sense placed on the final title by the commentary on the last stanza: "The Lord Jesus, the most sweet Bridegroom."

A diastolic rhythm of language, and therefore of experience, emerges. To a systolic moment centered on the two words of nuptial love there succeeds a diastolic moment in which the vocabulary, as it were, bursts open. Starting from the exclusiveness and concentration of love, the language soars into a fireworks of predicates, which sketch a nimbus of glorious qualifications around the core title of Beloved Bridegroom. A systolic moment returns when the nimbus fades away, letting all the strength of love throw light on the titles of Bridegroom and Beloved; then again, in another diastole the vocabulary blooms into a halo made by the names of Christ. Finally a last systole, reduced to "Jesus" as the supreme name of divine love, preludes to the definitive explosion of a mystical dying from love.

The title Wisdom of God is, for several reasons, in a category of its own. In the first place, the term is ambiguous since it may designate the wisdom acquired by the bride in her quest for the Beloved, or the essential wisdom that is counted among the divine attributes, or also the Word himself, Wisdom of God. In fact these three senses are found intertwined in the commentary on the *Canticle*. The first two come at the beginning of the commentary on stanza 36, when the bride enters "into this thicket of the wisdom of God, . . . into the thicket of knowledge and experience of trials of which we have spoken, . . . farther into this wisdom and these trials. . . . "[71] The wisdom of this passage is, first, the divine Word, then the mystical wisdom, gained from experience and given by grace. It consists precisely in "a knowledge of the lofty mysteries of God and man, which are loftiest in wisdom and hidden in God. . . . " Once she has entered this thicket, the soul may taste the knowledge of divine attributes, "such as justice, mercy, wisdom, etc." Generally, however, the personal sense, Wisdom being identical with the divine Word, is dominant in the *Canticle*: all things have been created by God, that is, by "his Wisdom, . . . which is the Word, his only-begotten Son."[72]

Undoubtedly, John of the Cross has inherited the tradition, deriving from Augustine, that opposes science and wisdom, science being pure knowledge, oriented to use and to the techniques of transformation and application, while wisdom is loving knowledge, turned to admiration and spiritual enjoyment. Yet the Mystical Doctor goes further. He builds up a two-sided dialectic of wisdom. In the *Ascent* the relationship between the bride and the Bridegroom, or rather, at this stage, between the bridegroom and the Bride, stems from the personal Wisdom of God, the divine Word. After the third night of Tobias there will take place "a union with the Spouse, who is the Wisdom of God."[73] As a designation for the Second Person, the divine Word, Wisdom creates the context for the position of the Word as Bride of the soul. In the light of this supreme, uncreated Wisdom, whose nuptial union with the soul will bring ineffable delights, "all the world's wisdom and human ability, compared to the infinite Wisdom of God, is pure and utter ignorance."[74] Comparison between these two wisdoms, one of which is and the other is not, can be made at the level of qualities or attributes. "Ignorance does not grasp what wisdom is." The human quality of wisdom misunderstands the divine attribute. In all this passage, "divine Wisdom" is associated to other attributes of God, like infinity, beauty, grace, goodness, lordship and freedom, delights, wealth, which themselves stand in contrast with the corresponding human qualities. Yet at the end of the chapter all these divine attributes, which are in reality predicates of the Being of God, belong to the personal Wisdom who speaks in the book of Proverbs,[75] announcing that what men seek when they place "their heart and affection" in the things of this world, can only be found in herself. The divine Wisdom proclaims "that the riches and glory they love are with her and in her, not where they think; and that lofty riches and justice are present in her."[76]

The Word, divine Wisdom, is thus shown as the golden monstrance of the divine attributes, and first of all of wisdom. Accordingly, wisdom is not a purely functional term,[77] its meaning relating only to the universe and the soul in quest of the divine Word. It is both an essential and a personal name; it expresses an aspect of the way in which the Word, second Person, owns the divine Being received eternally from the Father.

What is this aspect? The Mystical Doctor does not only affirm that the Word is the Wisdom: he also explains the ground for this identity. The Wisdom of God is explicitly opposed by him both to the radical limits of the human intellect and being, and to those other limitations that come from paying attention to contingent realities: "If a person will eliminate these impediments and veils, and live in pure nakedness and poverty of spirit, . . . his soul in all its simplicity and purity will then be immediately transformed into simple and pure Wisdom, the Son of God."[78]

Human intelligence is structured according to "limited mode and manner. But God's Wisdom, to which the intellect must be united, has neither mode nor manner, neither does it have limits nor does it pertain to distinct and particular knowledge, because it is totally pure and simple."[79] The two wisdoms are like "extremes"; as such they need a common element to be united, and this common element implies the soul's rejection of all distinct and particular knowledge: she "must be pure and simple, unlimited and unattached to any particular knowledge, and unmodified by the boundaries of form, species, or image." Only then can she receive from God the kiss on the mouth, being united to God, not "through the disguise of any imaginative vision, likeness, or figure, but mouth to mouth: the pure and naked essence of God (the mouth of God in love) with the pure and naked essence of the soul (the mouth of the soul in the love of God.)"[80] Analogously, an abyss separates the reception of lights that bring the soul "the wisdom of one, two, or three truths," and God's communication without manner or mode, in faith, when "all God's Wisdom is communicated in general, that is, the Son of God, who is imparted to the soul in faith."[81] Wisdom of God, as a name of the Word, Son of God, Bride of the soul, has thus a very precise sense for John of the Cross: it designates the Word as the divine essence beyond all modes, to which the soul who loves God must be united, beyond all human mode of knowing or being.

This meaning also underlies the texts of the *Dark Night* on the Wisdom of God. Indeed, the *Night*, continuing the *Ascent* in the latter's own line, adds nothing to the title "Wisdom of God" as this is used in the first commentary. Not "by human operation and way of acting"[82] does the soul love when it is united to divine love, but rather "by means of the divine Wisdom to which it is united." This union takes place in the darkness of faith. As soon as the soul has been "put to sleep and silence regarding earthly and heavenly things, divine Wisdom unites itself with the soul in a new bond of the possession of love."[83] A certain wisdom is still received in contemplation, since "this infused contemplation, as loving wisdom of God" purifies and illumines the soul.[84] Yet this is a secondary meaning of the word, stemming from the primary sense: Wisdom is the Word of God.

If the phrase "Wisdom of God" connotes the modeless mode of

the Word's eternal existence and of his identity with divine Being, and thereby demands adherence to *nada* from the created person that has been called to share his love, it follows that entrance into this divine Wisdom opens to the soul an entirely new vista on the divine attributes of the Word; it acts as a gesture of unveiling of the divine ineffability that has become the soul's Bridegroom. This doctrine of the commentaries on the poem of the *Dark Night* on the nature of Wisdom will in fact provide a key for reading the *Living Flame of Love.*

Let us return to the *Spiritual Canticle.* John of the Cross has declared, in regard to morning knowledge, that is, to the knowledge of the created universe in the Creating Word, that "the Word is the loftiest Wisdom of God."[85] All contingent entities are related to his beauty, in which he and the bride admire each other, as was said concerning the verse "And let us go to see in your beauty." Summing up this fullness, in which the Word is, in a transcendent way, all things, the poet of the *Canticle* exploited the wonderful ambiguity of the Spanish word *espesura:* "*Entremos mas adentro en la espesura,*" which may be rendered: "Let us enter farther into the thickness." Yet this translation is neither the only possible one nor the most satisfactory. *Espesura* means not only thickness but also and more precisely the thickness of the wood, the clump of trees, the thicket. Hence the translation: "Let us enter farther into the thicket." Let us therefore go into this living and rich forest of the splendors of the Word, who is the received Image of the Father and the archetype of the whole created universe in both its totality and its particulars. There shall the soul discover "the high mysteries of the Incarnation of the Word,"[86] which constitute for her "the highest and most delectable wisdom," "the lofty and high and deep mysteries in the wisdom of God which are in Christ," and also, never to be forgotten, "the thicket of the Cross, which is the road to life."[87]

This fullness of the Word, Wisdom of God, the soul's Bride, enables the Mystical Doctor, from the moment of the first discoveries of the spiritual espousal, to identify the Beloved, in a certain sense, with all things:

My Beloved, the mountains,
Lonely wooded valleys,
Strange islands,
Resounding rivers,
The whistling of breezes in love,

The tranquil night,
Close to the rising dawn,
Sounding rivers,
The banquet that refreshes and enamors.[88]

These are not simply metaphors and comparisons. The Beloved is not "like" the aspects and moments of nature that are evoked by the bride; he "is" this world of created nature: "The bride says that her Beloved is all these things, both in himself and also for her."[89] The theologian admittedly adds: "It must be understood that all that is expounded here is in God in an eminent and infinite manner." Yet he also goes on, lest the mystical insight be drowned in scholastic distinctions between the affirmative, negative, and eminent modes used by theological language: "Or, to express it better, each of these grandeurs which are spoken of is God, and they are all of them God; for, inasmuch as in this case the soul is united with God, it feels that all things are God in one simple being, even as St. John felt when he said: *Quod factum est in ipso vita erat.* That is to say: That which was made, in him was life."

The convergence of these two passages—stanzas 13–14 and stanza 35—justifies the identification of the Beloved: he is still the Word, Bride of the soul, Wisdom of God; yet as Wisdom he is also the created world, whose manifold contingent being is rooted in the Creator's simple, eternal Being. All the human experience of the world becomes, through mystical grace, an experience of the Beloved. The love that embarks on the infinite ocean of the uncreated Wisdom does not shed its own roots in the matter of this world, since the Beloved *is* mountains, valleys, islands, rivers, winds, night, music, solitude, banquet, as well as simultaneously being the most high mysteries of the Incarnation and the infinite mysteries of the relations of the Word with the Father and the Spirit. In all this the bride discovers her Beloved; loving him, she finds true joy in all things.

The journey of mystical love thus goes from the transitory being of creatures to their eternal being present in the Wisdom of God. This divine Wisdom is both eternal and incarnate; it has appeared on earth with the name and the features of the Son of God made man. The final message of the *Canticle* both assumes and grounds the condensed statement made in the romance on the Incarnation; "Three Persons, one Beloved." If the three Persons are, for their human lover, a single Beloved, this is because the divine Being, which is both Love and all the dimensions of this Love, is perceived such as it is in the Word, Wisdom of God, the soul's own Bridegroom. The Being which in God is Lover, Beloved, and Love, gives itself to the soul in the Wisdom coming to her under the name of "the Lord Jesus, the sweetest Bridegroom."[90]

CHAPTER 9

SPARKS OF LOVE

The present chapter will be a sort of parenthesis in our reading of the great tractates of John of the Cross. His work, one does not sufficiently notice it, is not limited to his major poems and commentaries. In prose as in poetry he also authored, after the internal and external trials of the Toledan nights, a number of so-called minor pieces, composed at the same time as the commentaries. The poetic part of what thus remains of the Mystical Doctor's writings is commonly neglected, these poems, like the saint's earlier compositions, being no more than transpositions *a lo divino* of popular songs or ditties. Yet just as his previous writings *a lo divino* occupy a sizeable place in the formation of the heart and mind of John of the Cross, likewise those of his Andalusian period offer privileged vantage points from which to measure and evaluate the state and the tone of his spiritual experience in this last decade of his life.

Yet it would be a mistake to look at these writings only by comparison with the major works of their author. Relationships are undeniable between the two kinds of compositions. But such relationships will emerge in full light only when the authenticity and originality of the minor productions of John of the Cross have been recognized. Each one has its own value, independently of what was written before or after. One should apply to them the principle from which John generally looked at the created universe: "All that was made was life in Him."[1]

We begin with the gloss that opens on the words, "Without support and with support."[2] In the productions of John as a poet, this is both the most prosaic as to its form and the simplest as to its meaning, which appears obvious in the framework of the general conceptions of the author. It would be tempting to translate the first verse "Anchorless and at anchor" if nautical metaphors could fit the human experience and the imagination of the Mystical Doctor. As a son of landlocked Old Castile, however, Juan de Yepes, who is attracted to water, who likes ponds, brooks, and rivers, has no experience of the sea or the ocean. He hardly ever evokes them. One may think of the "strange islands" of stanza 13 of the *Canticle* as somehow connected with the ocean and the discovery of the West Indies. No allusion in this *villancico*, however, connects it with a maritime context. One therefore has to fall back on a prosaic translation, which itself does not let through the rich ambiguity of the original, *Sin arrimo y con arrimo: arrimo* can indicate both abandon and support; it refers to the act of putting something aside, perhaps to forget it, but maybe to use it as support. Hence the translation, which is possible, yet unlikely, of "anchor." Yet this would also hide the connotation of abandonment. St. Thérèse de Lisieux, the "Little Flower" of recent hagiography, was particularly fascinated by this poem, of which she made a sort of paraphrase in verse. Her version of this verse, borrowed from a standard French translation of her time, may be put in English as "Leaning on no support."[3]

The form of the poem, itself rather artificial, comprises a three-verse envoy, each verse reappearing at the end of one of the three stanzas that make up the whole poem. Each stanza has nine verses of eleven syllables. The three stanzas are not entirely uniform. If the verses are put together in sequences according to meaning, the first stanza easily falls into the cadence 2, 3, 2, 2, which seems expressive of "position." The second follows the pattern 3, 2, 2, 2, which, being more rapid after a slower departure, indicates "passage." The third comes back to the first rhythm: "restoration."

What matters most here is not to find out how John of the Cross treated a preexistent text,[4] but rather to assess the final product. What does John sing in his personal version of a popular theme?

The heart of what he wishes to say clearly emerges in the envoy:

> Without support and with support,
> Living without light, in darkness,
> I am wholly being consumed.

This is undoubtedly another version of the motif of the mystical nights: life already deprived of the ordinary light of things and of mind, is now without the support of an expected light! Yet in such an exposed life, without support, the poet already discerns something more. He has experienced a hidden protection, manifested precisely in the fact that he is, in this life, "consumed." To be consumed is to diminish, to vanish, like wood engulfed in fire. Fire consumes away what it licks. We are near in time to the redaction of the *Living Flame of Love*, both as poem and as commentary. Whether "Without support . . . " is anterior or posterior to them, the image of the flame floats in the writer's mind, presumably because his own interior experience has brought it up. John is feeling a fire, which can only be of love, that is, it is the flame of the Holy Spirit, if not the Holy Spirit in person in his transforming action upon the soul.

The first stanza develops the paradoxical affirmation, familiar to the readers of John of the Cross, that is implied in the first verse, "Without support and with support." First, abandonment, the night of sense and of spirit, is suggested by the statement:

> My soul is disentangled
> From all created thing . . .

The two dimensions of created being (the past of accumulated things, and the future already implied in present detachment, yet placed here in reverse order) are succeeded by the three dimensions of supernatural being: the ascent, the access to a life in delight, and the participation in God. These themes of the following three verses constitute a Trinitarian symbol, since it is the Spirit who raises up, the Word who shares his divine filiation, the Father in whom the soul finds her ultimate support:

> And lifted above itself
> In a life of delight
> Supported only in God.

The last four verses act as counterpoint, picking up the initial assertion, yet at a level of joy and fullness that could not be suspected at the start of the envoy:

> So now it can be said
> That I most value this:
> My soul now sees itself
> Without support and with support.

The second stanza opens a perspective, as so often in the works of John of the Cross, on the darkness that is also light and the death that is life. Three verses evoke the night and its paradox of being painful without true pain:

> And though I suffer darkness
> In this mortal life,
> My pain has not increased so much . . .

The reason for this paradox follows, in four excited duos where the first verse stands in contrast with the next: lack of light / heavenly life; love and life / blindness; self-surrender / new life. These logical contradictions coexist in experience:

> For though I have no light
> I have a heavenly life,
> For love gives this life
> When it is all the blinder,
> Holding the soul surrendered,
> Living without light, in darkness.

This transition introduces the theme of love and the eschatological opening on heaven, though it does not pronounce itself on what holds the soul surrendered: is it love, or the new life? As far as meaning goes, the question is of no importance, since love is precisely the source of new life. Yet as regards rhythm, this hesitancy posits a moment of waiting, before one may continue without knowing. After the stanza of hope and ascent, this is the stanza of faith that, in the night, lasts and becomes life only if it is also love. Faith is love, according to the mystical perception of the one who nears the summit of Mount Carmel, when the paths of ascent dwindle and one must now follow a pathless way.

The third stanza unveils the scope of the faith that is now love. One enters the realm where the soul will be transformed by love into love. The whole universe feels the effect of such a transformation, for at this level, at the summit where all is love, the distinction of good and evil fades away. No doubt such a bold assertion could have proved embarrassing to the commentator if John of the Cross had commented on this poem, just as he may have been embarrassed, after the fact, by some expressions of his first commentary (A) on the *Canticle!*[5] The stanza opens on an affirmation of love and of its already long experiential knowledge by the poet. The three following verses unfold the outcome: beyond good and evil, that is, before the eating of sin under the tree of knowledge, as evoked in stanza 28 of the *Canticle,* all partakes of the same suavity, and the soul is metamorphosed by love into love:

> Love has done such work
> Since I have known it,
> That either good or evil in me
> It makes all one savor
> And transforms the soul into itself.

Two doublets close up the poem on a suggestion of its ultimate sense: love is a sweet flame that touches nothing without consuming it:

> And so in its sweet flame,
> Which I feel within me,
> Swiftly, leaving nothing,
> I am wholly being consumed.

Although it is not clearly stated at this point, John of the Cross thus locates the experience of the Spirit on top of the mountain. After the ascent of stanza 1 and the night of stanza 2, this is fruition in God, the theme of the *Living Flame.*

The authenticity of "For all the beauty" has been contested, not for extrinsic reasons (the poem is found in the Jaén manuscript along with the others), but for intrinsic reasons. The use of the word *beauty* (*hermosura*) in this poem would be, some authors have opined, contrary to the way it is employed in the commentaries on the *Canticle* and the *Living Flame.*[6] Such as it is explained in relation to stanzas 5 and 6 of the *Canticle*, beauty is a divine attribute in which creatures share. Catching a glimpse of this beauty here below is an integral part of the way to God. The beauty of creatures is a trace left upon them by a look thrown at them by the Beloved. There is therefore no danger to be lost in it. But, as has been suggested, the theme of the poem, as summed up in its envoy, would precisely be the danger of beauty:

> For all the beauty
> Never shall I be lost,
> But for I-know-not-what
> Which is found per adventure.

If one looks at it more carefully, however, two expressions in this stanza were such as to keep the Mystical Doctor's attention. First, the theme of beauty was dear to his heart. Indeed, John of the Cross need not use the term *hermosura* always in the same sense. He remained free from the constraints of his vocabulary. Nothing stands in the way of evoking creaturely beauty with its dangers at the beginning and at the end (envoy, and stanza 9), and divine beauty in the middle (stanza 5). Secondly, the theme of "I-know-not-what," this *no sé que* that appears prominently in the *Canticle* could not leave him indifferent: it offered a way to speak of the ineffable, a "stuttering," that did correspond well to the situation of language before the transcendence of the God who is loved and already, in some measure, known. I therefore see no persuasive reason to weed this poem out of the *villancicos* that John of the Cross rewrote *a lo divino*.

The poem is long, too long in fact for an inspiration that remains short of breath: nine stanzas of eight verses of seven syllables. The last verses of the envoy, picked up at the end of each, give the whole a circular tone that makes it apt to be sung by a group, even to be danced: in the Hispanic world, song is commonly paired to dance. Each stanza falls into two equal sections, the second of which draws the conclusion from the first, this conclusion remaining identical throughout, centered as it is on "I-know-not-what."

Several rhythms interlock. The dominant one is that of the refrain, itself borrowed from the envoy. But it is not constant: if stanzas 2 to 8 use the last two verses of the envoy, stanzas 1 and 9 use the last three.

Moreover, all the stanzas refer somehow to the first, which delimits the parameters of the poem as pertaining to the realm of taste. The following stanzas show a number of contrasts between the taste of the creaturely, symbolized by the palate and its desire for earthly foods, and the spiritual taste of divine realities, which pertains to faith.

Alongside this regular return to the first stanza, the stanzas go two by two in such a way that the second is both in continuity and in contrast with the first. These interlocking cadences give the poem a delicate structure. Yet they do not successfully endow it with the lightness that marks the envoy. The tone is too didactic, the images too rare; the absence of concrete setting for general principles hinders the fulfillment of the promises implied in the beginning. Yet the poem is not without merit. Above all, it puts the doctrine of John of the Cross in simple formulae, easy to understand and to remember.

The first two stanzas follow the logic of the *Ascent of Mount Carmel:* from the taste of the finite and its perils (first quatrain) it passes to the decision not to halt at this taste, but rather to hasten toward an "I-know-not-what" encountered per adventure, that is, by sheer grace:

> The savor of the finite good
> At the most can achieve
> Weanness of appetite
> And spoiling of the palate;
>
> And so for all sweetness
> Never shall I get lost,
> But for I-know-not-what
> Which is found per adventure.

This fundamental choice between the finite, which is known yet tiresome, and the Infinite, unknown but worthy of self-abandonment for its sake, brings about the invitation to go further. One must always reach ahead, never look back. What is difficult is alone worthy of attention (first quatrain of stanza 2). This is not Stoicism, a challenge to overcome obstacles, a will to power, a merely natural effort. It is already a self-transcendence through faith:

> The generous heart
> Never cares to delay
> Where it can pass,
> But at the most difficult:
>
> Nothing satisfies it,
> And its faith so ascends
> That it tastes I-know-not-what
> Which is found per adventure.

Stanza 3 and 4 also belong together. The third passes from faith to love, describing the lover, "touched by divine Being," as feverish, his taste and appetite being affected by fever (first quatrain), so that ordinary eating has become repulsive (second quatrain).

The heart of the poem lies in stanzas 5 and 6. Unlike the first one, these refer to divine beauty, known only by faith (st. 5), perceived "without form or figure" (st. 6):

> Now that the will has been
> Touched by the Divinity,
> It cannot be rewarded
> Except by the Divinity;
>
> But since its beauty is such
> That it is seen only by faith,
> It tastes It in I-know-not-what
> Which is found per adventure.
>
> Then of such a lover
> Tell me if you have pity,
> For he finds no savor
> In all that is created;
>
> Alone, without form or figure,
> With no support or foothold,
> Tasting there I-know-not-what
> Which is found per adventure.

With stanza 7 the theme of "with no form or figure" is prolonged and broadened. All that is worth tasting by the "inner man" is set "above all beauty," above the past, the present, and the future. Thus the poet, speaking in the first person, wants to turn to, and to enjoy, not what he has but what he has not yet gotten, yet which he hopes to have. Beyond the duration of this world he turns to the absolute future, symbolized by the "height" of stanza 8. He wants to dwell "above all beauty, / above what was, what is, what will be":

> And so for greater height
> Always I will turn
> Above all toward I-know-not-what
> Which is found per adventure.

Stanza 9 brings the poem to its conclusion. Still speaking in the first person, the poet returns to the theme of the beginning and the envoy: all that falls within sense experience, all that can be understood by the natural mind, and even grace and beauty, have to be left behind. The only thing worth loving may be neither known nor named. The lesson of the *Ascent of Mount Carmel* is epitomized in these few lines:

> For all that through feeling
> Can here be understood,
> And for all that can be grasped,
> Even if it is most high,
> Nor for grace and for beauty,
> Never shall I lose myself
> But for I-know-not-what
> Which is found per adventure.

Admittedly, this is not the best *villancico* among those that John borrowed from the folklore to shape them into hymns to the Beloved. Its pedagogical value is nonetheless noteworthy: it is a good reminder, for others and for oneself, of the nature of the ascent to God. The central topics of the *Ascent* are preserved in it, without the theological apparatus and the biblical illustrations of the tractate. Rather than the poet's voice, it is the voice of the novice master, the instructor of Carmelite nuns, and the spiritual director that resounds here.

The much shorter *villancico*, "Following a loving impulse" (*Tras de un amoroso lance*)[7] has higher poetic value than either "Without support and with support" or "For all the beauty." Its images, borrowed from the theme of the hunt, are particularly striking. The hunt in question is already metaphorical, symbolic of the quest of love. One should presumably think of falconry, of hunting with a hawk, for the action takes place up in the air, as well as of the pursuit of a woman by her lover, when everything happens in a dream no less than in reality.

A third level of attention is required. The poem deals with an upward flight, an ascending movement, a leap that is "so high, so high," a sudden entrance into darkness, a running forward beyond visible horizons. The hunter is after a heavenly prize. One may be tempted to hear this as a reversed echo of the poem by Francis Thompson (1859–1907), *The Hound of Heaven*.[8] Thompson perceives behind himself the footsteps of God, who is the Hound of heaven. With John of the Cross, the poet is the hunter, a bird of prey who has spotted a prey. This prey remains nameless, yet one cannot avoid identifying it with God. All happens in the context of love, in keeping with the tone given by the envoy:

> Following a loving impulse
> And not without hope,
> I flew so high, so high,
> That I caught up with the prey.

These last two verses act as a refrain at the end of all the four stanzas, though not without some alterations. John of the Cross remains free in regard to what he borrows: he may change a word or two in the burden, thus introducing diversity into uniformity. In this case the verse of the ascent, "I flew so high, so high," varies, though the next verse, that of arrival, remains unchanged. What varies, however, is less the assertion of the high level of the flight than the mode of this flight. John will replace "I flew" with other expressions: "But love was so high," then: "And I was so high, so high," again: "That I was so high, so high," and finally: "For I was so high, so high." In sum the entire poem is focused on the ascent to heaven, the evocation of which in recurrent monotone produces a haunting effect. The loving impulse of the beginning ends only once the poem closes up on its last line. In between, the four stanzas evoke four episodes of the love hunt, as was presumably the case in the original *villancico.*[9]

The rhythm is the same throughout. The lines in each stanza are grouped, first, four together, then two, and again two. The quatrain always describes an aspect or episode of the hunt; the first pair of lines, in contrast, suggests how the mystic reacts to the situation described in the quatrain; the final pair concludes, always in the same fashion: this special moment of the hunt has served as jumping point to reach "so high, so high."

Once transposed *a lo divino,* the four hunting episodes correspond respectively to the dangers of the hunt, to the night, to the necessity of *todo-nada,* and to the triumph of hope. If "Without support . . . " was the poem of love, we now read the poem of hope. The profane expectation of sexual congress has become the theological hope of mystical unity. Yet there are obstacles to overcome.

The first is to lose oneself in self-complacency. Admittedly, the poet does not say so in so many words. He proceeds by slight touches, hinting at such an exhilaration in hunting that others have already lost sight of him, thus leaving implied, unformulated, the unavoidable question: is he lost in reality?

> In order to catch up with
> This heavenly impulse,
> So much had I to fly
> That I was lost from sight.

To the peril of self-satisfaction in this flight, which is illustrated abundantly in the *Ascent of Mount Carmel,* the poet opposes the humility of recognizing one's fault in self-renunciation:

> And yet in such a danger
> In my flight I was failing.

This again stands in contrast with the power and totality of love, which is the true impetus in searching for God, as stated in the last two lines:

> But love was so high
> That I caught up with the prey.

At the end of this first stanza it is love that reaches "so high, so high." In the others it will be the poet. By not placing himself in evidence at the beginning, insisting more on the work of love than on his own, he suggests that the task of ascending and pursuing is not really his own; it is love's. And although the poet does not say what the theologian or commentator would have had to explain, this love can be no other than the attribute, identical with the divine Being, which is called agapè in the Johannine tradition, and which the theology of St. Augustine appropriates to the Holy Spirit. Born by the one who is Love, John of the Cross reaches the threshold of heaven, where he comes upon the one he has been seeking and pursuing, God. Yet, in the world of Carmel, such a meeting can take place only through the night:

> When higher I ascended
> My sight was dazzled,
> And the most powerful conquest
> In darkness took place.

What can one do in the dark night when one follows tracks, when, seeking, one can see no longer the point one has started from, nor yet the distant shadow of the Beloved? As John lets us know in the first stanza: one must then take a leap in the dark. And this can be done because love, acting as guide, does not need sight to have certainty:

> But this impulse being of love,
> I made a blind and dark leap . . .

Once more the burden recurs, cast now in the personal form, since the danger of taking it in a Pelagian, self-glorifying sense is past:

> And I was so high, so high,
> That I caught up with the prey.

The third stanza is that of "all-nothing," expressed in a way that

fits the image of the ascent toward the sky. As the stairs of the
Dark Night go down as much as they go up, and even go down
insofar as they go up, so the present ascent to the heights can
equally be a descent to the depths. The similarity of the opening
sounds of the second and third stanzas (*cuando, cuanto*) suggests
the identity of the two perspectives. The mystical night has opened
the way to a blind leap of the faith that is love. In this night the
ascent to the heights shows itself to be also a descent to the depths.
One does not know, since nothing can be seen, whether one is going
up or going down. In fact, ascent is descent, and conversely. The
higher the poet, and therefore the nearer to his prey and the closer
to his Beloved, the lower does he find himself in his aloneness and
his incapacity to go and reach his goal. The quatrain of this stanza
exposes this feeling of powerlessness that accompanies the experi-
ence of coming nearer to the goal:

> The higher I reached
> By so elevated an impulse,
> The lower and the more wearied
> And exhausted I found myself.

As the night gets darker as it is nearer to dawn[10]—according to
the *Ascent of Mount Carmel*—the impression of being low climaxes
when one is close to success. Whence the contrast between the last
pairs of lines. Yet there is more than contrast. The "all-nil" of the
Ascent takes the form of a "high-low." The hunt is a game where
the loser wins. From the low point of the first pair of verses there
arises a breakthrough to the goal, as sung in the last two lines, with
a repetition of *que* which is not without evoking the "I-know-not-
what" (*no se que*) of the *Spiritual Canticle:*

> I said: No one will catch up;
> And I fell so much, so much,
> That I was so high, so high,
> That I caught up with the prey.

With the last stanza the poet proclaims the triumph of the love
that carries him. Without naming it—but love has been named since
the "loving impulse" at the start of the *villancico*—John of the

Cross proposes, in an ecstatic cry, "In a strange manner," a paradoxical summing up of the ascent. He flies over a thousand flights; and he enters a realm in which neither may space be measured with the conventional standards of this world, nor can time be gauged according to the planets' revolutions. A thousand years are like one day. A thousand flights are less than one flight. The measurement is now that of hope, which is not merely waiting or desire, but is the measure of love, the measure of what is measureless:

> In a strange manner,
> A thousand flights I overtook with one,
> Because the hope of heaven
> Catches as much as it hopes.

The last four lines of the poem no longer form two pairs, the second of which would echo the envoy. "Following a loving impulse" gives way to "I hoped only in this impulse," the last verses facing each other as in the rest of the poem. This last recurrence of the burden achieves an infolding of the whole movement of ascent upon itself. The beginning was already the end; the crowning point is no other than the moment of initiation:

> I hoped only in this impulse,
> And in hoping I did not fail,
> For I was so high, so high,
> That I caught up with the prey.

John of the Cross recognized in 1584–85 what was not so clear in 1567 when he dreamt of joining the Carthusian Order: the beginning is already led by the promised breakthrough at the top. The first steps toward the high ground are already born by the impulse that will lead to reach the summit. The paths of approach, along which one enters the night, already draw the outline of the pathless way when, at the summit, there is no law and all is liberty.

As is now obvious, this exercise *a lo divino*, presumably composed fast, at the speed of the pen or the voice, to enliven a recreation in the gardens of the Carmels of Granada, Baeza, or el Calvario, or to illustrate a talk with the sisters at Beas de Segura, forms an echo of the great poems of John of the Cross, as it also sums up the teaching of his commentaries. It might be said that the Mystical Doctor is smiling as he applies to contemplative love what he knows is a popular love song. But such a smile is infinitely serious, for it celebrates the spiritual freedom where divine love leads. One may perceive in it a reminder of John's bold translation of the *Song of Songs*, 5:4: "Concerning this divine touch the bride speaks in the *Songs* after this manner: *Dilectus meus misit manum suam per foramen, et venter meus intremuit ad tactum ejus.* Which is to say: My Beloved put his hand through the opening and my bowels were moved at his touch."[11]

With the poem "A little Shepherd ..." *(Un pastorcico)*, John of the Cross moves to another genre. This is still a transposition *a lo divino*, of which a possible original is known.[12] Yet the piece seems quite different from the preceding ones in both tone and form. It is in fact unique in the works of the Mystical Doctor. The form—five quatrains, eleven syllables to each line—gives it a more classical aspect than is the case with John's other *villancicos* and makes it germane to the poem of the "Spring," composed in captivity. The pastoral scene reminds us of the *Spiritual Canticle*. At face value it seems to be a love poem in a pastoral setting. But this is intended to be symbolic of a deeper level, hidden beneath the symbols.

The "Little Shepherd" has been understood in a christological perspective. Then the shepherd is Christ in search of humanity, his beloved shepherdess, or perhaps the lost sheep. The young shepherd suffers from not being loved, finally dying as *desdichado*, in desperation. Such a reading of the poem has apparently not noticed the despair of its conclusion. Whence it runs into serious objections. Its christology would differ widely from that of the romance on the Incarnation and from that of the *Ascent of Mount Carmel*, 2:22. The romance, focused on the espousal of the divine Word with humankind, barely touched the theme of the death of Jesus (in its section 7), and rather celebrated the glory of God and of his Word. The *Ascent* depicted Christ as the only Word of God, at the same time the Personal, Trinitarian Word, and the word spoken to humanity, when he underwent "life and the first death."[13] On the contrary the "Little Shepherd" would be entirely turned to the death of

Christ, and, surprisingly, with no hint either of the salvific dimension of this death in love or of the resurrection on the third day. The death of the one who, in this short poem, climbs a tree to stretch his arms and die is reminiscent of a suicide, if not as an active taking of one's life, at least as a passive self-dereliction. One century later this text of John of the Cross will in fact inspire a notable passage in the christological theater of the Mexican nun, Sor Juana Inès de la Cruz: "divine Narcissus"—her name for Christ in one of her allegorical plays—will die in the branches of a tree, suspended over his own image reflected in the clear water well that is the Virgin Mary, herself representing perfect humanity.[14]

Furthermore, as the "Little Shepherd" does not seem to leave room for the rising of Jesus from the dead, an inescapable question is raised by the nature of the faith in the resurrection of Jesus. This question haunts the reader in the return of the last line, "The breast with love all injured." This verse is all but identical in couplets 1, 3, 4, 5: Did John place sorrowful self-pity at the heart of his christology? Indeed, he was attentive to the cross. In 1591 at Segovia, John perceived Christ carrying his cross—on a painting that is still preserved—speaking to him. Christ hanging from the cross he also drew in an unforgettable vision. In these two cases, life was triumphant over death; Christ was, in his own death, because it was a death through excess of love, source of life. But this would not be the case in the symbolism of the *Pastorcico*, entirely closed in on sorrow. One would have to admit, in this reading of the poem, that the Doctor of Carmel formulated an aberrant christology.

I would therefore propose another approach to the meaning of this delicate poem, whose texture is made of careful nuances. The shepherd is not Christ; he is the soul in love with God, whose whole thought goes out to his beloved shepherdess. God is this shepherdess in the meadows of love:

> A little shepherd, all alone, is in pain,
> A stranger to pleasure and contentment,
> With his thought on his shepherdess,
> The breast with love all injured.

The shepherd undergoes the travails of the night: night of sense in the first quatrain, night of spirit in the others, when he feels unloved, forgotten, abandoned, unfortunate:

> He does not weep for the wound of love,
> He has no pain in seeing himself so afflicted,
> Although in his heart he is wounded;
> But he weeps, believing that he is forgotten
>
> For only thinking that he is forgotten
> By his beautiful shepherdess, with great sorrow
> He lets himself suffer in a foreign land,
> The breast with love all injured.

The fourth stanza effects an unexpected change from the feminine gender of the shepherdess to the masculine. Projecting his own pain on his Beloved, the little shepherd sees her, like himself, as miserable. He thus finds himself made one with her, even in her absence, by the action of the one who comes to him—the Word incarnate—in what seems to be his absence. This is reminiscent of a similar inversion, though in the opposite sense, in chapter 2 of the *Ascent* (Book One), when God is the Bride of the soul before becoming his Bridegroom in the rest of the work and in the commentary on the *Canticle*:[15]

> And the shepherd said: Oh, unfortunate
> That one who has ignored my love
> And does not seek the joy of my presence!
> —The breast with his love all injured.

The poet reports his impression, not the deeper reality. God, his beautiful Shepherdess, has not forgotten him; the feeling of desperation surfaces in crossing through the night, when one is dazzled by overwhelming light. Hence the intriguing ambiguity of the last verse of this couplet. Is the injured breast male or female? Male in stanzas 1, 3, and 5, where the shepherd speaks of himself, would it be female in stanza 4? By placing the exclamation, as I have done, at the end of the third line, I have applied the fourth to the little shepherd; yet this verse, pertaining to the shepherd's discourse, could just as well refer to the shepherdess, who has suddenly been identified, in her very absence, with the shepherd who desires her. Is there still a distinction between them? This is the theme, already known to us, of the lovers' mutual identification.

The last quatrain describes the mystical death, a death by excessive love, which is also featured, at approximately the same time, in the commentary on the *Living Flame of Love:*

> And after a long time he climbed up
> A tree where he opened his beautiful arms,
> And, dead, he remained hanging from them,
> The breast with love all injured.

The picture of a man hanging by his arms evokes immediately John's drawing of the Crucified.[16] Christ is indeed hanging from his arms stretched out, tied to the horizontal wood. But, in the poem, this cannot be Christ: for the little shepherd is dead, and the Crucified of the drawing is alive; and moreover the Christ of faith did not remain hanging: he was untied, was buried, descended into inferno, rose from among the dead. The little shepherd hanging from a tree is no more than a man, if indeed, in the poet's vision, a man imaging Christ. The Christian who truly is one with the Word made flesh has become like him in the faith that is love.

With this conclusion the "Little Shepherd" adds delicate touches to the motif that has been at the center of John of the Cross's experience since his Toledan imprisonment: the night of abandonment is in its deeper reality a wonderful night of love.

If the minor poems of John of the Cross add nothing to the core of his doctrine, as this is expounded in his tractates, they nonetheless illustrate their author's virtuosity. Neither the inspired writing of his major poems, nor the labor of interpretation in his commentaries have taken from him the taste, presumably left over from his childhood, of folk poetry or, linked to his reading of Sebastian de Córdova, his liking for transpositions *a lo divino.* These secondary works reassure the reader as they underline and illustrate certain central themes: night, abandonment, love, quest, beauty, identification with the Beloved. They broaden the scope, if not of John's images as such, at least of the vistas that he has opened to the imagination of his followers. God is still an "I-know-not-what," to be reached through love rather than through intellection. Yet he is also a prey to be caught, a shepherdess to be tenderly loved. The author of the minor poems has lost nothing of the freedom, indeed, of the boldness, that characterize the poet of the *Canticle.*

Other poems may be lost. This is too bad for us. Yet one may catch a glimpse of a few of their colors in two isolated quatrains that have been preserved. Here is a motto for a Christmas card:[17]

> With the divine Word
> The pregnant Virgin
> Comes along the lane:
> Open her the inn!

And this is a cameo of the programme explained in the *Ascent of Mount Carmel:*

> Oblivion of the creature,
> Memory of the Creator,
> Attention to the inside,
> And now loving the Beloved!

This couplet gives the tone of the secondary works in prose authored by John of the Cross. The letters, filled with tender friendship, easily refute the objection that the Mystical Doctor, absorbed as he is in his relation to God, cares little for anyone. In fact, with others as with himself, he is primarily concerned that "Jesus be in their soul."[18] The *Sayings of Light and Love,* like the *Cautions* and *Advice,* may be placed in parallel with certain pages of the *Ascent* and of the commentary on the *Canticle,* whose ideas they reformulate succinctly. Thus the "all-nil," the perils of spiritual goods, the solitary thrush, the three signs of entrance into contemplation, the centrality of love, the suavity of the divine presence, the necessary mediatorship of Christ, the function of faith, the absoluteness of God, constitute the high points of these occasional writings and of the correspondence of John of the Cross.

Among these relatively short pieces, the *Cautions* and *Advice* belong to the orbit of the *Ascent of Mount Carmel,* whose teaching they put in lapidary formulas; the *Sayings of Light and Love,* which celebrate the mystery of the "solitary soul,"[19] the "most sweet love of God," the presence of "the face of God, clear and pure, in the soul," are more akin to the commentary on the *Canticle.* Above all one should read, written at the acme of love, the admirable page, filled with high poetry, that is known as the "Prayer of the Soul Aflame with Love."[20]

John has just stated once more that one should empty oneself of all ties to creatures, "and you will walk in divine lights, for God is not like creatures." From this point on a triple movement is sketched: offering up one's sins as the very realm of God's grace; the liberation of all "manners and limitations" in the "only Son Jesus Christ"; the repossession of all things in Christ. From the viewpoint of speculative theology one could identify here a threefold paradox. First there is the paradox of sin, concerning which John of the Cross comes remarkably close to Martin Luther:

> Lord God, my Beloved, if you still remember my sins in such wise that you do not do what I beg of you, do your will concerning them, my God, which is what I most desire, and exercise your goodness and mercy, and you will be known through them. And if it is that you are waiting for my good works so as to hear my prayer through their means, grant them to me and work them for me, and the sufferings you desire to accept, and let it be done.

Like Luther,[21] the Carmelite mystic has grasped that in itself sin is no match for divine grace. God, who can do all things, can make himself known, in his mercy, through my sins. If he wants works from me, let him perform them so that they will be mine! And if he does not want any, John of the Cross asks, what does he want? "But if you are not waiting for my works, what is it that makes you wait, my most clement Lord? Why do you delay? For if, after all, I am to receive the grace and mercy which I entreat of you in your Son, take my mite, since you desire it, and grant me this blessing, since you also desire that."

The mystical life is the theater of a "wondrous exchange" between God and the soul. God takes on himself the work of the soul, which is but sin and mite; and the soul receives the work of God, which is "grace and mercy." This dialectic of mystical exchange was celebrated at the ontological level by the Greek Fathers and applied by Luther at the existential. As to John of the Cross, he places himself at both levels without distinguishing between them, for they converge in the Son.

The second paradox relates to the modeless mode, the pathless way, the escape from the world of forms, which are so often described in the works of the Mystical Doctor. From the fact that God does everything there follows that man, limited by nature to the singular and contingent, must and can nonetheless live in the universal and absolute. Yet God, the Absolute, is beyond all form, figure, or image. Here again, it is the Son who hyphenates two positions that are otherwise incompatible. The Son, though named, in the world of forms, after the image of human filiation, is imageless, for he is the image of the One who, beyond all things, has neither form nor figure. John of the Cross therefore asks:

> Who can free himself from lowly manners and limitations if you do not lift him to yourself, my God, in purity of love? How will a man, begotten and nurtured in lowliness, rise up to you, Lord, if you do not raise him with your hand which made him? You will not take from me, my God, what you once gave me in your only Son Jesus Christ, in whom you gave me all I desire. Hence I rejoice that if I wait for you, you will not delay.

The dialectic of exchange continues in one of giving. Here, John—in a formula that has been favored in some Protestant theologies, which echo the profound intent of the most traditional Catholic piety—"pleads" the Son and his work before the Father. He presents and shows the only Son in such a way that henceforth he will himself be seen by God with the riches received from the Son. The one who is nothing is treated, in the Son, as though he were all. This is akin to Luther's formula: *simul justus et peccator.*[22] The saint is at the same time just and sinful. Sinful in himself, he is just in Christ. Whence the conclusion: let us not wait before praising God till we feel we are sinless. John of the Cross talks to himself: "With what procrastinations do you wait, since from this very moment you can love God in your heart?"

The third paradox of mystical life follows: already in this world such a life is a triumphal celebration of love fulfilled. In the victory of the double gift that has been received—being and having, by creation and by grace—all that belongs to God belongs also to me: "Mine are the heavens and mine is the earth. Mine are the nations, the just are mine, and mine the sinners. The angels are mine, and the Mother of God and all things are mine; and God himself is mine and for me, because Christ is mine and all for me."

One may easily recognize here the tone of stanzas 13 and 35 of the *Spiritual Canticle*. In Christ, seen once again as the one in whom God gives himself, there is no opposition between being and having. The necessary denudation has taken place in the ascent of the mountain; the central path has been followed through the night. But all has now been recovered in God through Christ. Morning knowledge has replaced evening knowledge. All is mine. And so John will conclude, turning once more to himself: "What do you ask, then, and seek, my soul? Yours is all of this, and all is for you. Do not engage yourself in anything less, nor pay heed to the crumbs which fall from your Father's table. Go forth and exult in your glory! Hide yourself in it and rejoice, and you will obtain the supplications of your heart."

Only at this point may God, who was so named at the beginning of this text because of his transcendence, be also called Father by the creature. In the depths of mystical experience the full reality of the Son's filiation and the Father's paternity is perceived. The Son is Son in that he receives all he is from the Father. At the moment when the human creature discovers in faith that it has received from God all that it is, and that this being is also absolute having, it may call God, Father.

The remaining pages of the *Sayings of Light and Love* enshrine in aphorisms the insights that have thus been grasped. Points for mental prayer, pious ejaculations, thoughts, desires, ecstatic utterances may be selected according to attractions, remembered according to needs, or simply forgotten in the ocean of infinite love.[23]

CHAPTER 10

THE *LIVING FLAME OF LOVE*

he poem of the *Living Flame of Love*, composed in Granada during the years 1582 to 1584, contrasts sharply with the transpositions *a lo divino* made in the same period. On the one hand, John of the Cross interprets folk poetry, adapting it, in keeping with the taste of his times, to the piety of Carmel. On the other, the poet listens only to his own inspiration to write four stanzas of a striking originality. In both cases, however, he claims no originality as to form. Indeed, the commentary on the *Living Flame* will remain unique among the Mystical Doctor's works in that it will specify with all necessary precision from what source the poetic form has been borrowed: it is made of *liras* with six lines on the model of "Boscán," that is, of Garcilaso as rewritten *a lo divino* by Sebastián of Córdova. As is duly noted by the commentator, "the fourth line goes with the first, the fifth with the second, and the sixth with the third."[1] In other words each stanza includes two triads of verses, which are parallel in both form and rhyme, following the pattern *a-b-c—a-b-c*. In Garcilaso de la Vega this is found in the Second *Canción*,[2] which is, however, twice as long as the *Flame*, and which diversifies its rhythm by alternating six-line and seven-line stanzas. John strictly follows as demanding but more monotonous a form as the means to express his interior freedom. Thus restraining himself to a given path, he makes a choice in the material utilized by Garcilaso and Sebastián.

Why the six-line stanza, which appears nowhere else in John's works, rather than the five-line one, as in the poems of the *Dark Night* and the *Spiritual Canticle*, that John had clearly mastered?

To this question one cannot answer before further examining the form of each stanza. Yet the change of form already suggests that we now have access to another level than with the other great poems. Admittedly, the approximately five years that separate the *Living Flame* from the *Dark Night* and the first thirty-one stanzas of the *Canticle* could suffice to explain the change of model. After a certain poetic silence, broken only by the production of the second *Canticle* and the rewriting *a lo divino* of some folk poetry, the author, newly inspired, starts again. It would then seem normal not to use the older patterns; a new medium is needed to say something new. In the same years, or maybe shortly before, John composes the last verses of his second *Canticle*, on the five-line *lira* model, which he uses as effectively as before. He has preserved his mastery of this form. If he now changes poetic pattern, this is not for a mere literary whim or because of a need for change or a desire to strike on a new path. John is neither doing literature nor sharpening a stylistic tool. He makes his choice because he is aware of doing something other than in *Canticle (A)*, which he has just finished or is finishing. Between the *Spiritual Canticle* and the *Living Flame of Love* there is literary continuity: the atmosphere remains that of the Italianizing poetry that has introduced into Spain some orientations of the Italian Renaissance. Yet there is also something new. The five-line stanza has become insufficient; it is literally left behind by a sixth verse that cuts the stanza in two equal parts.

But not all equalities are the same. The second triad of each sextet, though it is exactly parallel with the first in its form, is no mere repetition. We are not in the parallelism of Hebraic poetry, with which John of the Cross was acquainted through the biblical psalms and the *Song of Songs*. The triads of the *Flame* have been influenced by those that abound in the works of Garcilaso, where they control much of the shape of *Second Eclogue* and all of the *Third Elegy*. Garcilaso's triads are progressive. They describe action along with scenery. They move around in a kind of dance in which the dancers' steps never fall on their own tracks.

With Dante Allighieri (1265–1321) and his *Divine Comedy*, the triad had become a privileged form of Italian religious poetry. Yet Dante's *terza rima*[3]—of eleven syllables, solemn, hieratic even, repeating the same rhyme three times—is not that of the Spanish mystic. Here one passes from two five-syllable verses to one of eleven syllables. An ascending movement leads from the second to the third, so that the whole poem beats a wavelike march: up to the third verse, down on the first line of the next triad, and up again at the end. Rather than a dance in which one pivots on oneself or a group goes in a circle, the *Living Flame* leaps higher and longer on the third step, thus creating a diastolic motion. This is all the more remarkable as, from the standpoint of the rhyme, no three verses are complete. Over against the rhymes of the *Divine Comedy,* those of the *Living Flame* do not exist in the triad, but in the sextet. Joined two by two across two triads, the rhymes break the circularity of each and open a larger universe.

As regards the grammatical structure of the sentence, the *Flame* carries to an extreme a tendency that was already present in the first *Canticle:* the absence of prepositions is astonishing. Out of the four stanzas of the poem, only one contains a normally con-structed sentence, with a verb in the indicative form. The reader faces a sequence of exclamations that are merely strung together. If there is progress from the one to the next, this is not manifested by the grammar. It is of the paradigmatic rather than the syntagmatic order. It belongs to feeling or to being, not to thinking. Moreover, most of these exclamations are verbless. They are not sentences; they are cries. Yet these cries are not automatic reflex reactions; they have a recognizable sense. In fact John of the Cross explains their meaning very well:

> To extol the fervour and delight with which it speaks in these four stanzas, the soul begins each of them with the word 'Oh' or 'How,' which words signify affectionate exultation. Each time that they are used they show that something is passing within the soul beyond that which can be expressed by the tongue. And the word 'Oh' serves also to express a deep yearning and earnest supplication with the aim of persuasion; for both these reasons the soul uses that word in this stanza, intimating and extolling its great desire, and endeavouring to persuade love to set it free.[4]

John uses few subjects or verbs. Vocatives stand out: flame, burn, wound, hand, touch, are talked to. The poet conveys the impression that, if he does know where he wishes to go, he is not eager to let

184 · *The* Living Flame of Love

the reader into the secret too soon. The rare verbs explain but little. The first, "woundest," acts in fact as a predicate in relation to the flame to which the discourse is addressed. Such is also the case with the second verb, "thou art." Then the tempo suddenly accelerates: whereas the first three lines have only one verb, the second three have four. This is, however, illusory. For only the last verb, "Break," gives meaning to the movement: the poet asks, beseeches, or prays. Yet this prayer is reduced to a minimal expression, the chief effort bearing, not on the poet's desire, but on the identification of the flame to which the supplication goes. One request only is formulated in the entire poem: it comes at the end of the first stanza, the rest of the first three stanzas having no other effect than to multiply the qualificatives of the flame. This one petition, "Break the web of this sweet encounter," does little more than suggest a conclusion to what the flame has, by its very nature, already done. As is said in the second triad of the first stanza, the flame is not evasive. Already, the poet writes, it has deeply wounded the soul at its center. Let it then finish off what it has started. The request in question is hardly original: its content derives from what comes before. May the past, as is proper, lead to the future! Thus the only prayer of this poem does no more than elaborate and draw out the implications of the nature of the flame to which the poet is talking. The petition is included naturally in the exclamation.

The second stanza is the only one to end on a complete sentence, with what traditional grammar calls subject, verb, and complement: "Slaying, death into life you have changed." This statement, or perhaps this accusation, still addressed to the Flame, follows four exclamations, the first three of which constitute a progressive sequence:

> Oh sweet burn!
> Oh delectable wound!
> Oh soft hand! . . .

Burn, wound, hand: three moments in the poet's growing awareness of the depth of his wound! They go back from the burn—which is in fact the cauterizing effect of applying a hot instrument to the wound to be cauterized—to the hand that has caused both the wound and the burn. Yet perspectives are reversed within the very movement of discovery; each exclamation includes its antidote: the burn is sweet; the wound, delectable; the hand, soft. Comfort comes along with pain; health is given within the disease. At each level of this growing awareness of the wound there is a passage to the opposite, which smoothly brings about the last exclamation, when calling on the noun and its qualifier becomes a double affirmation of what the preceding adjectives mean. After the "sweet burn," the "delectable wound," the "soft hand," there comes, in continuity with the adjectives, a "delicate touch":

> Oh soft hand! Oh delicate touch
> Savoring of eternal life
> And paying every debt!

The triumph of the qualifier over the noun to which it is attached is full: the noun, "touch," is introduced by the adjective, "delicate." In the normal process of healing, a remedy is determined by the diagnosis, or the awareness of the wound. Here, however, the perspective goes in reverse: the remedy determines the form and nature of the wound. Such an inversion also reverses the order of grammatical functions: the noun becomes a predicate in relation to a subject shaped like an adjective. The "delicate touch" is in reality a touched delicacy, a delight communicated by contact. It brings into harmony the preceding disjunctions; it reaches beyond the horizon of the wound, be it profound, to include in one totality eternity and the restoration of the moral order in which every debt has been paid off. Without telling us, John of the Cross opens a vista on the jubilee or sabbatical year of the Old Testament, which, every seventh year, was to bring the People of God back to its ideal origin when they were crossing the Sinai desert in simplicity and equality of goods,[5] thus laying down the foundation for the later orientation of hope toward the expected Messiah and the ultimate transformation of the universe. As indicated by the last line ("Slaying, death into life you have changed!"), the matter is nothing less than a passage from death to life. The perspective is open on the resurrection.

As one may see, the structure of this second stanza, like that of the first, underlines the conclusive effect of the sixth verse. This is, in both cases, the line of the verb. And the verb bestows meaning on the whole stanza: "break" in the first; resurrection in the second. The action outlined in the sixth verse brings to a climax the ascent of the preceding lines. The undulating wave of the poem is a dance: the leap of the end reaches higher than the midway leap of each stanza.

The entire third stanza is a long exclamation, which is modulated in keeping with the structure of the first triad. The reader is led to the high points of the third and sixth verses, which are correlated. The "deep caverns of sense" of line 3, an image that evokes darkness, then the imperfection of creatures, give, in the paradoxical logic introduced by the second stanza, the "warmth and light" of line 6. The "lamps of fire" are identical with the "living flame"; they form an aspect of it, and more exactly the aspect by which the flame shows itself in the caverns of sense when it illumines it with its rays. Such a light, which is shared and is fecund, does not lie there like an alien body. Rather, the "caverns of sense" partake in its radiation, and radiate in turn "warmth and light":

> Oh lamps of fire,
> In whose radiations
> The deep caverns of sense
> That was dark and blind
> With strange beauties
> Warmth and light give close to their Darling!

Let us note at this point another remarkable dimension of the *Living Flame of Love,* which is particularly stressed here: John of the Cross does not only invert the grammatical structure; he also upsets the creaturely order. There is an ambiguity between the singular and the plural. The "lamps of fire" have transformed the "deep caverns of sense" to the point where these "warmth and light give close to their Darling!" In fact, however, "their Darling" (*su Querido*) could be just as well "his" or "its" Darling. Is this the darling of the caverns? Is he not rather that of sense, of which it is said that it was (formerly) "dark and blind?" Admittedly there is an identity of the caverns and the sense, and thereby of the plural and the singular. The Darling is clearly the Beloved of the *Spiritual Canticle.* If he is dear to sense and its deep caverns, this can only be, for readers of the *Ascent of Mount Carmel,* after a total mutation of sense. Just as the singular of the Flame is the same as the plural of the lamps, the singular of sense equals the plural of the caverns.

Together, sense and its caverns now have strange beauties, the role of which, in the on-going march of the poem, is to allow sense and its caverns to remain "close to their (its) Darling." They radiate, yet not on their own, only by their being near to the Beloved; they radiate with his light. After the evocation of the sabbatical year, the type of Messianic times, this evokes Pentecost. Yet there is a sharp difference between the Pentecost of the apostles and the present one: in the Acts,[6] the Beloved, having ascended to heaven, is absent. The Spirit, coming down in the image of fiery tongues, brought to the disciples the gift sent to them by the Beloved after his ascension. Here on the contrary the Beloved is not absent; the lamps of fire do not stand for him. He is here; and it is close to him that the caverns of sense radiate warmth and light in their strange beauties: they have been transformed in the likeness of the Living Flame of Love.

The tone of the last stanza differs noticeably from what has gone before. Like the third one it contains no statement in proper form. Each triad constitutes an exclamation dominated by "how" (*cuan*). The feeling of ambiguity or, if one prefers, the indifference between singular and plural, is taken one step further. The reader hesitates as to the identity of the addressee. To whom is the poet speaking in these lines? The logic of the first three stanzas would require that he speak, as he has done hitherto, to the flame. This was, at the second stanza, burn, wound, hand, touch. Passing to the plural, it became lamps at the third stanza. And now the poet changes the grammatical gender of the one to whom he speaks. At first in the feminine (yet both "burn" and "touch" are masculine in Spanish), the interlocutor is now put in the masculine:

> How gentle and loving
> You awaken in my breast
> Where in secret only you live!

Two hypotheses come to mind, though, from a strictly poetic angle, choice between them is by no means necessary. On the one hand, the poem is still addressed to the Flame. John has extended to grammatical gender the identity he had previously established in grammatical number. Plural and singular, masculine and feminine, lose their specificity and fade away. One enters a world without accidental differentiations. And if there is an instrument of this unification, whether defect or advantage, this can only be, in the structure of the poem, proximity to the Beloved. He it is who transforms what comes near him. He initiates into the new world envisioned by St. Paul in the epistle to the Galatians: "There is neither Greek nor Jew, neither slave nor free man, neither male nor female, but you are one in Christ Jesus."[7]

On the other hand, the poet does not address himself anymore to the Flame, but to his Darling. The Beloved, gentle and loving, wakes up in his breast, where he dwells secretly in solitude. The last three lines still evoke the Beloved:

> And in your perfumed breathing,
> With good and glory filled,
> How delicately you woo me with love!

Between the third and the fourth stanzas the addressee of the poem has acquired a face and been personalized. A flame, a burn, a wound, a hand, lamps of fire, are not in human experience, even that of Christian mystics, sources or objects of personal or interpersonal relations. They may be looked at, admired, received; by them one may be warmed and enlightened; one may even sing of them and celebrate their advent. But one scarcely comes to them to love and be loved. It is quite different with the Beloved and Darling. Being loved, he is already known as a person. Thus the topic of the *Living Flame of Love* is no other than the passage from the experienced Flame to the already known Beloved of the *Spiritual Canticle*. In theological terms it is the passage from the enlightening Holy Spirit to the Word, the soul's own Bridegroom.

Of all the poems of John of the Cross, the *Living Flame of Love* is the one in which the poetic expression best adheres to the theological content. Knowledge of its two commentaries is not needed to realize that the first three stanzas are focused on the one who enables us to know and love the Beloved, that is, in classical theology, the Holy Spirit. It is the Spirit who, as living flame of love in the soul, wounds, who is not evasive, who becomes burn, wound, hand, touch, who knows eternal life and who pays every debt. He it is who makes himself lamps of fire, who brings light to the caverns of sense to transform them and make them share his light. The

Spirit provides the theme, though not explicitly identified, of the first three stanzas: to him the task of tearing the veil of this sweet encounter, since he is transforming power, who, slaying, changes death into life. Through him the caverns of sense, henceforth filled with strange beauties, give warmth and light when one is close to one's Darling. The Spirit is love, but also strength, the one no less than the other. As strength he is, in the same proportions, gentleness. And since he is God, he is all this infinitely.

Before going further in theological analysis, one may note the basic lesson of the *Living Flame:* facing the Spirit and his works, the creature finds itself unable to speak. The limits of language have been reached. Hence the writer's recourse to exclamations. The lack of expected verbal forms lets the subjects, so to say, float in the air, without the stabilizing qualification that would accrue from a predicate. This undoubtedly points to the Spirit as the subject, and even as nothing other than subject: as lord of his acts he leaves the initiative to no other. When he acts upon a human person, the latter can only be passive. And this also emphasizes the radical impossibility of speaking of the Spirit and his action with the ordinary norms or conventions of language. We are at the extreme boundary of the possibilities of communication, outside the tales that can be told by men. The poet attempts a supreme effort, after which all is silence.

We should now be able to answer the question raised at the start of the present chapter: why did John of the Cross abandon the five-line *lira* featured in the *Canticle?* The reason was that he wanted to do something new, different from what he had begun in prison. He wanted to create the poem, no longer of escape to freedom, but of total freedom, when nothing constrains personal liberty, engaged as this is in the sovereign liberty of the Spirit. At face value the sixth verse is unnecessarily added to the first five. Contrasted with the *Spiritual Canticle,* the *Living Flame of Love* contains an element of superfluity, of gratuitousness, which hints at the Spirit's boundless generosity. Yet, if one looks closer, the opposite happens. The supplementary verse is not the last one; it is really the first. Placing one verse in front of a *Canticle* stanza would provide the precise form of the *Living Flame.* The former's second and fifth lines, like the latter's third and sixth, have eleven syllables, against the seven of the other lines. John of the Cross, in composing the *Living Flame of Love,* started earlier, taking one step back before jumping ahead. He literally prolonged the inspiration of his poetry (in Latin as in Greek, *pro* means *before*) by anticipation, not by complementation. Poetic inspiration, a phenomenon that John explicitly acknowledged at the beginning of the commentary on the *Canticle,*[8] started earlier. The new stanza testifies to a deepening and lengthening of experience. This inspiration is, if possible, steadier than in the *Canticle,* whatever perfection this already showed.

Indeed, the new stanza, like the older one, has its own integrity, which is not revealed by comparison. Yet comparison points to an element of gift, of gratuity, that underlies all the poem of the *Living Flame.* The sixth verse—which conveys the erroneous impression of being superfluous—brings each stanza to a conclusion that, Spirit-given, has been received by the mystical poet. Already at this moment, the poet is himself, literally, silence.

The Trinitarian theology of the Mystical Doctor would have to be discussed for a fuller grasp of this poem. Yet it is not necessary at this point to return to the analysis of the *Romance on the Incarnation,* in which John, in the nights of Toledo, had embodied his doctrine of the Trinity. Nor need we come back to the Trinitarian dimension of the *Spiritual Canticle,* the main aspects of which have already been pointed out, and which I have briefly analyzed elsewhere.[9] In any case the topic will retain us below, for it is broached again in the two versions of the commentary on the *Living Flame of Love.*

Let us simply remark, at the end of this short chapter, that the Holy Spirit, whose action in the soul in love takes up three stanzas of the poem, is himself the context for the soul's "sweet encounter" with the Beloved. The Beloved is other than, yet inseparable from, the Spirit. The experience of mystical love takes place in the Holy Spirit, even though this love is not for the Spirit but for the Word, the Son, the Shepherd of the *Canticle,* who emerges in the *Living Flame,* beyond all metaphors and symbols, directly as the Beloved. Having posited the Spirit's action, unconcerned with the effects and results of his own discourse, since it is now the Spirit who does all, John of the Cross has no more need for symbols. Or rather, he uses symbols—the burn, the wound, the hand, the touch, the lamps of fire—to designate the Spirit. But for the Bridegroom, the Beloved, he needs symbols no more. The Beloved is simply the one who both loves and is loved. He is the Darling, asleep on the bed of the soul, in secret, in the shared solitude of the soul and the one she loves. He is also, above all, the lover, since it is he who, at the last line of the poem, so "delicately woos" the poet "with love."

CHAPTER 11

THE DIVINE BEING

he circumstances in which
the commentary on the *Living Flame of Love* was composed are
fairly well known. Responding to a request from doña Ana de Mer-
cado y Peñalosa, a wealthy lady living in Segovia who had come to
know John of the Cross during a sojourn in Granada, and who had
evidently received high mystical graces, John wrote the commentary
in some two weeks' time, during the years 1584–87. He confesses
in the prologue that he hesitated and waited for some time before
acceding to doña Ana's wishes. Yet it appears immediately, as one
reads it, that the first commentary (A) remains quite close to the
poem as far as inspiration goes. In spite of the two or three years
that may have passed since the poem was written, both seem to
carry the same tune. On the one hand, the author "can say naught
that is of any value, especially in things of such sublimity and
substance."[1] On the other, he specifies: "And it is of this degree of
enkindled love that the soul must be understood as speaking when
it is at last transformed and perfected interiorly in the fire of love;
not only is it united in this fire but it has now become one living
flame within it."[2]

These two assertions are not contradictory. Nothing comes from
John of the Cross as to the substance and the content of the book.[3]
As to the form, it is dependent on the mediation of his whole
personality, in keeping with the scholastic principle, which he duly
recognizes: "Nothing can be received except according to the re-
ceiver's mode."[4] Yet, as to the expression, the writer is responsible
both for its substance and for its form. If all that the Mystical
Doctor wished to say in his commentary had passed through his

own experience in the higher reaches of mystical life, the substance in need of a form, and the form itself, which was poetic before it became theological, proceeded from the writer himself. The substance of the expression relates to his culture; the form derives from his own choice.

In this case the rapidity with which he wrote did leave traces in the commentary. The stanzas are not given equal treatment, the third being examined at greater length, the fourth taking up only a few pages. Large digressions break the poetic thread that may still be discerned in the commentary. Thus, speaking of the verse "And who pays every debt!" in 11:21–27, the author analyzes the reasons why few persons are raised to the high level of experience that is described here. Or yet, the explanations on the third stanza are interrupted by a long digression, presented as such, on the blind guides identified as the spiritual directors, the devil, and oneself.[5] Moreover, some passages do not seem to fit very well where they are. Examples of this are: a return to the subject matter of the *Ascent of Mount Carmel*,[6] and some lengthy exclamations that would be more appropriate at the beginning of stanza 2 than at the end.

This is no doubt the reason why John also composed a second commentary, (B), of the *Living Flame*. Being as good a writer as he was a poet, he picked up his work when inspiration had cooled down, added a few transitions, modified some formulations, introduced clarifications and developments, and took out certain lines. Between this version (B), done at an uncertain date in the last years of the author's life, and version (A), there is identity of content or, if one prefers, of doctrine. But the expression of (B), less spontaneous, is more studied than that of (A) in form as well as in doctrine.

From the start John of the Cross equates the "living flame of love" with the Holy Spirit. "This flame of love is the Spirit of its Spouse—that is, the Holy Spirit."[7] Yet the author's purpose is neither to explain the traditional Trinitarian doctrine, nor to construct a new one. It is to show how the soul is aware of the presence and action of the Spirit, how the Spirit dwells in her, and what he does. Here as elsewhere the Mystical Doctor's aim is to clarify experience rather than to build a theology, even though, in so doing, he may open important theological avenues. What he explains is simply that, through the Spirit in her, the soul that has come to this level becomes Spirit herself: "And this flame the soul feels within, not only as a fire that has consumed and transformed it in sweet love, but also as a fire which burns within and sends out flame, as I have said, and that flame bathes the soul in glory and refreshes it with the temper of divine life."

The doctrine of John of the Cross on the Holy Spirit is in fact hardly original. It comes from Thomas Aquinas, more remotely deriving from St. Augustine's understanding of the procession from the first two Persons *(Filioque)*.[8] The Spirit, and this is also a factor in Augustine's theology, is the love uniting the first two Persons, their "link." Being the Spirit of the Father, by whom he is sent, he leads to the Father. Being the Spirit of the Son, by whom he is also sent, he shows the Son, to whom he guides the faithful. As the expression and active channel of divine grace, he introduces the faithful into the divine life. Created participation in God hinges on the Spirit, who manifests his presence through his "unctions." And since his deeds in the created world cannot be separated from what he is himself in God and as God, he is the divine Being as capable of sharing with the creatures.

The originality of the Mystical Doctor is not of the order of doctrine or of speculation. It pertains to experience and symbolization. This is shown by the correlations that are established between the Spirit on the one hand, and a certain number of analogies and metaphors on the other. As the Spirit is flame, and more particularly flame of love, he takes on the characteristics of fire, throwing sparks, multiplying itself in smaller fires, engulfing in flame all it touches, and thus burning and wounding.

As it follows, the commentary on the *Living Flame* chiefly describes the human experience of the Spirit, who leads to the Beloved, assures the meeting of the two lovers, shows the Beloved to his bride, shares with her the beauties, grandeurs, sweetnesses of her Bridegroom. He acts as a revealer of what is properly ineffable, which man alone, at whatever degree of spirituality or perfection, would be unable to reach. The experience of the Spirit is pure grace. It is a time when "God is the craftsman of everything, the soul doing nothing of her own."[9]

Unlike the divine Word, the Spirit is not given many names. He is simply the Spirit, the Holy Spirit, "the Spirit of the Word,"[10] "the Spirit of her Bridegroom. . . . " Even the scriptural titles, Paraclete,

196 · The Divine Being

the other Paraclete,[11] are not used. A term that in the tradition and
the liturgy has sometimes designated the third Person—Wisdom,
Wisdom of God—is applied only to the Word, except when it simply
means wisdom as an attribute of the divine nature. It looks as
though the Mystical Doctor had decided to reduce the language
used of the Holy Spirit to what is strictly characteristic. Now, the
chief mark of the Spirit, in both the Western and the Eastern tradi-
tions, is to be Person in another way than the other two: the Spirit
has his consistency, not in himself, but in that he is the Spirit of
someone: he is Spirit of God, Spirit of the Father, Spirit of the Son,
and also, in the context of Augustinian theology, the Spirit of the
Father and the Son, proceeding from both as from one principle.

In these conditions it may seem surprising that the commentary
on the *Living Flame of Love,* just like the poem that is commented
upon, multiplies, if not direct appellations for the Spirit, at least
analogies and comparisons. In spite of what had been suggested by
reading the poem, the vocatives of the second stanza are not all
identified with the Spirit. He is indeed "flame" and "burn"; but he
is neither the "hand," for this is the Father, nor the "touch," for
this is the Word. He is not the "wound": this is the first of "three
great favors" extended to the soul by God: "The first is the delectable
wound, which the soul attributes to the Holy Spirit, wherefore it
is called a burn. The second is the desire for eternal life, which the
soul attributes to the Son, and therefore calls a delicate touch. The
third is a gift wherewith the soul is right well pleased, and this it
attributes to the Father, and therefore calls it a soft hand."[12]

This text throws light on the nature of the attributions that are
thus made. They are, in the theology deriving from Augustine,
"appropriations." The soul that has experienced the living flame of
love perceives several of its effects, which she attributes, the one
to the Spirit, another to the Son, a third to the Father. To each of
these attributions there corresponds a name for the Person involved.
Yet, far from being essential or personal names, they are given names
which express neither the one divine essence nor the properties of
the divine Persons: they merely translate the impact of an experience
upon the soul. These names are given "because of the properties of
their effects." It is strictly a linguistic phenomenon.

Undoubtedly, John of the Cross is acquainted with the theological
principle of appropriation, which he formulates in this way: "They

all work as one, and the soul attributes the whole of their work to one, and the whole of it to all of them." Moreover, John is the first to acknowledge that this is a linguistic problem. Speaking of the sweetness and delicacy of God, he admits that one cannot possibly speak of it adequately: "Nor would I willingly speak thereof, lest it should be supposed that it is no more than that which I say; for there are no words to expound and enumerate such sublime things of God as come to pass in these souls; whereof the proper way to speak is for one that knows them to understand them inwardly and enjoy them and be silent concerning them."[13]

Concerning the Spirit and his action in the soul, John of the Cross would say what he states of the Word, who is "alien to all mode and manner, and free of all volume, of form, figure, and accidents...."[14] For this reason one cannot speak of it. And yet one cannot entirely abstain from telling the story of the things of God of which one has obtained a certain experience. Yet one should carefully avoid being attached to "natural ability and reasoning... Yet it is something quite different when an effect of the spirit overflows in the senses."[15] To this principle John of the Cross traces St. Paul's "stigmata." It holds the key to mystical language as flowing from experience. One may then name the cause after its known effects. Nonetheless, when reading mystical literature one should remember that God, who is "formless and figureless, ... being what He is—unimaginable—cannot be grasped by the imagination."[16] This is undoubtedly the reason why John did hesitate to write his commentary at doña Ana's request.

The intent of mystical language is not to hand on a message. It is to express for oneself what has been experienced. Such language acts as a reminder; it may even be a memory of what has taken place. It may serve in later times to remember and feel the same joy once more.[17] It is a type for those who know the antitype, a symbol for those who are acquainted with the reality. It is an image, but one that proceeds by allusion and suggestion rather than by description. Only those who have made a similar experience will grasp it. In order to understand it one must find its meaning within oneself. Yet such a meaning does not correspond literally, point by point, to the image. It does not result from a geometric projection; but it points to a direction; it places on a path. And since, as John of the Cross said it abundantly in his previous writings, this path must eventually become a wayless way, petering out at the summit of Mount Carmel, this language cannot act as a guarantee of anything.

At the end of the work, having finished his brief explanation of the fourth stanza, the author will come back to this incapacity of language to communicate the most important points. He will confess that he has decided not to say anything more, because, in final analysis, it is really useless and may be dysfunctional: "I do not desire to speak of this spiration, filled for the soul with good and glory and delicate love of God, for I am aware of being incapable of so doing, and were I to try, it might seem less than it is."[18]

In these conditions one may understand why John of the Cross preferred to keep the name of the Holy Spirit that appears the most frequently in Scripture. He wished to formulate the faith, not to invent it. Yet as soon as he came to experience and to the way in which he had himself perceived the action of the Spirit, the Doctor of Carmel adopted a language that was, in final analysis, that of love. The Spirit had become, in his soul, a "burn"; at the same time He wounded him and cauterized the wound. In one movement of love, John of the Cross felt the delicate touch of the Word and the soft hand of the Father, who had touched him through the Word his Son.

Yet the Spirit is not only a burn. This is neither the most frequent nor the most significant appellation of the third Person under John's pen. The Spirit is called "flame of love," a title that is of course related to experiencing the burn: "This flame of love is the Spirit of its Spouse, that is, the Holy Spirit."[19] He is furthermore implicitly described as being love, in that what love does in the soul is the work of the Spirit: "Love unites the soul with God."[20] The "living flame" and "this divine Love" are identical.[21] The soul invokes the Spirit: "O love enkindled...." A wide range of symbols turns around this central identification. The Spirit is like the angel "who rose upward to God in the flame of the sacrifice of Manoah."[22] Center is itself a symbol, since it is the degree of love that determines the soul's center. As the soul goes through several degrees of love, it has several centers. Or rather, it has centers within one another, God dwelling in each one of them. Or, more exactly, God is himself all these centers. In an allusion to St. Bernard's seven degrees of love and to Teresa of Avila's seven mansions, John of the Cross presents the striking image of more and more interior centers, in which God, that is, in the context, the Holy Spirit, dwells and acts: "Love unites the soul with God, and the more degrees of love the soul has, the more profoundly does it enter into God and the more is it centered in Him; and thus we can say that, as are the degrees of love of God, so are the centers, each one deeper than another, which the soul has in God; these are the many mansions which, He said, were in His Father's house."[23]

The image of the feast also relates to the symbol of love. There is a "feast of the Holy Spirit,"[24] held in the substance of the soul. In this feast the Spirit, like a smouldering fire, bursts up suddenly in a flash of sparks. This is the game of love:

> It is a marvellous thing: for, as love is never idle, but is continually in motion, it is continually throwing out sparks, like a flame, in every direction; and as the office of love is to wound, that it may enkindle with love and cause delight, so, when it is as it were a living flame within the soul, it is sending forth its arrow-wounds, like most tender sparks of delicate love, joyfully and happily exercising the arts and wiles of love.[25]

Then the soul "is, as it were, keeping festival, and has in its mouth a great song of joy to God, and having knowledge of its lofty state."[26]

The image of the seraph's arrow belongs to the same keyboard. The seraph launches an assault upon the soul "with a dart of most enkindled love."[27] This is a clear allusion to Teresa's "transverberation" by a cherub, as recorded in her *Autobiography*.[28] It also evokes the experience of Francis of Assisi at La Verna, when, in 1224, the saint had a vision of a seraph "in the form of the Crucified One," who left him with the stigmata of the Passion. The seraph, John of the Cross writes, "wounded the soul of St. Francis with love, and in that way the effect of those wounds became outwardly visible."[29]

To the same register of Spirit-love one may relate several other images or symbols. The soul has the impression of feeling in itself, "at the center of the heart of the spirit," something like "seas of fire which reach to the farthest heights and depths of the machines, filling it wholly with love."[30] These "machines," which unexpectedly break the metaphor, nevertheless play an important role. They are nothing else than, in a ptolemaic view of the physical universe, three structural dimensions of the created world, corresponding to heaven, earth, and inferno.[31] Henceforth the soul realizes that the divine life fills not only the spiritual, but also the physical, universe. The world is both the work and the depository of the love that God is. John of the Cross has the boldness to assert that, at this level of spiritual experience, the very center of the universe as the ocean of divine love is located precisely in the soul, who "sees that it has become like a vast fire of love, and the point of its virtue is in the heart of the spirit."[32] The love at the soul's own center is nothing less than cosmic love; the heart of the universe is enshrined in the soul as bride of the creative Word.

Another image, no less bold, goes in another direction: John of the Cross borrows from the *Song of Songs* the image, already featured in the commentary on the *Spiritual Canticle*, of the bride's belly. There, her belly shivered under the caress of her fiancé.[33] Here, her belly is seen and admired, depicted as it is with the rural imagery of the biblical poem: "Who, then, can describe that which thou perceivest, oh, blessed soul, when thou seest thyself to be thus loved and to be exalted with such esteem? Thy belly, which is thy will, we shall describe as the heap of wheat which is covered and set about by lilies."[34] The soul, loving belly that formerly was thrilled at the Beloved's touch, is now filled with the Spirit of the Bridegroom. As he is flame, so too does it become flame. And this is not all: "Thus, though these are lamps of fire they are living waters of the Spirit ... And thus this Spirit of God, while hidden in the veins of the soul, is like sweet and delectable water quenching the thirst of the spirit in the substance of the soul."[35]

Love is therefore, in the *Living Flame*, the central symbol for the Holy Spirit, just as wisdom is, in the *Canticle*, the central symbol for the Word. In order to understand John of the Cross's experience of the Spirit, we therefore need to examine what love does in the soul. What is the nature of love that has such an importance in the life and works of St. John of the Cross?

The nature of love must show itself in its works. It should be manifested particularly at the way it works. These two related points can, in practice, be distinguished. As regards the way love acts, John of the Cross, who is not concerned about theory, provides no systematic analysis. Yet he distinguishes between three aspects or qualities or ways of acting. There is what I would call, for brevity's sake, love-strength, love-desire, and love-instant.

Love-strength is involved in the action by which love draws the soul toward its center.[36] Love-desire acts at the two planes of the will, which is also the faculty of appetition and of choice, namely, the spontaneous, basic orientation of created beings toward their goal, purpose, and ultimate end. At all degrees of its being, the bride's humanity finds itself transformed by the Beloved's touch. Understanding, will, memory, desire, "and finally all the movements and operations which the soul had aforetime, and which belonged to the principle of its natural life, are now in this union changed into movements of God."[37] Love-desire is both desire for God and desire given by God and belonging to him.

There also exists another dimension of love, which is itself dependent on love-strength and love-desire. One could call it, in keeping with the description provided by John of the Cross, love-instant, in which strength and desire reach their acme together. A long prayer addressed to the "flame of the Holy Spirit" at the end of the commentary on the first stanza, brings these aspects of love together. John begs the flame to infuse its power in him: " . . . with desire did my soul desire Thee when my impatient love would not suffer me to be conformed with the conditions of this life that Thou desirest me to live, and the past assaults of love sufficed not in Thy sight, because they had not sufficient substance."[38] Today, however, the soul is "so greatly strengthened in love" that "I entreat that which Thou desirest me to entreat, and that which Thou desirest not, that I desire not, nor can I desire it, nor does it pass through my mind to entreat it." The union of strength and desire may be called intensity. In examining the first stanza, the commentator wonders why the poet begs the flame to tear the veil rather than to cut it or to take it away, since these actions would have the same overall effect. He provides four reasons for this.

The first is merely tautological and of little interest: this better fits the nature of the encounter in question. The second argues from love-strength: "Love delights in the force of love and that of forceful and impetuous contacts, and these result in a breaking rather than in a cutting or a wearing away."[39] The fourth reason is related to the wish to die, symbolized by breaking "the web of life."

The third reason brings in a new element that deserves close attention. The Mystical Doctor introduces a distinction between the act and the dispositions that precede it and lead to it. Act and dispositions relate to each other like form and matter in the philosophy of Aristotle. Now, as John writes,

> Love desires the act to be very brief and quick. The strength and power of the act is commensurate with its brevity and spirituality, for virtue when united is stronger than when scattered. And love is introduced as form is introduced into matter; it is done in an instant, and until then there is no act but only dispositions toward it. Spiritual acts are produced instantaneously in the soul, because God infuses them. But those the soul makes of itself can better be referred to as dispositive acts by means of successive desires and affections, which never become perfect acts of love or contemplation, unless, as I say, when God sometimes forms and perfects them very quickly in the spirit.[40]

That "love desires the act to be very brief" is not self-evident, except in Western sexual conceptions and customs. Would John of the Cross have proposed a different analysis if he had lived in another civilization, in which, for instance, the practice of *amplexus reservatus* would be commonly accepted,[41] or in a context similar to that of the *Kamasutra?* However this may be, the Mystical Doctor attributes the rapidity of the act to its intensity, to the power of the loving strength in it. On account of this intensity, which, in unifying love, reduces it to a point, love reaches its goal in an instant. Its instantaneity in time is parallel to its punctuality in space. When God or the Spirit, entering the soul, infuses such a love into it, this is done at one point and in one instant. Undoubtedly we are near to the conception of the "fine point of the soul," the *scintilla animae*, of the Rhineland mystics.[42]

The condensed rapidity of the act of love corresponds also, for the Mystical Doctor, to experience. A testimony to this is provided by Scripture: "The Wise Man affirmed that the end of prayer is better than the beginning (Eccles. 7:9), and it is commonly quoted that the short prayer penetrates the heavens."[43] Above all he argues from what takes place in the well-disposed soul. This soul

> can make many and far more intense acts in a short time than someone undisposed can in a long time; and, by reason of his being so fully disposed, he usually remains for a long time in the act of love or contemplation . . . In the prepared soul, the act of love enters immediately, for at each touch the spark catches fire in the dry tinder, and thus the enamored soul desires the brevity of tearing more than the delay involved in cutting or destroying.

Is there a contradiction between the coincidence of point and instant, and the experience of the mystic in whom the act of loving continually enters? I would not think so, if at least this is not, properly speaking, a mystical "state":[44] at the summit of experience, continuity is itself discontinuous. Rather than being a prolonged period or state, it consists of a series of unseparated, contiguous moments.

The Spirit's action, since this is the subject matter of this discussion, shows therefore the three characteristics of power, of infusing desire, and of instantaneity. We know how this love that is the Holy Spirit acts. But what is its action? What does it do?

What love does amounts to one point, which belongs to John of the Cross's conception of all love and is presumably central to his own experience: love "touches." It is the meeting point of two beings: "Thou touchest me tenderly with thy love,"[45] does he write in commenting on the verse "Who tenderly wound." In the *Spiritual Canticle* as in the *Song of Songs* and the mystical theology of St. Bernard, love "kisses with the kisses of the mouth."[46] In the *Living Flame*, it caresses with the caresses of the flame, which licks what it burns. But since the touch, as is explained by the commentator, is not the Spirit but the Word, love is neither the initiator (which is the hand, or, the Father) nor the means of contact (which is the Word): love is the inner quality, the sweetness, and the power, the stream that flows through the lovers as they touch and kiss. For St. Augustine it is the weight that pulls with all its heaviness to the point where it tends: *pondus meus amor meus.*[47] In the language of John of the Cross, love-strength or, if one prefers, the strength of love, leads the soul to the point of encounter, which constitutes for human life a center. "We term the deepest center of a thing the point to which its being and virtue and the force of its operation and movement can attain, and beyond which they cannot pass."[48] John of the Cross adds, "The center of the soul is God."[49] The soul cannot journey any further within itself than where God is its center "by grace and by his own communication." Accordingly, "love unites the soul to God,"[50] taking it to its deepest center. Through love, God unites the human creature to himself.

The center in question is not empty; it is the scene of an action. There takes place in it a transformation, which is abundantly described in the commentary on the burn. At the exact point where the fire of love is "most intense and most concentrated,"[51] "so vehement and so consuming,"[52] full of "strength and heat," it "transforms the substance of the soul into itself";[53] it "delights and deifies."[54] At that moment, since the object of these communications "is to magnify the soul, this fire afflicts it not, but enlarges it; it wearies it not, but delights it and makes it glorious and rich. . . . " Then, the transformed soul "knows everything, tastes everything, does all that it desires, and prospers, and none prevails against it or touches it. For it is of this soul that the Apostle says: The spiritual man judges all things yet he himself is judged of no man."[55]

In more striking imagery, John of the Cross also writes that the soul reaches the state where the flame of love in it is water as well as flame. It is like "the fire of the sacrifice which Jeremias hid in the cistern."[56] "In the middle of the heart of the spirit" the soul is struck at "the intimate point of the wound."[57] It feels something like "a tiny seed of mustard"—an allusion both to the parable in the gospels and to the seasoning of Andalusian cuisine!—"in the middle of the heart of the spirit." This mustard seed, "tiny, very much alive, and enkindled," sends "into its surroundings a living and enkindled fire of love," which spreads "through all the spiritual and substantial veins of the soul," which thus believes it has in itself "a sea of love" of cosmic dimensions, brimming over with love. It has the impression that "the entire universe is a sea of love in which it is engulfed, for, conscious of the living point or center of love within itself, it is unable to catch sight of the boundaries of this love." This sort of liquefaction of the soul in the love which is the Spirit is germane to two aspects of the transforming action of love.

The first is tied to the tearing of the veil: "Tear the veil of this sweet encounter." In reality, however, as the commentary brings it out, there are more than one veil between the soul and God; there are three: "the temporal, which comprises every creature; the natural, which comprises the operations and inclinations that are purely natural; and the sensual, which comprises only the union of the soul in the body, which is sensual and animal life."[58] Mystical life takes the form of a dance in which the dancer strips, taking away all her veils one by one. Tearing the first two is needed "in order that we may attain to this possession of the union of God through love," for these veils are equated with the earthly and human ties of the soul to this contingent and imperfect world. At the moment of which the poet speaks, however, these two veils have been removed. The third, which keeps one in the present life, remains. But the tearing away of this web of death does not take on frightening colors for the mystic. On the contrary, this desired tearing will be sweet: "There is now no other web than this, which, being already so delicate and fine and so greatly spiritualized by this union, is attacked by the flame, not in a severe and oppressive way, as were the others, but sweetly and delectably. And thus the death of such souls is ever sweeter and gentler than was their whole life."

If tearing away the veil of death must be sweet and delectable, this is because the mystical death is neither merely natural nor accidental. It is a death in love: such souls "die amid the delectable encounters and impulses of love, like the swan, which sings most sweetly when it is about to die and is at the point of death." Then, "the rivers of love of the soul are about to enter the sea, and they are so broad and motionless that they seem to be seas already."

Death in love, the ultimate destiny of the Christian mystic, is tantamount to entering the kingdom. At this moment, the soul "sees itself to be pure and rich and prepared for this, because God permits it in this state to see its beauty and entrusts it with the gifts and virtues that he has given it, since all turns into love and praises, as there is no more leaven to corrupt the mass."[59]

The last veil is torn at the final moment of the soul's deification. This theological term, which comes from the second epistle of Peter through the oriental patristic theology known in the West chiefly in the translated works of Denys, is familiar to John of the Cross,[60] who does use the verb, to deify, at least as much as, and perhaps more than, the noun, deification. These words sum up for him the Spirit's acting upon the soul. There is, as he explains, a meeting of the soul and the Spirit: "God makes certain assaults upon it that are glorious and divine and after the manner of encounters—indeed, they are encounters—wherewith He penetrates the soul continually, deifying its substance and making it divine."[61] Then, by the Spirit's action the soul is absorbed "above all being in the Being of God, for He has encountered it and pierced it to the quick in the Holy Spirit, whose communications are impetuous when they are full of fervor, as is this communication." The wish for death in love is identical with the desire for God's kingdom and glory. The soul now knows by experience that its movement toward God, just as the Spirit's intimacy with it, cannot reach its highest point "until the time comes for it to depart from the sphere of the air of this carnal life and enter into the center of the spirit of the perfect life in Christ."[62]

As one may see, Spirit, love, deification, access to glory, penetration to the center, intimacy, mutually imply one another. The Spirit, who is love, works out all this in the soul, which lets itself be transformed. The soul experiences such a transformation here on earth insofar as it lives at the center of love, in this sea of love that is the deepest reality of the universe and its true being in God.

In John of the Cross's experience, the effect of the love that transforms the soul by conforming it to God reaches all the levels of creaturely being. The movement by which the soul enters into as full a participation in God as is possible to the human creature entails an interior transformation. Under the assaults of the flame of love that is the Holy Spirit the soul enters "the perfect spiritual life, the possession of God through union of love."[63] It then lives with "the life of God," when its understanding,

will, memory, natural appetites, and even all its "movements, oper-
ations, and inclination" are divinized. The soul is now "like a true
daughter of God."[64] John develops powerfully, in a way that is truly
original, what pertains to the sublimation of the intellect. At this
moment a new interior horizon opens around two inseparable foci.
On the one hand, intimacy with the three Persons reaches its zenith.
On the other, the soul acquires a new knowledge of the divine Being
and its attributes.

There is no need to come back at this point to what was previously
said about the Father and the Word. As usual in classical Trinitarian
theology, according to which the first Person does not reveal itself
directly, but only through the Word and in the Spirit, the Mystical
Doctor says little of the Father as such. Yet, in relation to the image
of the hand, identified with the Father, he formulates a beautiful
prayer: "Oh hand, as generous as thou art powerful and rich, richly
and powerfully dost thou give me thy gifts! Oh, soft hand, softer
still for this soul, and softly laid upon it, for if thou wert to lean
hardly upon it the whole world would perish."[65]

If John of the Cross thus places himself before the Father, this is
because he has first sensed the Father's touching. And so this prayer
continues as addressing the Word: "Oh, delicate touch, Thou Word,
Son of God, who, through the delicacy of thy divine Being, dost
subtly penetrate the substance of my soul, and, touching it wholly
and delicately, dost absorb it wholly in thyself in divine ways of
sweetness which have not been heard of in the land of Canaan nor
seen in Teman."

This delicate touch renews for the mystic the experience of the
prophet Elijah, when the Word made himself known in the "whistl-
ing of a soft breeze": "Oh, gentle breeze, that art so delicate and
gentle! Say, how dost Thou touch the soul so gently and delicately
though Thou art so terrible and powerful!"[66]

The Word of God, "touch of the divinity,"[67] is, as in the *Canticle*,
the Wisdom of God. He is the Bridegroom, the Beloved, the Darling.
He is also the "great Emperor,"[68] the "Prince," the "King of
heaven."[69] Yet the unique contribution of the commentary on the
Living Flame relates, not to the names, titles, or qualities of the
Beloved, but to a new unveiling of the divine Being. In fact, the
experience depicted by John of the Cross transcends the scholastic
discussions on what constitutes the summit of the mystical ascent.

Would this be a growing intimacy with the three Persons? Or a deeper discovery of the divine Being in its oneness? Some mystics have at times been opposed to others, for instance, blessed John Ruysbroeck, the great mystic of the *devotio moderna*, to St. Mary of the Incarnation, the Ursuline of Quebec. The former would have presented the discovery of divine Unity as the high point of mystical contemplation.[70] For the latter, on the contrary, to see God "face to face and openly" would designate a created participation in the Trinitarian relationships.[71] The language of John of the Cross does not encourage such an opposition. At the summit of mystical experience the intimate knowing of the Word and the Spirit, and therefore of the Father who is manifested through them, brings about a more profound understanding of the divine Being in its oneness and in its attributes.

God's Being is now known from the fact that the delicate touch sensed by the soul in its own depths is precisely the touch of the divine Being. What dwells and acts beyond "every mode and manner, and free of all volume, of form and figure and accidents,"[72] can only be the infinitely simple Being of God, his "most simple substance and most pure Being, which, as it is infinite, is infinitely delicate and, as such, touches so subtly and lovingly and eminently and delicately." The Word's touch unveils the divine Being in its sheer simplicity beyond all real, possible, or imaginary division. As one enters the simplicity of divine Being, one reaches beyond all that is in itself manifold or complex. By the same token, one comes to face the simplicity of one's own being, which, as taught in the *Spiritual Canticle*, is simple, if not in the present life, at least in the "other day" of stanza 37, which commentary (B) identifies with the eternity that is anterior to creation.[73] Such as God thinks it in the eternal Word, created being shares in the simplicity of the Word's Being. My rediscovery of this being that I have in God before my coming to the world presupposes my participation in the infinitely simple Being of God. The divine Being is therefore, in the highest mystical knowledge, inseparable from its eminent simplicity. It is in this perspective that the third stanza of the *Living Flame of Love* is commented upon. Knowing the divine Being implies knowing what theology has commonly called the attributes of God.

By virtue of the divine touch, the soul "in such a state tastes of all the things of God, and there are communicated to it fortitude, wisdom, love, beauty, grace and goodness, and so forth. For as God is all these things, the soul tastes them in one single touch of God."[74] Having brought up the question of the divine attributes in his commentary on the second stanza, the Mystical Doctor devotes to them most of the third.

The lamps of fire are, precisely, the divine attributes. These are neither appendixes to the Being of God, nor adjunctions that would cover it up like so many coats of paint; they are the divine Being itself, in such a way that God is both totally simple in his Being and infinitely diversified in his attributes. But this is not exact language, since the manifoldness of the divine attributes is itself absorbed in utter simplicity. There is an identity of Being with its attributes, singular with plural, one with many:

> God in his one and simple Being is all the virtues and grandeurs of his attributes; for He is omnipotent, wise, good, merciful, just, strong and loving, and has other infinite attributes and virtues whereof we have no knowledge here below . . . And, as each of these things is the very Being of God in one single simple reality, each attribute being God himself and God being infinite light and infinite divine fire, . . . it follows from this that in each of these attributes, which, as we say, are innumerable, and are his virtues, He gives light and burns as God.[75]

As he communicates himself to the soul, God is therefore as many "lamps of fire" as there are attributes. Each one of these is perceived and sensed distinctly, even though "all these lamps are one lamp which, according to its power and attributes, shines and burns like many lamps."[76] From each "the soul has knowledge and by each is given the heat of love, in its own way and all in one simple Being." Each is distinguished from and implies the others. All these attributes open, as it were, a window on the divine Being: "The splendor given it by this lamp of God's Being, insofar as He is omnipotent, imparts light to the soul and the warmth of his love according to his omnipotence. God is then to the soul a lamp of omnipotence which shines and bestows all knowledge in respect of this attribute."

The case is the same with all the divine attributes, known or unknown: God is lamp of wisdom, lamp of goodness; he is "neither more nor less, a lamp of justice, fortitude, and mercy, and of all the other attributes which are represented to it together in God." Now, these openings onto the divine Being are not perceived only in succession. At the same time, in one movement, by one grace, God presents himself to the soul as being "all these things."[77] Whence the soul's ineffable delights and its wonder before the Being of God and his unmeasurable simplicity![78] The soul also perceives, at the same stroke, that God is still an infinite number of other lamps of fire, knowledge of which will be revealed beyond one's own death by love. The Word acts in keeping with what he is. "And thus since thy Spouse, who is within thee, is omnipotent, he gives thee omnipotence and loves thee therewith; and since he is wise, thou perceivest that he loves thee with wisdom."[79] And so forth with his infinite goodness, holiness, justice, mercy, piety and clemency, strength, light and the delicacy of his Being, his purity and limpidity, his truth, his liberality, his supreme humility and bounty, his supreme esteem, with which he "makes you his equal, gladly revealing himself to you in these ways of knowledge, in this his countenance filled with graces, and telling you in this his union, not without great rejoicing: I am yours and for you and delighted to be what I am so as to be yours and give myself to you."[80]

The soul who shares all this reflects it back, becoming in turn a radiating fire and a sea of love. It is transformed into a flame of the Spirit. It partakes of all the divine attributes. John of the Cross proposes the suggestive image, inspired by the annunciation to Mary (Luke 1:35), of "adumbration" or overshadowing.[81] The shadow is a sign of nearness, since one has to be near something to reach it with one's shadow. Thus the Virgin was close to the Holy Spirit who overshadowed her. Now, John of the Cross remarks, the shadows of darker objects are dark; those of lighter objects are light. The shadow and what is being overshadowed wear the tonalities of the shadow's source:

The shadow of life will be light: if divine, divine light; if human, natural light. What then will be the shadow of beauty? It will be fresh beauty, of the nature and proportions of that beauty. So the shadow of strength will be fresh strength, of the nature and quality of that strength. And the shadow of wisdom will be fresh wisdom; or, more correctly, it will be the same beauty and the same strength and the same wisdom in shadow, wherein will be recognized the nature and proportions of which the shadow is cast.[82]

Partaking of the divine attributes, the soul is therefore more than their reflection. It is not only a shadow of the wisdom of God; it is this very wisdom as shadow. It is not only a shadow of God's Being; it is the divine Being that has become shadow in it. The soul becomes all the divine attributes known to us, as later it will participate in the divine glory, will become this very glory, and thereby will partake of attributes of the divine Being that are unknown here below. Being a divine lamp, it shines with many divine flames. "For the attributes of God and his virtues are lamps which, resplendent and enkindled as they are, will cast shadows that are resplendent and enkindled according to his nature and proportions, and will cast a multitude of them in one sole being."[83]

Being clothed with the luminous shadow of the divine Being with its innumerable attributes, the soul now shines by virtue of its participating in God in "the deep caverns of sense." These caverns being "the faculties of the soul, memory, understanding, and will,"[84] the soul feels itself lying passively under the action of the Spirit, in what it is (memory), in what it thinks (understanding), and in what it loves (will). One may then truly say: "All its acts are divine."[85] This transformation into God reaches so far that the soul, though passive under the loving flames of the Spirit, having become flame of the Spirit, can be involved in a marvelous exchange with the divine Being. The caverns of sense,

> With strange beauties,
> Warmth and light give close to their Darling.

Or also, according to the commentary, the splendors that have been received are lamps "sending back God into God"; they "turn to God in God and become themselves lamps enkindled in the splendors of the divine lamps, giving to the Beloved some of the same light and heat of love that the soul receives; for in this state, after the same manner as they receive, they are giving to the Giver with the same brightness that he gives to them."[86] Moreover, the gift in this wondrous exchange is not of some superfluous object. It is a gift of one's very being and of the divine Being who lets be. For the attributes and the Being of God are not two distinct realities. The one cannot be apart from the other. Each is all that God is. Thus the wondrous exchange takes place at the level of being. As it is wisdom, the soul gives wisdom to God; having become the goodness of God, it "gives to God in God the same goodness; for the soul receives it only to give it again":[87]

> According to the brightness of the other divine attributes which are here communicated to the soul—fortitude, beauty, justice, etc.—are the manners of brightness wherewith the sense, having fruition, is giving it to its Beloved in its Beloved that same light and heat that it is receiving from its Beloved; for, since in this state it has been made one and the same things with Him, it is after a certain manner God by participation; for, although this is not so as perfectly as in the next life, the soul is, as we have said, as it were a shadow of God.

In the soul God lives the Trinitarian life, radiating all the dimensions of the attributes of the divine Being. And thus the soul itself "does in God and through God that which He does through himself in the soul, in the same way as He does it." As the soul pronounces the Word and breathes the Spirit, being at the same time spoken as Word and breathed as Spirit, it also gives back to the Being of God all the divine attributes and this very Being. Hence the first three verses of the last stanza:

> How gentle and loving
> You awaken in my breast,
> Where in secret only you dwell!

The commentary of these three verses, and indeed of the entire last stanza, is dominated by the symbol of awakening. The Beloved wakes up in the soul in which he has been at rest. There are, as John of the Cross points out, numerous awakenings of the Beloved in the soul, so many in fact that their description would be inexhaustible. This leads him to select "one of the most elevated" for special attention: it consists in

> a movement of the Word in the substance of the soul, containing such grandeur, dominion and glory and intimate sweetness that it seems to the soul that all the balsams and fragrant spices and flowers of the world are commingled, stirred, and shaken so as to yield their sweet odor, and that all the kingdoms of the world and all the powers and virtues of heaven are moved; and not only this, but it also seems that all the virtues and substances and perfections and graces of every created thing glow and make the same movement all at once.[88]

In other words the entire universe takes part, in the soul, in the Word's awakening. Once again the soul transcends itself and escapes its bounds to embrace and feel the fragrances of the whole universe. Yet this is not caused by the soul. No meditative technique or ascetic practice has the capacity to blow open the limits of the soul and expand it to the confines of the world. The Word's awakening is a motion, at the soul's center, of the one in whom the universe is created: "When, within the soul, this great Emperor moves, . . . he bears on his shoulder . . . the three spheres, celestial, terrestrial, and infernal, and the things contained in them . . . All things seem to move in unison. . . . " In the medieval language, which was still familiar to the Mystical Doctor, this awakening of the Word illumines the soul with morning knowledge, by which it "knows creatures through God and not God through creatures. This amounts to knowing the effects through their cause and not the cause through its effects. The latter is knowledge *a posteriori*," or evening knowledge, "and the former is essential knowledge."[89] This type of knowing does not take place without intense spiritual delights.

John of the Cross investigates further: this motion of the Word, his awakening, is not really a movement of the Word in himself. What makes it "a wonderful thing" is precisely that God does not move, that he is immutable, and yet that, in the soul's eyes, at that moment all seems in motion, including God. What has happened is that

> as the soul is renewed and moved by God that it may behold

this supernatural sight, and there is revealed to it in this great renewal that divine life and the being and harmony of every creature in it which has its movements in God, it seems to the soul that it is God that is moving, and thus the cause takes the name of the effect which it produces, according to which effect it may be said that God is moving.[90]

God is "the beginning and the root of all movement," and therefore too of this motion in the soul. It is not the Word who wakes up; it is the soul who, moved by the Word, rises to a new day. God is then known as the source of all being and all life, as acting in all that is and in all that lives. The soul discovers that divine wisdom "is more active than all active things." It experiences, along with the divine presence in all things, the presence of all things in God the Word. This presence, as John specifies in the didactic manner that he occasionally assumes, is "virtual, presential, and substantial."[91] The soul sees at one glance that God is in himself and that he is in his creation.

The commentary on the last stanza depicts the highest reaches of the mystical ascent as an awakening to another life than that of daily empirical existence. A hitherto unseen horizon opens, inviting one to go out of oneself and embrace the whole visible and invisible universe. Yet this horizon is at the center of one's own self, where the divine Word "in secret dwells."[92] There, "in the substance of the soul, ... there is heard in the soul the immense power of the voice of a multitude of excellences, of thousands upon thousands of virtues." Wide awake, the soul opens its eyes.[93] The fullness of such an awakening can be no other than entrance into glory. Already "everything is perfect; for it is He [the Spouse] who is its sole cause."[94] Then the soul feels "the breathing of God," which she celebrates in the last three verses:

> And in your fragrant breath,
> With good and glory filled,
> How delicately you enamor me!

When he reaches this point in his poem, John of the Cross finally gives up any further commentary. More he cannot say. Language has reached its ultimate boundaries. Yet the Mystical Doctor is not loathe to explain why this is so, and this explanation serves as a conclusion to all his writings:

> For it is a breathing of God himself, wherein, in that awakening of lofty knowledge of the Deity, the Holy Spirit breathes into the soul in proportion to the knowledge wherein he most profoundly absorbs it in the Holy Spirit, inspiring it with most delicate love for himself according to what it has seen; for, the soul being full of blessing and glory, the Holy Spirit has filled it with goodness and glory, wherein he has inspired it with love for himself, which transcends all description and all sense, in the deep things of God. And for that reason I leave speaking of it here.[95]

It seems to me, however, that for the sake of those readers who have not reached far enough in the mystical pilgrimage "in the depths of God" to understand the full scope of his text, John of the Cross has provided a most valuable teaching in the *Living Flame of Love*. This has to do with the relationship, in Trinitarian theology, between Person and divine attribute. The Word has been perceived as Wisdom, the Spirit as Love. For the more common theology, these are appropriations: our own process of thinking assigns to one divine Person an attribute that really belongs to all three. But, as it clearly emerges from the text of the *Living Flame*, what the mystic perceives is not, and cannot be, an appropriation: in the fire of the highest experience, the mystic is not aware of scholastic disputes and theories. He has entered into God's own life, and the living God has entered him. Mystical participation, which gives the mystic authentic humanity, since to be human is, according to John of the Cross, to be "God by participation,"[96] brings in the experience of a divine reality that is set far beyond theological speculation: the Word is Wisdom; the Spirit is Love. Undoubtedly one ought to add: the Word is the Father's Wisdom and also the Wisdom of Love; the Spirit is the Father's Love and also the Love of Wisdom (in the two senses, originary and objective, of "of"). This is something other than appropriation in the Augustinian sense of the word. Symbolization aims at what the Word truly is in relation to the mystic, and therefore at what He is in himself, since what the Word does expresses what he is; this symbolization well shows what the Spirit is in his overshadowing the soul, and therefore what He is in himself.

In God, each Person is the whole divine Being, and the divine Being is each and all of the attributes. Strength, wisdom, love, and the infinity of attributes that we cannot even conceive, are not superadded to what God is: God is each of them and each of them is God in totality. It is true indeed that the Word is Wisdom and the Spirit is Love. The point where human language inevitably fails is that experience does not seem to allow for what thought would require: the Word is not perceived as Love, yet he is also Love; the Spirit is not perceived as Wisdom, although he is wisdom too. At the climax of experience, and presumably also in the beatific vision beyond dying love, each Person is perceived both in its identity with divine Being (each is all that God is) and in its constitutive relation to the other Persons.[97] The coincidence of these two relationships justifies using a term of nature, an attribute, to designate a Person, and this Person in particular, to the extent that the Person is known as such. Yet this is not, as an appropriation would be, merely a view of the mind and a phenomenon of speech. It is a symbol in the true sense of the term:[98] it unites (*sym* in Greek means *with*) in reality what the created mind conceives separately. Using a term that is not alien to John of the Cross, we would say that there is, in this perception, a fruition. The fruit received from God in his self-gift breaks appropriation down, just as it tears the veil, all the veils, of merely human life and thought. Fruition is participation in the divine Being at all levels that may be shared: simple Being, numberless and infinite Attributes, Persons.[99] By the same token, the fruition of God, of his Wisdom and of his Flame, suggests that these are not three successive or simultaneous planes. If the Word makes himself known as Wisdom and the Spirit as Flame this by no means implies that the Father and the Spirit are not wisdom, and that the Father and the Spirit are not flame. But the Word makes himself known as Wisdom and the Spirit as Flame. What will be revealed of them beyond the veil of dying in love we may discover at that point: it must transcend all that may be thought, imagined, or said.

CHAPTER 12

THE THIRD *CANTICLE*

ohn of the Cross might have drawn a lesson in humility from the subtle irony that emerges from a paradoxical dimension of the study of his writings: even though it may be focused on his poetry and his mystical experience, such a study is in danger of ending on considerations of textual criticism. As it appears in the Jaén manuscript, the *Spiritual Canticle* contains forty stanzas. The eleventh stanza is new, and the order of the subsequent ones has been considerably modified. Is this version authentic? By the same token, is the commentary on this version, called commentary (B), authentic? The double question has been raised since the publication of Jean Baruzi's major thesis on the Mystical Doctor: Baruzi was the first scholar of importance to reject the full authenticity of version (B). Yet he was prepared to admit the authenticity of the new stanza 11 while refusing the new ordering of the rest of the poem.[1] Since 1921 the authors who have been interested by the works of John of the Cross have adopted opposite stands. Yet the problem is more complex than appears at first sight. Some respected critics, such as Dámaso Alonso, reject the Johannist authorship of the poem for literary reasons: even if the authenticity of stanza 11 is granted, the reorganized work would be, as they think, disastrous from the standpoint of poetry.[2] In other words arguments of internal criticism have carried the conviction of some. But such arguments are extremely difficult to use, especially when they run afoul of impressive arguments of external criticism. The chief reason why a number of theologians reject the Johannist authorship of commentary (B) pertains also to internal criticism: the substance of version (B) would be too different from that of version (A), unless one admits that the author contradicted himself on important points of mystical theology or even of speculative scholastic theology. Such is the line followed by one of the recent opponents of the Johannist authorship of version (B), Max Huot de Longchamp.[3]

In contrast the arguments in favor of version (B) derive primarily from external criticism: allusions to this version of the poem and of its commentary are provided by visual witnesses who personally knew John of the Cross and his works.[4] Yet this is not all. At least one author argues from internal criticism: the first commentary, (A), would have been theologically so unsatisfactory that John of the Cross himself was led to redo it, even though this redoing necessarily entailed reorganizing the poem in a way that was bound to make it far inferior to its original presentation. Thus, according to Eulogio de la Virgen del Carmen, John of the Cross in the last years of his life would have had to make a difficult choice between a good poem accompanied by a bad commentary, or a good commentary on a bad poem. He would have opted for good theology at the expense of poetry.[5]

In the context of the present study it is not necessary to consider in detail all the arguments pro and con. Nor do we need to analyze some complementary theories, like that of Jean Krynen, who has proposed that version (B) was the work of a Carmelite priest in the seventeenth century.[6] I have not myself been persuaded either that the forty-stanza poem is unsatisfactory, nor that the theology of commentary (B) would be unacceptable to the Mystical Doctor, and still less by the opposite thesis that the theology of version (A) would be highly doubtful.

It presumably was in Granada, in the years 1584–86, that John of the Cross started again on his great poem. One could discuss indefinitely whether redoing the commentary led the author to compose an additional stanza and to reorganize the poem, or on the contrary a new redaction of the poem brought about redoing the commentary. In any case the question seems badly put. For at any rate it was the poet in John of the Cross who rewrote the poem, and the theologian who composed the new explanations. The reverse would of course be an absurdity. Moreover, I refuse to admit that the poet could agree to bow to the theologian's demands: poetry is not an outer garment that one sheds at will! In addition such a claim would introduce a wedge between poetry and theology,[7] a move that would not be justified by anything in John of the Cross's life, and that is contradicted by the clear testimony of the prologues to his commentaries.

In other words we face, in the *Canticle* of Jaén, a writing that is no less poetic than the previous two *Canticles*. I therefore intend to treat the forty-stanza poem, not as a new version of what was begun in the Toledo jail, but as a new piece, made with material furnished by the previous *Canticle*. The insertion of a new stanza and the complete change of order in what follows transformed the borrowed material. The third *Canticle* thus produced neither replaces nor abolishes the others. It simply follows them in time. It should also be taken such as it is found in the manuscript. And it would make no sense, in my view, to bastardize it by producing a version that would feature the new stanza 11 where the author placed it, yet preserve the unchanged order of the rest of the poem.[8]

In order to grasp the structure of the new *Canticle*, let us briefly refer to what was said above about the previous ones. The basic structure, that of the first *Canticle*, emerged as follows:[9]

Search (I)	st. 1–4
Preliminary answer (1)	st. 5
Search-desire (II)	st. 6–11
First full answer (2)	st. 12
Encounter (I), responding to search (I)	st. 13–16
Encounter (II), responding to search-desire (II)	st. 17–27
Second full answer (3), which crowns	
the previous answers (1) and (2)	
the search (I) and encounter (I)	
the search-desire (II) and encounter (II)	st. 27–30
Conclusion	st. 31

Starting from this point, and taking account of the additions introduced in the second *Canticle*, we were able to determine the topical structure of version (A), as follows:

Quest (I)	st. 1–4
Preliminary answer (1)	st. 5
Quest-desire (II)	st. 6–12

First full answer (2)	st. 12
First encounter (in creatures) (A)	st. 13–16
Second encounter (in himself) (B)	st. 17–26
Second full answer (3), made	
by the chorus	st. 27
by the Bridegroom	st. 28–30
Sleep and awakening of the bride	st. 31–32
Third encounter (C)	st. 33–34
New quest	
(invitation to a last encounter) (D)	st. 33–34
Final rest	st. 39

After this topical structure we discovered a dramatic structure that presents itself as follows in version (A):

bride	st. 1–4				
chorus (I)	st. 5	chorus (II)	st. 27	chorus (III)	st. 39
bride	st. 6–12	Bridegroom	st. 28–30		
Bridegroom	st. 12	bride	st. 31–32		
bride	st. 13–26	Bridegroom	st. 33–34		
		bride	st. 35–38		

In the third *Canticle*, or version (B), this dramatic structure has been slightly modified, the new order of the stanza bringing in an additional intervention of the Bridegroom, at the end of what one may call the zone of influence of the first chorus:

bride					
Chorus (I)	st. 5	chorus (II)	st. 22	Chorus (III)	st. 40
bride		Bridegroom			
Bridegroom		bride			
bride		Bridegroom			
Bridegroom		bride			

As a result the topical structure of version (B) has been changed in its second section, or zone of influence of the second chorus:

Quest (I)	st. 1–4
Preliminary answer (1)	st. 5

Quest-desire (II)	st. 6–13
First full answer (2)	st. 13
First encounter (in creatures) (A)	st. 14–19
appeal to creatures	st. 20–21
remembrance	st. 22–23
Second encounter (in himself) (B)	
described by the bride	st. 24–33
described by the Bridegroom	st. 34–35
Desire for the eternal encounter	st. 36–39
Final rest	st. 40

This double modification of the topical and dramatic structures of the poem was not made haphazardly. John of the Cross worked on his text. The kind of work done clearly emerges if we divide *Canticle* (A) in a certain number of units, each one comprising from one to three stanzas. For simplicity's sake we can omit the poem of thirty-one stanzas, which would only be a shorter version of our first column. Let us group these units into four blocks, the first and the last of which were neither reorganized nor relocated in the rewriting of the poem, except insofar as the first received the additional stanza 11. The second block was moved toward the rear, and the third was both moved toward the front and interiorly reshuffled. The sequence of the two versions (A) and (B) may then be seen as follows *(see overleaf)*, the blocks being indicated with roman numbers, the units with capital letters.

One glance suffices to show that the constant units stand at the beginning, with a block going from A to H (counting the addition of stanza 11 in unit H), and at the end, with a block of four units, R to U. The transformation of the two intermediate units starts with the displacement of a long block, I-M: stanzas 15–24 of version (A) become stanzas 24–33 of version (B). Whereas they follow block I in 1582–84, they immediately precede block IV in 1586. They still belong to the central core of the poem. But, being originally closer to the initial movement, which they then echoed, they later become propaedeutic of the final movement. John of the Cross has reversed their orientation. From witnesses to the past he has made them heralds of the future. The verbs of the units that have been displaced in this way generally remain in the past, yet stanza 25 is in the present and 30 in the future, 29 and 33 mixing the tenses in a subtle

(A)			(B)		
BLOCK I	A	(st. 1–2)		identical	
(constant)	B	(st. 3–4)		identical	
	C	(st. 5)		identical	
	D	(st. 6–7)		identical	
	E	(st. 8–9)		identical	
	F	(st. 10–11)		(st. 10–12)	
	G	(st. 12)		(st. 13)	
	H	(st. 13–14)		(st. 14–15)	
BLOCK II	I	(st. 15–16)	BLOCK III N	(st. 16–17	= 25–26 of [A])
(moved)	J	(st. 17–18)	Q	(st. 18–19	= 31–32 of [A])
	K	(st. 19–20)	P	(st. 20–21	= 29–30 of [A])
	L	(st. 21–22)	O	(st. 22–23	= 27–28 of [A])
	M	(st. 23–24)			
BLOCK III	N	(st.25–25)	BLOCK II I	(st. 24–25	= 15–16 of [A])
(moved,	O	(st. 27–28)	J	(st. 26–27	= 17–18 of [A])
inversed	P	(st. 29–30)	K	(st. 28–29	= 19–20 of [A])
from O on)	Q	(st. 31–32)	L	(st. 30–31	= 21–22 of [A])
			M	(st. 32–33	= 23–24 of [A])
BLOCK IV	R	(st. 33–34)	BLOCK IV	(st. 34–35	
(constant)	S	(st. 35–36)		(st. 36–37)	
	T	(st. 37–38)		(st. 38–39)	
	U	(st. 39)		(st. 40)	

and delicate balance. But this is neither an objection nor a reproach: as the future is naturally rooted in the past, the latter may be perceived as an anticipation of the former. Moreover, these stanzas are now set in a new context, defined by what comes before, and on which they depend.

A second great block, N-Q, has also been moved, but toward the front, where it occupies the place vacated by the relocation of block II. It does this with a change of its internal sequence: after N, which remains at the beginning, units O and Q will be inversed, the sequence O-P-Q being turned into Q-P-O. Here again the change has taken the shape of a reversal of direction. Just as block II (units I-M), once transposed to a subsequent locus, is reoriented in a teleological sense, so block III (units N-Q), being displaced toward the beginning to occupy the place left vacant by the removal of block II, is nonetheless interiorly reversed. Altogether, the remaking of the poem has thus taken place under the sign of the poet's tension toward the future, which, at this moment of John of the Cross's life and experience, could scarcely be less than the eschatological future.[10]

Let us find out what has resulted from this reshaping.

What we began to call the dramatic structure of the poem when we studied the second *Canticle* included in fact the two structures that have just been designated as topical and, in a somewhat more restricted sense, dramatic. The more global structure has now been profoundly transformed. The first part of the poem, in the zone of influence of the first chorus, passes from three to four sections. Instead of the sequence of narrators-actors—bride, Bridegroom, bride—we now go through a four-actor sequence: bride, Bridegroom, bride, Bridegroom. The second intervention of the bride has been modified by the new stanza 11:

> Unveil your presence;
> Let your sight and your beauty kill me!
> See what is the sorrow
> Of love, that is not healed
> Except by your presence and your image!

By inserting these lines shortly before the end of the discourse in which the betrothed (who, however, has not yet gone through the betrothal) expresses her deep desire for the Beloved, the poet marks this discourse, and by the same token the desire it formulates, with a new orientation. The theme is not without similarities with the last line of the first stanza in the *Living Flame of Love*: "Tear the veil of this sweet encounter." So striking is the resemblance with "Unveil your presence" that one should presumably think of an influence of the commentary on the *Living Flame* upon the rewriting of the *Canticle*. If the poem of the *Living Flame* dates from 1582–84, its first commentary (A) was composed in 1586–87, and the second, (B), followed a fairly short time later.[11] The eschatological orientation of the *Flame* was precisely what must have brought about the new teleology of the third *Canticle*. The wish for love-induced dying, which constitutes the central theme of the

Living Flame, now becomes part of the quest for the Beloved and the desire for him that the betrothed feels in the second phase of her search, after vainly pursuing him among the fields of creatures and finding herself turned, by the creatures, toward the Beloved in person. There then emerges in her soul the hope for a face-to-face encounter, without any intermediaries. The profound realism that is born of mystical love now reveals to the bride that her Beloved is not totally unveiled this side of death.

The discourse of the new stanza 11 formulates the desire for this death in love, which must coincide with the sight and the beauty, the presence and the image, of the Beloved. This substantially alters the meaning of the next stanza, "O crystalline fountain," along with the sense of the beginning of stanza 13. Joined to the wish for love-induced dying, the perception of the Beloved's image and, above all, of his eyes in the crystalline fountain within the soul gives the betrothed the impression that she has already passed through the veil; yet this "already" comes too soon: she is not yet ready for the passage. She has not reached the proper level of love. And therefore, although she still wishes to see the Beloved's own eyes, she also begs him to turn them away from her:

> st. 12 O crystalline fountain,
> If on these your silvered surfaces
> You would suddenly form
> The desired eyes
> Whose sketch I bear in my inside!

> st. 13 Pull them away, Beloved,
> For I am taking flight!

To the desire expressed by the betrothed her Beloved answers, as in version (A), by providing a clue, in stanza 13, as to his own reciprocal desire for her. Yet instead of now hearing the bride's long monologue of version (A), we listen, before the chorus's second intervention, to a reciprocal chanting of the bride and the Bridegroom. As in (A) she starts by praising the identity of the Beloved with all the things of nature "My Beloved, the mountains . . . "). She evokes the image of a fox hunt in a fanciful landscape of vineyards in which one might leisurely make a pine cone with roses.

She calls on the warm south wind, asking it to blow in the garden and spread the scents that will attract the Beloved to the flowers (block N, st. 16–17). The theme of flowers and fragrance flows happily into the evocation of the nymphs of Judea. And finally the betrothed directly turns to her Beloved, inviting her "Dearie" to look toward the mountains and, in secret, to see her own companions, who cannot be other, at this point, than the nymphs of Judea (block Q, st. 18–19). Thus will he know that she is not the only one who loves him: they all seek for him. He is the Beloved of women.

The Beloved's response, which is made of the former block P, perfectly fits what now precedes it. It is addressed to the betrothed's companions, who have now become all the scenic manifestations of created nature, asking them to keep silence as long as the bride sleeps in quiet. These two stanzas, 20–21, which end the first part of the new poem (zone of the first chorus), echo the betrothed's words in stanzas 14–15: two evocations of nature face each other, the second echoing, though it also is contrasted with, the first. By the same token, the Bridegroom confirms the bride's previous request.

In these appeals to nature, the creaturely horizon brings about a double peal of music. John of the Cross, who was a master at drawing, a craftsman of words and verses, shows himself also, at least by implication and suggestion, as an artist of the voice and musical instruments. In the betrothed's parlance, the identity of the Beloved with creatures looms so large over the horizon that it lifts up the "silent music" of stanza 15. In the Beloved's language, the creatures' friendship for the bride and their respect for her mystical slumber end up by beseeching the same creatures in the name of the "pleasant lyres" and "the song of sirens" of stanza 21. Seen by the Beloved, in whom all has been created, the creatures are not God. They cannot be identical with himself: all of them together, the betrothed and her companions pertain to the contingent order. Yet this contingence is itself supported by the creating Love, which endows them with infinite value. To the eyes of the creature enamored of her Maker, all that is not herself is naturally identified with him, since it finds consistency only in that it is his work and nothing but his work. In each case music acts as the means of union. Escaping the limits of language, music breaks through the barriers of analogy and witnesses to the oneness that joins together the created betrothed and her creating Beloved (st. 15), and which, in stanza 21, already unites the Creator and the obediential potency of the creaturely world.

By moving the second chorus from stanza 27 (A) to stanza 22 (B), John of the Cross divided his poem in two parts that are just about of equal length: first, all that comes before the bride's entrance to the mystical garden; then the description, by the bride and the Bridegroom, of this experience in the garden, followed by the expectation and already the anticipation of the more profound union to be reached by the bride's death through love. If one imagines the mystical journey as being a straight line going from left to right, with a certain number of wayside stops, from the initial quest for the Beloved in the creaturely fields to their ultimate encounter beyond the veil, the descriptions of the third *Canticle* have been displaced along this line in the direction of the final nuptiality in heaven. By borrowing from the second part of *Canticle* (A) its description of the states and experiences of the new first part, the first zone of action has pushed the poem toward the right. If the four blocks of stanzas correspond to four long stretches in the pilgrimage toward the top of Mount Carmel, the first stretch is, as far as stanza 11, identical with what it was in the second *Canticle*. Beginning with stanza 11, the whole description slides suddenly up toward the top. Already the poet places himself at the degree of ascent reached in the *Living Flame of Love*. Whence, although he still describes the same stretches as in *Canticle* (A), he constructs their description in the light of the more advanced stretches, those that are closer to the Beloved's ultimate unveiling in the death of love. Starting from the beginners' quest, the third *Canticle* describes more what may be foreseen, this side of dying by love, of what will happen beyond. Block II of version (A), once it has been shifted further along the line of walking, acquires a new character since it now belongs to a more advanced phase of experience. Yet when it changed its place within the mystical movement, and thus acquired another content than that of version (A), this block of stanzas 24–33 (B) [15–24 in (A)] lost nothing of its poetic flavor. It simply needs to be read at another level than formerly. From the standpoint of pure poetry, there is of course no valid objection against the idea that a text may potentially apply to other situations and contexts than those of its original composition, that it must be read, in diverse contexts, at different semiotic levels, and that it has, consequently, several senses. What was, in patristic and medieval exegesis, the basic principle of the three spiritual senses of Holy Scripture,—themselves latent within the historical and literal meaning[12]—obtains also as regards poetry in general and the poems of John of the Cross in particular. Now, the context of version (B) is all but entirely outlined by stanza 11: "Unveil your presence. . . . "[13] It is this stanza that, in the reading of the *Spiritual Canticle* that I propose, entailed the reworking of the whole poem.

Let us return to stanza 11. It opened on a delicate call to the Beloved to "unveil his presence." It continued with lines in which initial M sounds (in Spanish of course: *y mateme . . . , mira que . . . , de amor que . . .*) led to a redundance of guttural sounds (*que . . . que . . . con . . .*), which fit well in the sequence of *que* that marks the betrothed's whole discourse in stanzas 6 to 13. Taking account of such words as *quien, quiero, aqueste,* the guttural sound recurs five times in stanza 6, three times in stanza 7—with its famous line, "*un no sé qué que quedan balbuciendo*"—three times in 8, four times in 9, twice in 10. It occurs twice inside stanza 11, once being grammatically redundant, though one could disagree on which one. The breathing of the request seems to halt, to stutter, after syllables articulated on M and on R sounds (*mira que . . . / amor que . . .*). Awe brings about hesitancy before the desired presence; yet such hesitancy can only feed the desire and its prayer. Only the "presence" and the "image" can bring to fruition the bride's stammering. The solitary *que* featured at the last line of stanza 12 precisely acts as a hyphen between the desire and its fulfillment, the outline of which is already being drawn in the soul:

> The desired eyes
> Whose sketch I bear in my inside!
> (*Que tengo en mis entrañas dibujados!*)

Shall we say, with Dámaso Alonso and others, that the forty-stanza *Canticle* is a poetic disaster?[14] Not only do I not agree with this judgment; I even think that the poem is remarkably well put together from a poetic point of view. But, and this point has been commonly overlooked in the Johannist literature, it is not the same poem as the thirty-nine stanza *Canticle*. To read the one with nostalgia for the other would make no more sense than, in the hypothesis of the primacy of Mark among the synoptic gospels, to regret the gospel of Mark when reading that of Matthew! The poet of stanza 11 and of the *Canticle* as reworked under the impact of "Unveil your presence" is the same as the poet of the dark nights of Toledo when the first *Canticle* took shape with thirty-one stanzas. But he is this man at a later moment of his religious and mystical experience. If the first *Canticle* is a subdued song of hope hoping against hope, if the second is a chant of the nuptial union that is called betrothal and marriage, the third is once again a poem of hope. Yet this is at a higher level: relatively to eternal life and the vision finally glimpsed, all the present life is the poet's jail in Toledo. The third *Canticle* reaches, yet does not cross, the threshold of eternity as already and also, as the commentary will show,[15] as still, sensed here below. Only a poet of genius could, by reworking one text without repudiating the previous stages and versions of it, make out of one poem the three poems that John of the Cross left with the Carmelite nuns, his daughters and sisters.[16]

CHAPTER 13

THE THRESHOLD OF ETERNITY

As we have already indicated, some theologians are just as negative about version (B) of the *Spiritual Canticle* as some literary critics are before the forty-stanza poem. Yet the theologians' negation goes further than that of the literary critics, since, taking their clue from Jean Baruzi and Philippe Chevallier, they simply reject the Johannist authorship of version (B) of the commentary.[1] Admittedly, such a judgment intends to be as honest as it is radical; its purpose is generally to serve and to protect the Johannist theology and interpretation of the mystical experience. Indignation would not be an appropriate response,[2] for these critics highlight a real and important question. If John of the Cross is indeed, as I think, the author of the two commentaries on his major poem, why did he produce the second one? It is not enough to remark that there already are two versions, universally recognized as authentic, of the commentary on the *Living Flame of Love.* For these differ from each other superficially, in expression, not in substance and doctrine. By contrast, there really is, between the two commentaries on the *Canticle,* a substantive difference: a change of direction in the way the experience is described and explained justifies the notion that the Mystical Doctor's theological orientation has changed profoundly.[3] The entire version (A) confines itself within the parameters of the present life, whereas version (B) includes an evocation of eternal life and of the beatific vision, which are presented as connatural follow-up on the highest mystical experience here below. Now, one could debate at length on the relationships of mystical experience through grace in this life to the beatific vision in heavenly glory.[4] The connections between grace and glory are as certain as they are difficult to investigate. Undoubtedly, one may finally fall back upon theories and hypotheses; yet as long as these cannot be shored up with solid experiential data, every hypothesis can be contradicted or made obsolete by another hypothesis. It is therefore with serenity, without being tied to a patrimony to be defended at any cost, whether national, poetic, or theological, that one should look at the problems in which a good part of modern Johannist scholarship has floundered.

The central objection is that, in the words of Huot de Longchamp, from the first commentary to the second there would be "a destruction of the global architecture of the *Spiritual Canticle* in fundamental points."[5] And again: "ALL THE INCARNATIONIST DYNAMICS of the work tumbles down." The architecture and dynamics would pertain to the fullness of mystical union that is possible in this life at the level of spiritual marriage. According to version (B) the full union would be reserved for the next life, after the passage of death. Indeed, the conclusion of version (A) evokes the interior quiet that is characteristic of spiritual marriage,[6] the high point of the mystical life here below, whereas the second commentary ends with the passage from spiritual marriage "in the Church Militant to the glorious marriage of the Church Triumphant."[7] The emergence of the name of Jesus at the end of the commentary leads, on the one hand—(A)—to a more profound experience of spiritual marriage, and on the other—(B)—to eternal glory.

Before going further one should give up the belief that John of the Cross was bound to consider the text of the first commentary as being perfect and immutable. If one remembers the prologue to the *Ascent of Mount Carmel*, the opposite seems obvious. As he professes it there, the Mystical Doctor does not wish to "rely on experience or knowledge";[8] he will remain close to Holy Scripture, taking it as his guide lest he fall in error and delusion. He even adds: "If I should misunderstand or be mistaken on some point, whether I deduce it from Scripture or not, my intention will not be to deviate from the true meaning of Sacred Scripture or from the doctrine of our Holy Mother the Catholic Church. If this should happen, I submit entirely to its decision or even to anyone who judges more competently about the matter."

In other words John of the Cross is not adamant about his insights and explanations. He does not renounce his own thought at the first level of judgment, at least as regards the interpretation of his experience and the sense of his poems. Yet, as a member of the Church Militant, as the son of his "Holy Mother the Catholic Church," as being in solidarity with all those who also attempt to understand Scripture and who live from mystical grace, he places his thoughts in the public domain, where anyone who should happen to be better informed in experience or doctrine, or more able to provide good formulations of the ineffable, can be found to be a better judge than himself. There would be no reason to place the *Canticle* outside the field of application of this principle. This is a general principle, not a particular statement that would only be relevant to the *Ascent*. In fact John of the Cross repeats the main point in the prologue of the *Canticle:* he desires "to subject to better judgement and to submit entirely to that of Holy Mother Church."[9] One cannot therefore dismiss the possibility that a Carmelite nun, or one of his colleagues among the Discalced, or someone else, may have suggested, in the course of some conversation on spiritual matters, what will be the central point of version (B): why not show the correspondence of the Johannist scheme with the better-known classical division of the spiritual ascent in three ways?[10] Without necessarily finding that this is a "better judgement" than his first conception of his work, one may think that the Doctor of Carmel discerned such pastoral and spiritual possibilities in this approach as to make a recasting of his work worth while. Without taking the place of the first commentary, a second one that would be focused on this idea would add a further dimension to his own doctrine.

A glance at the additions that give version (B) its consistency shows that these additions are of two kinds. First there are some marginal notations found in the Jaén manuscript; they affect stanzas 1, 5, 7, and all those from 14–15 (commented together, as in the first version) to 39. The printed editions usually locate these either at the end of the previous stanza or at the beginning of the one they introduce. Generally, these additions sum up the commentary that follows. An "argument" placed at the end of the prologue, where it serves as introduction to the beginning of the commentary, belongs in the same category.[11]

Second, another kind of change consists in more or less extensive alterations of the text, complements, that are at times substantial, placed here and there in the commentary. One can make no generalization on their intent. Some of them alter the expression to make it milder or more subdued. Others, on the contrary, seem to show a theological audacity that is not found in version (A).

One has not sufficiently averred to the fact that two passages in version (B) seem destined to outline its intention and its plan. In the first place, the "argument" at the end of the prologue is relevant, though it has not failed to intrigue the students of the thought of John of the Cross. The author begins by remarking that the *Spiritual Canticle* sketches the journey of the soul from the first moment of its serving God to "spiritual marriage, the ultimate state of perfection."[12] Yet he also introduces a new element: he will correlate the itinerary described in the poem and its commentary with the traditional tripartite division of the spiritual life in three ways or states: purgation, illumination, union. Yet this is not all. For the author also points out the general correspondence of the *Canticle* and the doctrine of the three ways. The first stanzas speak of the beginners, who are in the purgative life; those that follow "deal with the state of proficients, in which the spiritual espousal is effected, that is, the illuminative way."[13] Still further into the poem, the stanzas that follow "refer to the unitive way, that of the perfect, where the spiritual marriage takes place."

Although he does not provide exact references to the transitions from one way to the next, the author clearly makes his intention clear. This is simply to suggest certain correspondences between his categories and those that are presumably already familiar to his readers, since they appeared in many a volume on the spiritual life. The distinction of the three ways in fact has its remote origin in the "hierarchies" of Denys, who already distinguished between purgation, illumination, and union.[14] Yet two divergent interpretations of the ways had developed in the spiritual literature of the West. The more common line had described the ways as successive moments or stages that follow one another. The other view, especially illustrated by the works of St. Bonaventure, where it constitutes the very structure of a popular pamphlet, the *De Triplici Via* ("The Threefold Way"), identified the three ways as parallel aspects of the spiritual life, each of which would lead from the starting point to the summit, yet each with its own tonalities and exercises.[15] John of the Cross speaks only of the successive conception, which was presumably better known in Spain, where it had served the Benedictine García Jiménez de Cisneros in what may be called his *Spiritual Exercises,* and where the Franciscan Francisco de Osuna (1492–1540) had incorporated it into the *Third Alphabet,* a work that was familiar to the great Teresa.[16]

Yet John of the Cross does not merely provide an easy concordance between the categories used in his work and some more common presentations of the spiritual life. He adds another dimension by introducing a fourth "way." This one refers to the beatific vision and eternal life: "The final stanzas speak of the beatific state, that sole aspiration of a person who has reached perfection."[17] Otherwise stated, the author plans to touch all the consequences and implications of the mystical ascent. This is not only a pilgrimage that takes place on this earth. It leads to eternal life, to which it already introduces, in the perspective of the argument, by way of aspiration. Yet again, no precision is given as to the exact stanzas where this is to be found. Now this aspiration calls to mind a point that was noted concerning the third poem: the eleventh stanza orients the reader toward eschatological hope. One should therefore expect a similar orientation to be also the main originality of version (B) of the commentary. The meaning of the forty-stanza poem and the direction given the commentary by the new prologue and the argument that follows it go in the same direction.

A later passage in the commentary provides more precise references to the articulations of the Johannist itinerary in relation to the three ways and the beatific vision. In fact the text of stanza 22, 3, is very clear. It deserves to be quoted extensively, in spite of its length:

> To offer a more lucid explanation of the order of these stanzas and of what the soul usually passes through before reaching this state of spiritual marriage, which is the highest (that which, with the divine help, we will now speak of), it should be noted that before the soul reaches this state she first exercises herself both in the trials and the bitterness of mortification and in

meditation on spiritual things. This is referred to from the first stanza until that which says: /Pouring out a thousand graces/. Afterwards she embarks upon the contemplative way. Here she passes along the paths and straits of love about which she sings in the sequence of the verses until that stanza which begins, /Withdraw them, Beloved/, where the spiritual espousal is wrought. Afterwards she advances along the unitive way, in which she receives many remarkable communications, gifts, and jewels from her Bridegroom, and, as one betrothed, learns of her Beloved and becomes perfect in loving him; this she relates starting at the stanza in which the espousal was made (/Withdraw them, Beloved/) until this one beginning with, /The bride has entered/, where the spiritual marriage between this soul and the Son of God is effected.[18]

Admittedly, the expression, as is often the case with John of the Cross's prose, seems heavy. Yet the meaning emerges clearly:

purgative life:	st. 1 to 5;
illuminative life:	st. 5 to 13;
unitive life:	st. 13 . . .

No precision is furnished here on the beatific vision and glory. A perspective on the vision, however, is opened in the commentary on stanza 37:

> The bride states in this stanza that once she has entered further into the divine wisdom (further into the spiritual marriage she now possesses, which will be the face to face vision of God in glory as well as union with this divine Wisdom, who is the Son of God), she will know the sublime mysteries of God and man. These mysteries are exalted in wisdom, and the soul enters the knowledge of them, engulfing and immersing herself in them. And both the bride and the Bridegroom will taste the savoriness and the delight caused by the knowledge of these mysteries together with the powers and attributes of God uncovered in them: justice, mercy, wisdom, power, charity, etc.[19]

The bride thus expects to enter deeper into the divine attributes manifested in the Incarnation, such as this will be understood in the eternal union of the beatific vision. The perspective of commentary (A) is limited to the present world; the deeper penetration in wisdom takes place during the spiritual marriage rather than in a heavenly prolongation of the mystical marriage. Yet the complicated sentence that has just been cited is so typical of John of the Cross's prose that it would be difficult to deny his authorship of it. The least artistically sensitive rewriter would have straightened it up.

To tell the truth, the plan is not so clear as the author suggests. The notes or annotations that are characteristic of version (B) show the text swinging back and forth between the sequence of three ways and some experiences or graces that may be anterior or posterior to the state of the soul that is being considered. One gets the impression that the narrative comes back several times to already bygone moments of the spiritual journey, or at times jumps ahead toward states that are yet to come for the soul.

The reason for this must be that no exact point-by-point correspondence can be found between the three ways and the categories of betrothal and marriage. In fact the argument of the prologue did not affirm the absolute equivalence of the two systems. It only posited that the betrothal takes place in the illuminative way, and that the spiritual marriage happens in the unitive way.

The three signs of entrance into mystical contemplation, which were abundantly explained in the *Ascent of Mount Carmel*, the *Dark Night*, and the *Living Flame*, are briefly mentioned in the annotation to stanza 10.[20] Now, there is no doubt that this entrance precedes the spiritual betrothal. Only at the beginning of stanza 14 is the betrothal mentioned with full clarity: "Before commenting on these stanzas [i.e., 14–15] we should call to mind for the sake of a clearer understanding of them and of those that follow, that this spiritual flight denotes a high state and union of love, in which, after much spiritual exercise, the soul is placed by God. This state is called spiritual espousal with the Word, the Son of God."[21]

The flight in question being that of stanza 13, this stanza corresponds to the initiation to the soul's espousals. As one recalls the bride addresses the Bridegroom, asking him to withdraw his eyes:

> Withdraw them, Beloved,
> I am taking flight.

To which the Bridegroom answers:

> Return, dove,
> The wounded stag
> Is in sight on the hill,
> Cooled by the breeze of your flight.

The spiritual espousal must therefore take place toward the end of the illuminative way.

Likewise, the spiritual marriage is anticipated in the "state of peace and light and gentleness of love"[22] in which the soul enters when, in the betrothal, it discovers that the Beloved is all the things of created nature, as stanzas 14–15 sing it: "My Beloved, the mountains." The soul then begins to take part in the Beloved's qualities and attributes. Commenting, in a most beautiful passage, on the line "The supper that refreshes and deepens love," John introduces a verse from the book of Revelation: "Behold, I stand at the gate and I knock; if anyone opens, I shall enter and dine with him, and he with me." John comments: "In this text he indicates that he carries his supper with him, and it is nothing but his own very delights and savors that he himself enjoys. In uniting himself with the soul he imparts them, and she likewise enjoys them."[23] We are indeed in the espousal; yet the commentary on stanzas 14–15 end on a note that, announcing what will come later, clarifies the chief difference between betrothal and marriage: the former spreads its peace only at the higher level of the soul; the latter diffuses it also in the lower or sensory part.

The spiritual betrothal is described in stanzas 13 to 21, 14–15 already forming something like an anticipation of the marriage, 20 and 21 constituting a transition expressed in terms of desire and prayer. It is in stanza 22 that, the bride having "entered the garden,"[24] the spiritual marriage is consummated. This state of marriage will be described in principle until the end of the commentary,[25] since the last stanza will still speak of it: the soul will then be hidden and protected from the devil (Aminadab) in "this fort and hiding place of interior recollection with the Bridegroom."[26] And the curiously suggestive image that brings the poem to an end directly relates to marriage: the "cavalry" that at the sight of the waters descended "is no other", as the commentary makes it clear, than the total quiet of all the soul's motions in its lower part, for it is already "in this state of spiritual marriage . . . purified and spiritualized. . . . "[27]

At this point John of the Cross opens a long parenthesis in the description of spiritual marriage: stanzas 36 to 39 speak of the beatific vision and eternal life. This comes at the right moment, since the soul that is in the state of marriage desires eternal life and the vision face-to-face of its Beloved, who, however, due to the creaturely condition of the bride, cannot yet be seen clearly and definitively. The soul finds itself now at the "peak of perfection and freedom of spirit in God,"[28] where it has nothing to do but "surrender to the delights and joys of intimate love of her Bridegroom." Yet delighting in the Bridegroom's beauty, which has now become her own, as the commentary explains it in describing in unforgettable language the dialectics of the espoused soul's divine-human beauty, makes it impossible for the soul not to go further. The Beloved's beauty that is henceforth known and shared inspires the desire for eternal life beyond the veil. Let the Beloved "discover his presence," as the eleventh stanza says it. Hence the parenthesis on the beatific vision, as an experience of beauty (st. 36), as a knowledge of the divine attributes at work in the Incarnation (st. 37), as a transformation of the bride by the Bridegroom in "the beauty of his created and uncreated Wisdom,"[29] and finally as the equality and identity of their mutual love (st. 38). All this is epitomized in the five points of stanza 39: spiration of the Holy Spirit; jubilation and fruition in God; (morning) knowledge of the creatures; "pure and clear contemplation of the divine essence";[30] "total transformation in the immense love of God."

The authors who deny the Johannist authorship of version (B) have argued from these passages. John of the Cross could not, it is said, have contradicted his clear teaching in version (A), according to which the experiences described in stanzas 35–38 [36–39 in version (B)] belong entirely to the present life; they are not located in heaven but here below in the high reaches of mystical experience.[31] That this is the teaching of version (A) is undoubtedly correct. Yet it proves nothing against the authenticity of version (B). For this is supported by the annotation to stanza 39 (B), according to which the soul in the spiritual marriage has a foretaste of what has been described as belonging to the beatific vision: "Yet since the soul in this state of spiritual marriage knows something of this 'what,' she desires to say something about it, for by her transformation in God something of this 'what' occurs within her. She now feels within herself the signs and traces of the 'what'."[32]

Said differently, the mystical life at its highest level anticipates on certain dimensions of the vision face to face. Such an anticipation is what enables the soul to aspire intensely, totally, to the vision. The distinction between spiritual marriage and vision is similar to that between betrothal and marriage, which is not so neat, in the poem and its commentary, as is suggested by the analogy of the three ways as proposed in the prologue. One should take account of the author's project in its integrity. Without putting forward a program or blueprint, the prologue of version (B) offers a key for reading. Yet this is not the only key: the schema of the three ways runs parallel to that of the betrothal and marriage. By the nature of things, the two schemata cannot coincide exactly. One therefore finds, in commentary (B), references that send one back to the past as well as those that refer forward to the future; there are transitions and parentheses that would lose all meaning had John of the Cross been content with patterning the account of his experience on the theoretical mold of the three ways. The same thing obtains as regards eternal life and the new eschatological dimensions that characterize version (B): the experience of the spiritual marriage calls for the fulfillment of this dimension in eternity, even though it gives a foretaste of it in a real experience of the present life.

The following schema sums up the relationships of the two planes of version (B):

Purgative way	1 to 4	quest	1 to 12
Illuminative way (signs of entrance to contemplation)	5 to 13 10		
Unitive way	13 to 40	betrothal (foretaste of marriage)	13 to 19 14 to 15
		transition	20 to 21
		marriage	22 to 40
Vision	36 to 39	(foretaste of the vision)	36 to 39

The contrast with the structure of version (A) is striking. This first commentary introduced the betrothal at stanza 13 ("My Beloved, the mountains") and mystical marriage at stanza 18, when the soul, who has just entered the interior cellar and drunk, announces what has taken place: "There he gave me his breast." From this moment on, the two descriptions of spiritual marriage diverge, the second starting from other verses than the first.

Admittedly, reorganizing the commentary in keeping with what had become a different poem, and therefore according to another structural pattern, did not go without difficulties. The author did not consistently produce the needed transitions. He should have struck out some expressions, like a reference to "the two preceding stanzas," that was proper in stanza 15 (A), where it sent back to 13–14, but is out of place in stanza 24 (B), preceded by what was 27–28 in (A). Also, the clarity of the text would have been improved if the meaning of several "etc.s" had been clarified, as the reader is no longer sure of what should complete the list; such is the case in stanza 3, 1; stanza 17, 2; stanza 18, 5; stanza 20, 14, and elsewhere. But what can one conclude from this? John of the Cross, as an author, has not changed drastically from what he was when he gave up writing the *Ascent to Mount Carmel* and the *Dark Night*: he was not concerned about putting the final touches to his texts. As a writer he chiseled his poetry more than his prose. As a mystical author, he stopped writing as soon as he had said what he had to say, even if the original plan remained unfinished, even if loose threads were kept hanging.

Let us return to the annotation to stanza 39 with its repetition, which may sound awkward, of two "something of this 'what'," *(algo de aquello)*, that are separated by a "something of him" *(algo de ello)*. On the one hand, this passage introduces the very beautiful stanza 39:

> The breathing of the air,
> The song of the sweet nightingale,
> The grove and its grace
> In the serene night,
> With a flame that is consuming and painless.

On the other hand, it implicitly sends the reader back to the preceding verses:

> There you would show me
> What my soul has been seeking,
> And soon you would give me,
> There, you, my life,
> What you gave me the other day.

Several elements conspire toward painting these lines with the shades of *chiaroscuro*, filling them with soft music that sparks imagination without filling it up. The singing tone of this stanza fills the heart. It would make John of the Cross a romantic poet before the time if his poem merely evoked, like some pieces by Wordsworth or Lamartine, a vague nostalgia, as may grasp the soul when leaves are falling in autumn, or when one walks meditatively along the bank of a lake.[33] But this is not the point here. What is then the "what" desired by the soul, which has already been given to her?

The answers of the two commentaries are totally diverse, which is all the more surprising as the stanza falls at the same spot in the poems of thirty-nine and of forty stanzas. According to version (A), the soul calls "the 'other day' . . . the estate of original righteousness, wherein God gave to her, in Adam, grace and innocence; or the day of baptism, wherein the soul received total cleanness and purity, which the soul says here in these lines that he would give her at once in the same union of love. And this is that which is understood by what she ways in the last line, namely, 'That which thou gavest me the other day.'"[34]

"What" or "that which" *(aquello)* designates the original justice that, being given to the whole humanity in Adam and lost by him through original sin, was restored to the soul in the sacrament of baptism. The mystical life at its acme would be tantamount to a return to baptismal innocence, itself identified with the paradisaic garden of the creation of Adam and Eve. Such a precision on the place of mystical experience in sacramental life and in the history of salvation is not without value. John of the Cross belongs here to an older theological tradition: baptism implies, as Bonaventure wrote, "the restoration of innocence."[35] Moreover, the notion that the mystical life entails a certain return to paradise or, perhaps better, an access to a new paradise, was not unknown in spiritual literature: it forms the heart of a short tractate, traditionally ascribed to Bonaventure, and which, although it may be unauthentic, well reflects his teaching, the *On the Plantation of Paradise*.[36]

If John of the Cross may thus be related to a theological tradition that was well represented in the scholastic theology with which he was acquainted through his studies at the University of Salamanca, the point made in version (B) belongs to a different school, or to another level of thought. Neither original justice nor baptismal innocence is mentioned in the second commentary on the present lines. This commentary, which is longer, goes in another direction. The sense of "what" follows on the identification of "the other day." What is the "other day" in which "that" was revealed or given to the soul? The response of John of the Cross is well in line with a spiritual context that is usually associated, in the history of Christian spirituality, with the mysticism of the Rhineland and the Netherlands.

Are we hearing an echo of the doctrines of Meister Eckhart (1260–c. 1328) on "the day of God," the "Now-moment," the eternity in which "the Father begets his only begotten Son and the soul is reborn in God," the "one present Now" in which "God created the world and everything?"[37] John of the Cross was probably not directly acquainted with the writings of Eckhart. Yet blessed John Ruysbroeck (1293–1381) well illustrates the idea that we have in God, "outside of ourselves," an eternal life that is an eternal going out of oneself. As Ruysbroeck the Admirable states it, the human being already has, in God's eternity, a preconscious experience of eternity:

And this everlasting being and life which we have and are in the eternal wisdom of God, that is like to God . . . For even though, as the reason is concerned, all is here discretion and difference, this likeness is still one with that same image of the Holy Trinity which is the wisdom of God, in which God contemplates himself and all things in an eternal instant before which nothing came, after which nothing goes . . . . In this image like to God, all creatures have an everlasting life, outside themselves, as it were in their everlasting exemplar. And the Trinity made us in this everlasting image and in this likeness.[38]

The Rhineland mystics were known in Spain, at the time of John of the Cross, through the Latin translation of their works by the Carthusian Laurentius Surius (1522–78), whose publication began in Cologne in 1548.[39]

Whatever the literary and theological sources of the thought of John of the Cross in his explanation of stanza 38, the doctrine of the eternity in which the soul shares is expressed with care. The soul aspires to "essential glory, consisting in the vision of God's being."[40] The Mystical Doctor thus faces an objection inspired by the Thomism he has inherited. For, in the Thomist conception of eternal life, "essential glory lies in seeing God and not in loving."[41] Yet in this case, why did John write, when explaining the first two lines, that the soul wishes to love with the purity and perfection with which it is loved of God? In other words why did he convey the impression that eternal life resides in loving God? Would there be a contradiction between the first two and the last two lines of the stanza, or even between the author's theology and his mystical doctrine? The explanation is simple. "The ultimate reason for everything is love, . . . whose property is to give and not to receive,"[42] whereas "the property of the intellect (which is the subject of essential glory) lies in receiving and not giving." This is undoubtedly the reason John writes in *Sayings of Light and Love*: "At the evening of life you will be examined in love."[43] Urged on toward love by love, the soul aspires to give rather than to receive. Yet such an attitude finally includes the other too: one can give but what one has received. The soul cannot possibly love as it is loved before first receiving "the perfect vision of God."[44]

This response to the Thomist objection already implies an identification of "what" and of "the other day":

By "that other day" she means the day of God's eternity, which is different from this temporal day. In that day of eternity, God predestined the soul to glory, decreed the glory he would bestow on her, and gave it to her freely from all eternity before he created her. And this "what" is so proper to the soul that no event or adversity, whether great or insignificant, will suffice to take it from her. But she will attain the endless possession of the "what" to which God predestined her from eternity. And this is the "what" which she says he gave her on that other day, and which she now desires to possess in glory.[45]

There is thus an eternity, anterior to creation, that already belongs to the soul and in which it shares. The soul has no eternal being: this expression, which appears under the pen of the northern mystics, is not found in the works of John of the Cross. Yet the soul partakes, even before it is, in one of the divine attributes, eternity.

The rest of the explanation on stanza 38 remains most interesting, with John's interpretation of the seven letters of the Apocalypse, in which he discerns this eternal gift expressed in seven complementary ways. But most has been said. "Since it has no name, the soul calls it 'what'. The 'what' is in point of fact the vision of God, but that which the vision of God is to the soul has no other name than 'what'." The book of Revelation suggests a context rather than the nature of the vision. No name taken from this world is appropriate to it. Yet such an apophatic perspective can hinder neither desire nor prayer:

> Let us keep this term "what" which the soul uses, and explain the verse in this way: What You gave me (the weight of glory to which You predestined me, o my Spouse, on the day of your eternity when You considered good to decree my creation), You will give me then on the day of my espousals and nuptials and on my day of gladness of heart, when loosed from the flesh and within the high caverns of your chamber, gloriously transformed in You, I shall drink with you the juice of the sweet pomegranates.[46]

This comparison of the two interpretations of the same passage points to the true relationship between the two versions of the *Canticle:* far from contradicting, they complete each other. The second is entirely open on the dimension of eternity and oriented toward the desire for eternal life. It unfolds in a perfectly consistent way, despite some defects of redaction, the eschatological logic of stanza 11: "Unveil your presence."

As could be expected from this stanza, the commentary thickly underlies the soul's fundamental nisus of hankering after God. Yet this is less a desire to love God than a need to be loved by him. Love for God can only stem from the love with which God has loved us first. Therefore the soul asks for the divine presence in her: this intimate indwelling will manifest God's eternal love; it will be the precondition for the human response of love. But the divine presence follows three modes: there are the Creator's presence to what he has made, his natural presence; the spiritual presence wrought by the gift of grace; the presence in felt love, or "by spiritual affection, for God usually grants his spiritual presence to devout souls in many ways, by which he refreshes, delights, and gladdens them."[47] Although the desire for the divine presence could refer to any of these three modes, it is the last one, the most elevated, that draws the mystic's attention. The soul wishes, and asks, that God show himself "in his divine being and beauty."[48] Yet it also knows that such a presence can be perfect only in the state of heavenly glory, which cannot be experienced in this life. It therefore asks further for the grace of passing beyond the veil and seeing God in his glory. This is not a death wish, which would be, as John of the Cross remarks, with the common sense that never leaves him, "a natural imperfection."[49] Rather does it express the realism of mystical love, which measures the limitations of its present condition and hankers after the total fulfillment of union with the Beloved. Already living, as it were, in heaven, insofar as "the soul that loves God lives more in the next life than in this,"[50] echoing the belief that death is inseparable from the vision face to face as promised in the New Testament (and not as conceived in the Old, since the just of the time before Christ had to wait for his opening of heaven to them at his resurrection),[51] it prays for the completion of the conditions that will permit its full participation in the being and the beauty of God.

This passage is closely related to the commentary on stanza 36, and especially on the line "And let us go to see in your beauty." This passage being practically identical in version (A), it would be inconceivable that these three texts [versions (A) and (B) on the mutual beauty of the bride and her Beloved, and the commentary of (B) on stanza 11] would not come from the same hand.[52] John of the Cross had concluded his memorable passage on created participation in divine beauty: " . . . and I shall be You in your beauty, and You will be me in your beauty, because your very beauty will be my beauty." This is repeated in version (B). At stanza 11, however, John opens a similar perspective on the divine beauty which becomes that of the soul: "The soul is right in daring to say, may the vision of your beauty be my death, since she knows that at the instant she sees this beauty she will be carried away by it, and absorbed in this very beauty, and transformed in this same beauty, and made beautiful like this beauty itself, and enriched and provided for like this very beauty."[53]

A system of spiritual aesthetics could be drawn from these texts, which could lead to an elaboration of the principles that ought to inspire and structure Christian, and even simply religious, art. Yet this cannot be our theme at this point. From the Johannist view of the divine beauty becoming the very beauty of the enamored soul, let us nonetheless retain in what profound realism the experience and the thought of John of the Cross have steeped the eschatological dimension of Christian life. Desire for the beatific vision, for life beyond the veil, and thus the nisus of hope and of prayer toward the transformation to be wrought by dying through love, are no abstractions. They do not aim at a dream or at a mirage. They are grounded in actual participation in God, in the already shared experience of the joint beauty of God and self. The idea of the soul's twofold eternity and that of its participation in divine beauty go in the same direction, converging as they do on a discernment of the beyond as being somehow already known. In the unavoidable break between the two slopes of the mystical love-wrought death, this discernment preserves the continuity of grace and glory, not as a classical point of scholastic theology, which it also is, but and above all as an immediate datum of God's intimate presence. The explanation of this continuity in version (B) confirms the previous statements and implications of version (A) on mystical partaking of divine beauty.

The Mystical Doctor has now reached the ultimate point of his writing career. Admittedly, no one knows for sure if his last work is version (B) of the *Spiritual Canticle* or of the *Living Flame of Love*.[54] But this matters little. The point is that John of the Cross can now, whether before or after revising the *Living Flame*, formulate bold propositions that were not featured in version (A) of the *Canticle*. After reaffirming that the divine beauty has been given to the soul, he affirms the soul's twofold eternity, before its creation, and after its ascent to heaven. Above all, the annotation to stanza 27 ("There he gave me his breast") opens a new vista on God making himself the soul's slave and, by the same token, making the soul his God:

In this interior union God communicates himself to the soul with such genuine love that no mother's affection, in which she tenderly caresses her child, nor brother's love, nor friendship is comparable to it. The tenderness and truth of love by which the immense Father favors and exalts this humble and loving soul reach such a degree—O wonderful thing, worthy of all our awe and admiration!—that the Father himself becomes subject to her for her exaltation. And He is as solicitous in favoring her as He would be if He were her slave and she his God. So profound are the humility and sweetness of God![55]

This is, in a slightly different vocabulary, the perspective of the *Sayings of Light and Love:* "Mine are the heavens and mine is the earth. . . . "[56] Tenderness, sweetness: these are the attributes the unveiling of which is promised to the bride of "the Beloved, the Son of God," who is also "the most sweet Jesus, Bridegroom of faithful souls." Today already may "all who invoke his Name" aspire to this unveiling.[57] In the language of the *Living Flame,* the soul is filled with "delicate love of God . . . , with divine excellence and delicacy."[58] These come to the soul from the "spiration filled with good and glory," in which "the Holy Spirit has filled the soul with good and glory, in which he has enkindled it in love of himself, above all language and feeling, in the depths of God."

At this level the Beloved is not only mountains, solitary wooded valleys, strange islands, sonorous rivers, the whistling of breezes in love. He also makes himself, most particularly, the espoused soul. As the crowning of the creature's ascent, who from nature-mirror has already become nature-icon, the soul turns, in its eternal being, into deified nature, or nature-transformed-into-God.

CONCLUSION

book on St. John of the Cross, his experience, and the expression he gave it in poetry and theology, needs no other conclusion than that of each reader. The hoped-for result of such a study as the present one is only to bring some readers to see and understand John of the Cross in a new perspective. Those who care enough about his message to devote part of their life to investigating it and to sharing their findings can only look forward to throwing upon it some light that, even if not entirely new, will have been hitherto less noticed. Admittedly, the present time may seem to be unpropitious for the contemplative vocation. Despite the existence of marginal or even underground subcultures that are concerned about some, often illusory, forms of contemplation, our age pays more attention to the social and political divergences of the end of the twentieth century; and it is more eager to dominate the world through technology in order to transform it by planning and action, than to listen to the voice of the mystics of Christianity. The churches themselves are pulled in several directions by fashionable secular enthusiasms for the liberation of oppressed peoples. The Catholic Church also, which is still shaken by the ripple effect of Vatican Council II, is deeply torn by opposite movements, interpretations, and projects. Yet beyond all such agitation and the divisions between and among castes, classes, cultures, nations, continents—to mention only a few of the current antagonisms—there must be, if we do not wish modern society to sink in endless conflicts, a vision of unity, even if such a unity is not yet realizable. Precisely, John of the Cross proposes such a vision in what is at the same time its most profound level and its most universal scope. Although he does not speak of social conflicts, not even of those of his time, the Mystical Doctor provides an ultimate key to the solution of all conflicts: this is a conception of the human that sees each man and woman as participating in God to the point where they may be called "God by participation." Such a conception can be at the source of a liberation that will be, not only spiritual, but indeed total, and that will encompass all of humanity. More profound than the liberation of one's homeland from foreign military, political, or economic forces, more radical than the liberation of oppressed classes and downtrodden minorities, such a total liberation lies ahead of us all, calling us on, though obscurely, to itself as the fulfillment of theological hope.

John of the Cross invites all of humankind to know itself as destined to participate in God; he invites believers of all religions to seek for the ways of this participation; he especially invites all Christian believers not to rest satisfied with a receding vision in which the summit to be reached would remain hidden in permanent darkness, but rather to climb along the lanes of ascent of the mountain, in both their light and their night, until they reach the point where paths dwindle and there is no more law, because, in union with the Beloved, all is liberty.

The following abbreviations have
been used in the notes

A.   *The Ascent of Mount Carmel*

BAC   Biblioteca de Auctores Cristianos, Madrid

C. S.   *Commentary on the Sentences*

DS.   *Dictionnaire de Spiritualité*, Paris

D.-S.   Denzinger-Schönmetzer, *Enchiridion Symbolorum*

F.   *The Living Flame of Love*

L.   *Letters* of John of the Cross

N.   *The Dark Night*

NAPNF   Nicene and Post-Nicene Fathers

P. L.   J. P. Migne's *Patrologia Latina*

R.   *Romance on the Incarnation*

S.   *Sayings of Light and Love*

S. C.   Collection, *Sources chrétiennes*, Paris

S. T.   *Summa Theologica*

NOTES

INTRODUCTION

1. This is of course Emperor Charles V, Philip's father; see Daniel Olivier, *The Trial of Luther* (St Louis: Concordia, 1978), 169.

2. P. P. Ottonello, *Bibliografia di s. Juan de la Cruz* (Rome: Teresianum, 1967); Max Huot de Longchamp, *Lectures de Jean de la Croix. Essai d'anthropologie mystique* (Paris: Beauchesne, 1981), 33–34.

3. Emmanuel d'Alzon, *Ecrits Spirituels* (Rome: Maison généralice, 1956), 213; in *The Weight of God*, p. 28.

4. Allison Peers, *Complete Works of St. John of the Cross* (London: Burns, Oates and Washbourne, 1947); Kieran Kavanaugh and Otilio Rodriguez, *The Collected Works of St John of the Cross* (Washington: ICS Publications, 1973). Already in 1950, during this sojourn in England, I published an article on John of the Cross: *The Mystery of the Holy Spirit* (*Downside Review*, 1950), 255–70.

5. Henri Wasser, *La Septième vague* (Paris: St-Germain-des-Prés, 1976); *Le Silence d'une demi-heure* (Paris: St-Germain-des-Prés, 1980); *Sentiers de la demeure* (Paris: St-Germain-des-Prés, 1984); *Song for Avalokita* (Philadelphia: Dorrance, 1979).

6. I shall occasionally use this term to designate the works of John of the Cross; the convenient adjective often used in French, *sanjuaniste*, has no accepted equivalent in English writings devoted to Carmelite spirituality.

CHAPTER ONE

1. The general chapter of the Carmelites at Piacenza had decided, on 15 April 1575, to end the reform movement and to close the houses of the discalced.

2. *C.*, Prologue, n. 1. For the *Spiritual Canticle* and the *Living Flame of Love* I will specify the version only when quoting version (B).

3. *C.*, Prologue, n. 2.

4. *C.*, Prologue, n. 1. The reference will cover all following citations until the next footnoted reference.

5. This of course refers to the first commentary, version (A). I will generally keep this nomenclature regarding the versions (A) and (B), even though it does not quite fit the notion that the poem itself exists in three forms, the second one being commented upon in version (A), the third in

version (B). On Anne of Jesus (1545–1621), see L. Van der Bossche, *Anne de Jésus* (Bruges: Desclée de Brouwer, 1958).

6. See *C.*, st. 7, line 5: "an I-know-not-what which they keep stammering."

7. *S. T.*, I, q. I, a. 8, ad 2.

8. On these poetic forms in Spanish literature, see Dámaso Alonso, *La Poesía de San Juan de la Cruz*, 3d ed. (Madrid: Aguilar, 1958), 78–112.

9. Alphonsus the Wise became king of Castile in 1252.

10. See Peter Droncke, *The Medieval Lyric*, 2d ed. (London: Cambridge University Press, 1977), 70–74; 86–90.

11. At the time of John of the Cross, Arabic words had vanished from the language but for the many that had been completely incorporated into it. *Medina* means *city*. On Medina del Campo, see Jean Baruzi, *Saint Jean de la Croix et le problème de l'expérience mystique*, 2d ed. (Paris: Alcan, 1931), 73–78.

12. The customs of the Medina Carmel are unknown to us, nor do we know what form of the breviary and office was used by John of the Cross. The liturgy of the Holy Sepulchre, of Gallican origin, had been chosen for Palestine in 1210 by St. Albert, Latin patriarch of Jerusalem. The hermits of Mt. Carmel presumably used it. Confirmed by the superior general Sibert of Beka in 1312, the breviary was simplified in 1580 but was officially replaced by another in 1584. Finally, the Roman liturgy and breviary were adopted in 1586. One cannot know how fast these sudden changes were followed in the communities; see Jean (Cardinal) Vilnet, *Bible et Mystique chez saint Jean de la Croix* (Paris: Desclée de Brouwer, 1949), 12–18; Crisógono de Jesús, *The Life of St. John of the Cross* (New York: Harper, 1958), 23.

13. On the influence of Luis de Léon, see Francisco García Lorca, *De Fray Luis a San Juan. La Escondida Senda* (Madrid: Castalia, 1972), where the influence of Garcilaso is also discussed. Fray Luis's influence on John's poetry is extremely doubtful; John is by far the better poet. But an influence of Luis's commentary on the *Song of Songs* on John's commentary on the *Spiritual Canticle* is highly probable. The original version of Luis's commentary, composed in 1561–62, circulated in manuscript form before the printing of a Latin translation in 1589. On Garcilaso, see Alonso, *La Poesía*, 24–36; Dámaso Alonso, *Poesía Española. Ensayo de Metodos y Límites Estilísticos* (Madrid: Editorial Gredos, 1862), 42–108. The classical edition of Garcilaso is by Elias Rivers, *Obras Completas*, 2d ed. (Madrid: Castalia, 1968).

14. *F.* This passage, just before the commentary on the first stanza, is not numbered in Simeon (p. 1010; A. Peers, *Complete Works, St. John*, 18). The work of Sebastián of Cordoba is entitled *Las Obras de Garcilaso y Boscán trasladadas a materias cristianas y religiosas* (Granada, 1575); The

modern edition by Glen Gale, *Garcilaso a lo divino* (Madrid: Castalia, 1971), does not include the poems of Boscán.

15. Allison Peers, *The Complete Works of Saint Teresa of Jesus,* vol. 3 (London: Sheed and Ward, 1946), poem, p. 277–79, n. 1.

16. Alonso, *La Poesía,* 86–88.

17. Clearly, neither the writer nor the reader is a fish. The distance between reality and its metaphor will soon be called "night" by John of the Cross. See María Jesús Fernández Laborans, *Luz y Oscuridad en la Mística Española* (Madrid: Cupsa, 1978), 153–221.

18. These "elements" are air, earth, water, fire.

19. Alonso, *La Poesía,* 95; 170–72.

20. This is due to the rather prosaic form of the poem.

21. *C.,* st. 7.

22. *C.,* Prologue, n. 1.

CHAPTER TWO

1. Alonso, *La Poesía,* 48–53. There are few studies in English of John's poetry; see Gerald Brenan, *St. John of the Cross. His Life and Poetry* (Cambridge: University Press, 1973); Colin Thompson, *The Poet and the Mystic. A Study of the 'Cántico Espiritual' of San Juan de la Cruz* (Oxford: University Press, 1977).

2. Droncke, *Medieval Lyric,* 86–105. Galicia, a province of Spain located north of Portugal, is, of course, far enough from the Old Castile of John of the Cross, as also the eleventh to thirteenth centuries, the time of flourishing folk songs, are far from the sixteenth. Yet old traditions still underlay the culture of John of the Cross's period. Moreover, dialectical forms have no absolute boundaries. Travelers from Galicia crossed the plateau of Old Castile on the way to Toledo and Madrid, and Galician merchants attended the fairs of Medina del Campo.

3. A popular ballad, "Fontefrida, fontefrida / Fontefrida y con amor," may lie at the origin of John's poem, which is nonetheless structured differently. This same ballad has been seen as a source for stanzas 33–34 of the *Spiritual Canticle,* the word *tortolica* being used in both, as also in Garcilaso; see Thompson, *The Poet and the Mystic,* 79.

4. Should we accept Gerald Brenan's surmise *St. John of the Cross,* (113) that the Mystical Doctor is indebted here to two spiritual authors, Francisco de Osuna (c. 1497–1542), the author, among other works, of *The Third Alphabet,* and Bernardino de Laredo (1482–1540), the author of *La Subida del Monte Sion,* who both had used the Trinitarian image of the Source, the River, and the Stream (or the Sea)? This does not seem likely. In his

major tractates, John of the Cross does not allude to this analogy, which in any case is much older than these writers and could have been known to him from other sources. See Mary Giles, ed., *The Third Spiritual Alphabet* (New York: Paulist, 1981).

5. Bonaventure, *C. S.*, I, d. 27, p. I, a. un., q. 2 ad 3; *Breviloquium*, 1:chap. 3, n. 7, in José de Vinck, *The Works of Bonaventure*, vol. 2, (Paterson, N. J.: St Anthony Guild Press, 1963), 39.

6. *S. T.*, I, q. 33, a. 4, ad 1.

7. "The Tree of Life", trans. José de Vinck, *Works of Bonaventure*, 1:1960, 142.

8. Gonzalo de Yepes fell ill a few months after the birth of his third son, Juan, the future John of the Cross; he died some two years later, in 1544; he is buried, along with the second son, Luis, in the parish church of Fontiveros.

9. On this aspect of the Trinitarian experience, see George H. Tavard, *The Vision of the Trinity* (Washington: University Press of America, 1981), 93–118.

10. Droncke describes the French romance as "a song with monorhymed stanzas with refrain, generally with a simple narrative love-theme" (*Medieval Lyric*, p. 29, n. 1); Brenan specifies that "the same rhyme or assonance runs all through the poem," which is easy to achieve in Spanish "by ending each alternate line with a verb that is in either the imperfect or the conditional tense" (ibid., 105). See note 19, below.

11. Alphonsus X the Wise was the collector, and presumably also the author, at least in part, of Marian hymns in the Galician dialect: these are divided in *cantigas de loor* (praise) and *cantigas de miragos* (miracles). The poetry of Lull is composed in Catalan; see Droncke, *Medieval Lyric*, 72–74.

12. The romance on the Incarnation is subdivided in nine numbered sections that are sometimes presented as nine different romances. Some translators divide it also in stanzas (Kavanaugh and Rodriguez, *Collected Works*, 724–32; Lynda Nicholson, in Brenan *St. John of the Cross*, 87–207). Willis Barnstone thinks it is too prosaic to be translated in verse form (*The Poems of Saint John of the Cross* [New York: Indiana University Press, 1968], 107–20).

13. *Romance on the Incarnation*, n. 1.

14. Ibid., n. 2.

15. Ibid., n. 4.

16. Ibid., n. 5.

17. Ibid., n. 7.

18. Ibid., n. 8.

19. The Spanish conditional ends in *ia*, thus rhyming with the imperfect. Hence, what would normally be in the future is placed in the conditional

here. This stresses the tone of controlled nostalgia, of desire, that transpires through the whole poem.

20. *R.*, n. 1.

21. See Kurt Weitzmann et al., *The Icon* (New York: Knopf, 1982).

22. See below, chap. 9,

23. See George H. Tavard, *Images of the Christ* (Washington: University Press of America, 1982), 60–62.

24. See George H. Tavard, *Die Engel* (Freiburg, Herder, 1968).

25. *R.*, n. 1.

26. On the attributes of God, see below, chap. 13.

27. 1 John 4:16.

28. *R.*, n. 2.

29. See above, note 23. The perspective of sin is not absent from the works of John of the Cross; it underlies the entire attempt of the *Ascent of Mt. Carmel* to gauge the dimensions of the interior purification that is necessary for union with God.

30. *R.*, n. 5.

31. Ibid., n. 7.

32. Some translators divide also this romance in stanzas of four or more lines: thus Kavanaugh and Rodriguez, *Collected Works*, 733–34.

33. See below, chap. 4,

CHAPTER THREE

1. On the composition of John of the Cross's writings, see Eulogio de la Virgen del Carmen, *San Juan de la Cruz y sus escritos* (Madrid: Cristiandad, 1969), where the debate on the authenticity of version (B) is summed up. The author's position, which favors authenticity, seems correct to me. On the strictly mystical aspects of John of the Cross, see Alain Cugno, *St. John of the Cross. The Life and Thought of a Christian Mystic* (London: Burns and Oates, 1982).

2. Admittedly, the poem of thirty-one stanzas is known to all, but it is generally assumed that this poem is incomplete. Some authors reduce the original writing to twenty-seven stanzas, but this need not detain us.

3. Among the studies devoted chiefly to the *Canticle*, one should mention Thompson, *The Poet and the Mystic*; Cristobal Cuevas García, *San Juan de la Cruz. Cántico Espiritual. Poesías* (Madrid: Alhambra, 1979); Roger Duvivier, *La Genèse du 'Cantique spirituel' de saint Jean de la Croix* (Paris: Belles Lettres, 1971); Roger Duvivier, *Le Dynamisme Existentiel dans la poésie de Jean de la Croix: lecture du Cántico Espiritual* (Paris: Didier, 1973). Fernande Pépin, *Noces de Feu. Le Symbolisme nuptial du "Cántico*

espiritual" de saint Jean de la Croix à la lumière du "Canticum Canticorum," (Montreal: Bellarmin, 1972).

4. Alonso, *La Poesía,* 123–45; Alonso, *Poesía Española,* 291–305.

5. Alonso, *Poesía Española,* 291.

6. Ibid., 281.

7. *C.,* Prologue, n. 1.

8. On the de Yepes family, see Francisco Piferrer, *Nobiliario de los Reinos y Señoríos de España,* vol. 3 (Madrid, 1857), 189–99. The coat of arms described here is also substantially that of the town of Yepes, province of Toledo, which was later modified by King Carlos III (1716–88): the color purpure was changed to gules; the lion rampant held a monstrance between his front paws; the bordure disappeared; the shield was surmounted by a crown and a trumpet-blowing angel.

9. The child was in fact mistreated by Francisco de Yepes's wife.

10. *Journey of the Soul into God,* chap. 7, n. 1; in de Vinck, *Works of Bonaventure,* 1:55, which alludes to the *Song of Songs,* 3:9 (throne), rather than 3:7 (bed or litter).

11. On literary connections between the biblical *Song* and the Johannist *Canticle,* see Alonso, *La Poesía,* 113–22; Thompson, *The Poet and the Mystic,* 61–68.

12. The spiritual journey described by medieval authors commonly passed from "outside" to "inside," then to "above."

13. The Hebrew word for *eye* also means *spring;* although John of the Cross knew neither Greek nor Hebrew, he may have been acquainted with this detail.

14. *Song of Songs,* 4:1.

15. See the meaning of *soma* in vedic sanskrit: fire, sacrifice, inebriating drink; this may be related to the cults of Dionysios in Greece and Bacchus in Rome.

16. The bouquet is a *piña,* that is, an arrangement shaped like a pinecone.

17. Most editions locate this stanza in the bride's discourse, which then goes from stanza 27 to stanza 30. Yet this does not tally with the clear meaning of the passage. The Beloved's discourse starts only with stanza 28. Here the commentator ("in this stanza, where the Bridegroom speaks. . . . ": st. 27, n. 1) is misleading. The meaning of the poem contradicts the author's commentary. This is an obvious case in which the text stands by itself, independently of what the author has said about it.

18. The reference is to the Latin Vulgate; the Hebrew text has, "It was there that your mother conceived you. . . . ": 8, 5G in the *New American Bible.* Luis de León had noted the difference between the two texts (*Obras Completas Castellanas,* BAC, 1959, 189).

19. Those at least who can understand something of mystical experience and its creative power.

CHAPTER FOUR

1. The chapter of Almodóvar (October 1578), which John of the Cross attended shortly after escaping from prison, was the second chapter of the discalced. Unlike the first (also at Almodóvar, in 1576), the second was of dubious canonicity, since at the time the discalced no longer had an independent superior. In any case it was this chapter that sent John of the Cross to southern Spain.

2. This is the model of version (A) of the *Canticle*. Besides marginal notations, which could be from John's own pen, it includes the first collection of his poems; photographic reproduction in Silverio de Santa Teresa, *Cántico Espiritual y poesías de San Juan de la Cruz según el codice de Sanlúcar de Barrameda*, 2 vols. (Burgos: Monte Carmelo, 1928). Baruzi calls *Canticle (A)* the text itself and *Canticle (A')* the text with the marginal annotations. The critics who conclude to the authenticity of version (B) see these annotations as proofs of an intermediate state in which the author began to revise his work; see Cristobal Cuevas García, *San Juan de la Cruz*, 13–15.

3. Simeon de la Sagrada Familia (*Juan de la Cruz. Obras Completas*, 2d ed. [Burgos: Monte Carmelo, 1982], 54).

4. Kavanaugh and Rodriguez, *Collected Works*, 709.

5. St. 4, 5, and 8.

6. St. 5.

7. St. 7.

8. St. 4.

9. St. 1.

10. St. 8.

11. St. 3.

12. Alonso, who provides no folk model for this *villancico*, sees it as being "fundamental in the thought of St. John of the Cross" (*La Poesía de San Juan de la Cruz*, 171) and also as formulating "one of the best definitions of our national irrationality" (*Poesía Española*, 288). In opposition, Lucien Florent, who translated the poetry into French, thinks little of it: "Why not admit it? In spite of some fine lines, this poem is one of the least poetical of the saint. The abstract way of treating a difficult topic, the absence of images, everything leaves it distant from the lyricism in which the author of the *Dark Night* excels" (*Poèmes mystiques* [Paris: Le Centurion, 1975], 37.).

13. One may propose hypotheses: the last pages were lost (suggested by the puzzling fact that the book ends in the middle of a sentence, at 3: chap. 45, n. 5); or, chaps. 44–45 were added by someone else (since the manuscript of Alcaudete, copied by Juan Evangelista, companion of the

saint, ends with chap. 43); or also, there were two redactions of the *Ascent* (hazardous suggestion made by Baruzi, *Saint Jean*, 14–15, systematically supported by Jean Orcibal, *La 'Montée du Carmel' a-t-elle été interpolée?* in *Revue d'Histoire des Religions*, 1964, pp. 171–213). But none of these solutions is really convincing.

14. As is done by Brenan, *St. John of the Cross*.

15. Some authors are mentioned by Max Huot de Longchamp, under the heading, "How not to read John of the Cross"! Among well-balanced studies, one may mention Trueman Dicken, *The Crucible of Love. A Study of the Mysticism of St Teresa of Jesus and of St John of the Cross* (London: Darton; Longman and Todd, 1963).

16. *N.*, st. 1.

17. *C.*, st. 12.

18. This is the deacon's chant during the Easter vigil, called the *exsultet* from its first word in Latin.

19. *N.*, st. 1.

20. Ibid., st. 3.

21. Ibid., st. 4.

22. Ibid., st. 5.

23. The *castillo de la Mota*, today an impressive ruin, is a short distance from town; the fairs would have been held along the way going from the town to the castle (Baruzi, *Saint Jean*, 73–74).

24. *N.*, st. 5.

25. *Song of Songs*, 5:7; 8:8–10 (walls); 2:1–2; 6:2 (lilies), 4, 16 (the cool of the breeze). On the influence of Garcilaso, especially in his Second . Eclogue, see Alonso, 54, 56, 166–67.

26. Eulogio, *San Juan de la Cruz*, 263–68.

27. *The Way of Perfection*, chap. 5; *Autobiography*, chap. 14.

28. Among others by Dicken, *Crucible of Love*; Richard Hardy, *Search for Nothing. The Life of John of the Cross* (New York: Crossroads, 1982).

29. *A.*, 1:chap. 4, n. 3; chap. 13, n. 11.

30. *A.*, 2:chap. 1, n. 2; chap. 2, n. 1.

31. María Jesús Fernández Laborans, *Luz y Oscuridad*, 151–221.

32. On analogy, see George H. Tavard, *La Théologie parmi les sciences humaines* (Paris: Beauchesne, 1975), 77–90.

33. *A.*, 2:chap. 2, n. 1.

34. See chap. 5, below.

35. *A.*, 2:chap. 2, n. 3.

36. Ibid., chap. 3, nn. 4–5.

37. *N.*, 1:chap. 13, n. 15; chap. 13, below.

38. *A.*, Prologue, n. 3.

39. Ibid., n. 4.

40. Ibid., 1:chap. 5, n. 6; see chap. 14, n. 3.

41. Ibid., 2:chap. 7, nn. 1–3.

42. Ibid., 2:chap. 7, n. 1.

43. Ibid., n. 7.

44. Ibid., n. 8.

45. Ibid,. n. 9.

46. Ibid., n. 10.

47. Ibid., n. 11.

48. *M.*, 2:chap. 7, n. 13.

49. Michel Florisoone, *Esthétique et Mystique d'après sainte Thérèse d'Avila et saint Jean de la Croix* (Paris: Le Seuil, 1956), 113–21.

50. *A.*, 1:chap. 13, n. 11.

51. *L.*, n. 33 (Simeon, 1601); the letters are not numbered in the same way in all editions or translations; for this reason I will refer only to their place in Simeon's Spanish edition.

52. *A.*, 1:chap. 13, n. 11.

53. The drawing of the *Ascent of Mt. Carmel* is reproduced in most editions and translations, though it is sometimes modified in keeping with the artistic taste of the day. The BAC edition (1959) of Lucinio del SS. Sacramento shows the authentic copy, the printed version of 1618, in the baroque genre, and two modern stylized versions, pp. 297, 554, 601, and 720.

54. *A.*, 1:chap. 13, n. 12.

55. *N.*, Prologue, declaration.

56. Ibid., 1:chap. 9, n. 9.

57. Ibid., chap. 10, n. 2; chap. 9, n. 7.

58. *A.*, 1:chap. 13, n. 15.

59. *N.*, 1:chap. 10, n. 14.

60. *N.*, 1:chap. 12, n. 6. This touches on the question of the "signs" of the entrance into contemplation; see *A.*, 2: chap. 13–14; *N.*, 1:chap. 9; *F.*, st. 3, n. 30–34; *S.*, n. 117 (Simeon, p. 139–40).

61. *N.*, 2:chap. 16, n. 8.

62. Ibid., chap. 17, n. 6.

63. Ibid., n. 7.

64. Ibid., n. 8.

65. Ibid., chap. 18, n. 2.

66. Ibid., chap. 25, n. 2.

67. Ibid., n. 4.

68. *A.*, 2:chap. 26, n. 18.

69. *sinsabor* (*A.*, 2:chap. 7, n. 5; chap. 14, n. 3).

70. *A.*, 2:chap. 26, n. 18; chap. 8, n. 2.

71. On John's use of erotic and sexual symbols, see Eugene Maio, *The Imagery of Eros. A Study of the Influence of Neoplatonism on the Mystical*

Writings of St. John of the Cross (Thesis, University of California at Los Angeles, 1967).

72. *N.*, 2:chap. 11, n. 1.

73. Ibid., chap. 21, n. 2; chap. 23, n. 10; see *A.*, 2:chap. 14, n. 11.

74. *A.*, 2:chap. 24, n. 11.

75. Ibid., chap. 4, n. 4.

76. *A.*, 2:chap. 3, nn. 2, 4, 5; chap. 6, n. 2; chap. 14, n. 11.

77. *N.*, 2:chap. 16, n. 8.

78. Ibid., chap. 24, n. 3.

79. *A.*, 2:chap. 14, n. 11.

80. Ibid., chap. 4, n. 2.

81. Ibid., chap. 28–31.

82. Ibid., chap. 26, n. 18. In the context this principle is applied to feelings, but it has validity for "locutions."

83. Ibid., chap. 27, n. 7.

84. Ibid., chap. 30, n. 7.

85. Ibid., chap. 31, n. 2.

86. Ibid., chap. 3, n. 5.

87. *A.*, 2:chap. 2, n. 1.

88. *N.*, 2:chap. 16, n. 10.

89. Poem, n. 4 (Simeon, p. 54–56).

90. *A.*, 2:chap. 24, n. 9.

91. Ibid., chap. 17, n. 7.

92. See *C.*, st. 36, n. 2; *N.*, 2:chap. 17, n. 2.

CHAPTER FIVE

1. See chapter 6, note 9.

2. One could follow the tracks of mystical unknowing, for instance, among the English mystics, in Rhineland and Netherland mysticism, and in Oriental theology, to say nothing of Asian religions.

3. 2:36; 2:57.

4. Ibid., 10:13; see also *In Cant. Cant.*, chap. 1, n. 17 (*P. L.*, 79, 486); *In Ez.*, 2, hom. 27, n. 4 (*P. L.*, 76, 1207).

5. E.g., in *P. L.*, 180, 953.

6. *De gradibus humilitatis*, 7:21 (*P. L.*, 182, 953).

7. René Rogues, *Structures Théologiques. De la gnose à Richard de St. Victor* (Paris: Presses Universitaires, 1962), 313–19.

8. Chap. 7, n. 6 (De Vinck, *Works of Bonaventure*, 1:58).

9. de Osuna, *Third Alphabet*, pp. 97, 113.

10. James Walsh, ed., *The Cloud of Unknowing* (New York: Paulist, 1981)

chap. 3. The anonymous author wrote between the times of Richard Rolle (c. 1300–49) and Walter Hilton (d. 1396).

11. Walter Hilton, *The Ladder of Perfection* (London: Penguin, 1957), 2:chap. 25; the English original is from 1494; the Latin translation, *Scala perfectionis,* which had eight printings from 1500 to 1550, does not seem to have spread in Spain; see J. E. Milosh, *The Scale of Perfection and the English Mystical Tradition* (Madison: Wisconsin University Press, 1966).

12. On this school and its influence on John of the Cross, see Jean Orcibal, *Saint Jean de la Croix et les mystiques rhéno-flamands* (Bruges: Desclée de Brouwer, 1966). Nobody seems to have argued for an influence of Meister Eckhart; the influence of Ruysbroeck and Tauler does seem probable.

13. See Henry Bett, *Nicholas of Cusa* (London: Methuen, 1932).

14. *The Vision of God* (New York: Ungar Publishing Co., 1960) chap. 10.

15. Eulogio, "Illuminisme et illuminés," in *DS.,* vol. 7/2, col., 1367–92; citation, col. 1385. On the *alhumbrados* one may refer to Ronald Knox, *Enthusiasm* (Oxford: Clarendon, 1950).

16. See my studies on this mystic of the eighteenth century: *Lorsque Dieu fait tout. La doctrine spirituelle du bienheureux Jean-Martin Moye* (Paris: Le Cerf, 1984); George H. Tavard, *L'Expérience de Jean-Martin Moye. Mystique et mission, 1790–93* (Paris: Beauchesne, 1978).

17. Ewert Cousins, *Bonaventure and the Coincidence of Opposites. The Theology of Bonaventure.* (Chicago: Franciscan Herald, 1978), 207, with my critique, "The Coincidence of Opposites: a Recent Interpretation of Bonaventure" in *Theological Studies,* vol. 41 (September 1980), 576–84.

18. *A.,* 1:chap. 4, n. 2.

19. See the article in note 37.

20. *C. S.,* 3, d. 1, a. 1, q. 1, ad 4.

21. See note 17.

22. *S. T.,* 1, 2, q. 54, a. 2, ad 1.

23. Thomas Aquinas, *Commentary on Aristotle's De Anima,* 3:1, 4 e.

24. *S. T.,* 3, q. 46, a. 8, ad 1.

25. On these two types of knowledge, see Bonaventure, *C.S.,* 3, d. 4, a. 3, q. 1–2; Thomas Aquinas, *S. T.,* 1, q. 58, a. 6–7. The scholastics applied this distinction chiefly to the angels' cognition; by analogy it may be applied to mystical experience. The origin of the distinction will be found in St. Augustine, *City of God,* 11:chap. 7.

26. *John* 1: 3–4; *C.,* st. 13–14, n. 5; along similar lines John of the Cross writes: "God works, and his work is God" (*S.,* n. 106; Simeon, p. 138); see below, chap. 9, note 23.

27. *A.,* 1:chap. 4, n. 1.

28. Ibid., n. 2.

29. Ibid., nn. 3–4.

30. Ibid., nn. 4–5.

31. Ibid., nn. 6–7. One may note that the Spanish language has two words of different genders (*señorío, señoría*), which mean equivalently the same thing: "lordship." At this point John uses the masculine for the creature, the feminine for the Spirit of God.

32. *A.*, 1:chap. 4, n. 3.

33. Ibid., nn. 4, 5, 6, 7, 8.

34. *La Théologie parmi les sciences humaines*, p. 77–81.

35. See chap. 13, below.

36. *C.*, Prologue, n. 1.

37. *A.*, 1:chap. 6, n. 1.

38. "The means and the extremes are of the same genus" (*S. T.*, II II, q. 1, a. 2, *sed contra*).

39. *A.*, 1:chap. 6, n. 1.

40. "God is not in any genus" (*S. T.*, II II, q. 3, a. 5, *sed contra* and c).

41. *A.*, 1:chap. 6, n. 3.

42. Ibid., n. 4.

43. *N.*, 2:chap. 5, n. 4.

44. Ibid., chap. 6, n. 1.

45. *A.*, 2:chap. 16, n. 7.

46. Ibid., chap. 7, n. 9.

47. *R.*, 7 (Simeon, p. 70).

48. *N.*, 2: chap. 9, n. 2.

49. Ibid., n. 3.

50. Ibid., chap. 15, n. 1.

51. *A.*, 2:chap. 2, n. 3.

52. *C.*, st. 8, n. 2.

53. *C (B).*, st. 8, n. 3. On this version (B), see chap. 13, below.

54. *F.*, st. 1, n. 18.

55. *F. (B)*, st. 1, n. 22.

56. *A.*, 1:chap. 4, n. 2.

57. Ibid., n. 3.

58. Ibid., n. 4.

59. Ibid., n. 5.

60. Ibid., n. 6.

61. Ibid., n. 7.

62. Ibid., n. 8.

63. Ibid., chap. 6, n. 1.

64. Ibid., n. 3.

65. *N.*, chap. 5, n. 4.

66. Ibid., chap. 6, n. 1.

67. Ibid., chap. 9, n. 2.

68. *C.*, st. 8, n. 2.

69. *C. (B)*, st. 8, n. 3.

70. *F. (B).*, st. 1, n. 22.

71. On the structure of Christian love, see George H. Tavard, *A Way of Love* (New York: Orbis, 1977).

CHAPTER SIX

1. See chap. 2.

2. *R.*, 4 (Simeon, p. 67).

3. Poem, n. 13 (Simeon, p. 83).

4. Poem, (Simeon, p. 84).

5. *N.*, st. 3 (p. 52).

6. *A.*, 2:chap. 1, n. 2.

7. *N.*, 2:chap. 25, n. 4.

8. Thomas Aquinas analyzes the object of faith (*S. T.*, *II II*, *q.* 1), the interior assent of faith (q. 2), the exterior confession of faith (q. 3), the subjects or persons who believe (q. 4), the cause or origin of faith (q. 5), the effects of faith (q. 6), hence he passes on to the gifts of intelligence (q. 7) and knowledge (q. 8), which, in his theology on the gifts of the Holy Spirit, bring faith to perfection. He studies next the sins against faith, that is, infidelity (q. 10), heresy (q. 11), apostasy (q. 12), blasphemy (q. 13), and blindness (q. 14). He ends his tractate on the precepts of faith in the Old Testament (q. 15).

9. On the Johannist faith, see Karol Wojtyla, *Faith according to St. John of the Cross* (San Francisco: Ignatius Press, 1981).

10. *A.*, 2:chap. 3, n. 1.

11. *S. T.*, II II, q. 4, a. 1, c.

12. Ibid., II II, q. 2, a. 1, ad 3; q. 4, a. 1, ad 2.

13. Ibid., II II, q. 4, a. 1 c.

14. *A.*, 2:chap. 3, n. 1.

15. Ibid., chap. 6; see St. Augustine, *"On the Trinity,"* Book 14.

16. Ibid., n. 3.

17. *N.*, 2:chap. 21, n. 3–10.

18. Ibid., n. 11.

19. *S. T.*, 2, 2, q. 1, a. 1–2.

20. Ibid., 2, 2, q. 2, a. 2.

21. *A.*, 2:chap. 3; Rom. 10:17.

22. *C.*, st. 7, n. 6–7.

23. *A.*, 2:chap. 17, n. 1.

24. Ibid., chap. 24, n. 8.

25. Ibid., chap. 27, n. 4.

26. Ibid., chap. 3, n. 2.

27. Ibid., n. 4.

28. *S. T.*, 1:q. 1, a. 8 c.

29. At this point John of the Cross is closer to Martin Luther than to Thomas Aquinas; see George H. Tavard, *Justification. An Ecumenical Study* (New York: Paulist, 1983). Hans Urs von Balthasar thinks that the reformers of the Carmel gave "a Carmelite response to Luther" (*La Gloire et la croix. Les aspects esthétiques de la révélation*, 2/2 [Paris: Aubier, 1965], 8). This seems doubtful if it implies that John and Teresa intended to reply to Luther, whose doctrine they could have known only from hearsay and quite inaccurately. It is not at the level of faith and its nature that one can oppose John to Luther, but at that of the consequences and implications that they drew from a conception of faith that was very similar in both of them. See Daniel Olivier, *Luther's Faith. The Cause of the Gospel in the Church* (St Louis: Concordia, 1978); Jared Wicks, *Luther and His Spiritual Legacy* (Wilmington: Michael Glazier, 1984).

30. *A.*, 2:chap. 4, n. 2.

31. *C.*, st. 11, n. 3.

32. Ibid., n. 4.

33. Ibid., n. 3.

34. Ibid., n. 4.

35. Ibid., n. 3.

36. Origen, *The Song of Songs. Commentary and Homilies* (Westminster: Newman Press, 1957), 79–80.

37. *C.*, st. 13–14, n. 14.

38. Ibid., n. 15.

39. *De veritate*, q. 10, a. 6.

40. *C.*, st. 13–14, n. 14.

41. *A.*, 2:chap. 4, n. 4.

42. The expression is presumably inspired by Heb. 11:6.

43. See note 8, above.

44. *C.*, st. 11, n. 6.

45. This is the tendency of the theologian Garrigou-Lagrange, the philosopher Jacques Maritain, and others; see Huot de Longchamp, *Lectures*, 391–99.

46. *A.*, 1:chap. 2, n. 3.

47. *N.*, 2:chap. 18, n. 4.

48. Ibid., n. 5.

49. *A.*, 2:chap. 9, title.

50. Ibid., chap. 6, n. 1.

51. Ibid., n. 4.

52. Even some descriptions in the *Living Flame of Love* are made in the scholastic framework of the faculties and the theological virtues (e.g., st. 3, n. 41–43).

53. *A.*, 2:chap. 31., n. 1.

54. Ibid., chap. 5, n. 1.

55. Ibid., n. 2.

56. Ibid., n. 3.

57. *C.*, st. 32, n. 3.

58. Ibid., n. 4.

59. *F.*, st. 2, n. 16.

60. Ibid., n. 17.

61. Ibid., n. 18.

62. *N.*, 2:chap. 23, n. 12.

63. One may recognize here the theological method of Bonaventure in the *Breviloquium*; see George H. Tavard, *Transiency and Permanence. The Method of Theology according to St Bonaventure*, 2d ed. (St. Bonaventure, N. Y.: Franciscan Institute Publications, 1974), p. 112–13.

64. *A.*, 2:chap. 4, n. 5.

65. Ibid., title.

66. Ibid., Prologue, n. 9.

67. Ibid., 1:chap. 2, n. 3.

68. Ibid., 2:chap. 4, n. 1.

69. Ibid., n. 6.

70. *N.*, 2:chap. 2, n. 5.

71. *A.*, 2:chap. 8, n. 3.

72. Ibid., chap. 2, n. 1.

73. Ibid., chap. 8, n. 5.

74. Ibid., n. 2.

75. Ibid., chap. 9, n. 1.

76. Ibid, chap. 30, n. 5.

77. *N.*, 2:chap. 2, n. 5.

78. *A.*, 2:chap. 24, n. 8.

79. *D. S.*, n. 806.

80. *A.*, 2:chap. 8, n. 2.

81. Ibid., n. 3.

82. Ibid., n. 4.

83. Ibid., chap. 4, n. 5.

84. Ibid., chap. 9, n. 1.

85. See above, chap. 5, note 2.

86. Daniel Olivier, *Luther's Faith*; Tavard, *Justification*.

87. In 1516 and 1518, Luther had two versions printed, a short and a long one, of this anonymous work; he had found them in manuscript form

in a library and gave them their current title; see Bengt Hoffman, ed., *The Theologia Germanica of Martin Luther* (New York: Paulist, 1982).

88. Daniel Olivier, "Salvation in Jesus Christ," *LCA Partners* (February/ March 1984), 24.

CHAPTER SEVEN

1. See chap. 3, above.

2. Crisógono, *Life of St. John*, 134; A. Peers, *Spirit of Flame* (London: Burns and Oates, 1945), 62–63; Thompson, *The Poet and the Mystic*, 28–29.

3. Thompson, *The Poet and the Mystic*, 29–30; I have rendered *Carillo*, as "Little Dear," and *Querido* as "Darling," and reserved "Beloved" for *Amado*.

4. The jail in Toledo "had a small opening just over two inches wide high up in the wall, looking out on to a corridor" (Crisógono, *Life of St. John*, 103).

5. Simeon, 128.

6. *C.*, st. 32, n. 2.

7. On love and beauty in the Johannist faith and experience, see von Balthasar, *La Gloire et la Croix*, vol. 2/2 (Paris: Aubier, 1972), 33–56.

8. *C.*, st. 37, n. 5; on the reinterpretation of this verse in version (B), see chapter 13, below.

9. *C.*, st. 35, n. 3.

10. Ibid., n. 6.

11. See chapter 5, n. 25, above.

12. Ainsi dans *C.*, st. 13–14, n. 5. This punctuation of the verse was common in the Middle Ages.

13. de Léon, *Obras Completas Castellanas*, p. 140; see Lorca, *De Fray Luis a San Juan*.

14. On the nudity of Christ in Renaissance art, see Leo Steinberg, *The Sexuality of Christ in Renaissance Art and in Modern Oblivion* (New York: Pantheon, 1983).

15. On these events, see Crisógono, *Life of St. John*, 5–8.

16. Ibid., 210.

17. *C.*, st. 38.

18. Garcilaso, *Second Eclogue*, "filomela suspira en dulce canto"; see Alonso, *La Poesía*, 35.

19. For an extensive study of the prologues, see Georges Morel, *Le Sens de l'Existence selon saint Jean de la Croix*, vol. 1 (Paris: Aubier, 1960), 187–255.

20. *A.*, Prologue, n. 9.

21. *N.*, Prologue, declaration.

22. *C.*, fol., n. 3.

23. *F.*, Prologue, n. 3.

24. *A.*, Prologue, nn. 3–4.

25. *C.*, Prologue, n. 3.

26. *A.*, Prologue, n. 8.

27. St. Thérèse of Lisieux is not exempt from this in her poetry.

28. John occasionally borrows a "scale of love," like the ten degrees of love of an opusculum that was then attributed to Thomas Aquinas; see *N.*, 2:chaps. 19–20, which should be compared with the remark made in *F.*, st. 1, n. 13, where the degrees of love are more and more interior centers of the soul: "And thus, if the soul has one degree of love, it is already at its center in God; for one degree of love is enough to be in God by grace."

29. *F.*, Prologue, n. 2.

30. *A.*, Prologue, n. 1.

31. *C.*, Prologue, n. 1.

32. *F.*, Prologue, n. 1.

33. *A.*, Prologue, n. 2.

34. *C.*, Prologue, n. 1.

35. Ibid., n. 2.

36. Ibid., n. 4.

37. *F.*, Prologue, n. 1.

38. Ibid., n. 4.

39. See Vilnet, *Bible et Mystique.*

40. *A.*, Prologue, n. 2. This text places John of the Cross well in his own time, the question of the relationships between Scripture and the Church being then at the center of theological concerns, both for the Catholics and for the Protestants; see Tavard, *Holy Writ or Holy Church. The Crisis of the Protestant Reformation* (New York: Harper, 1959).

41. *C.*, Prologue, n. 4.

42. *F.*, Prologue, n. 1.

43. Such is the interpretation of José Nieto, *Mystic, Rebel, Saint: A Study of St. John of the Cross* (Geneva: Droz, 1979). To my mind, however, this point of view is improperly biased by a Calvinist prejudice against Christian mysticism (which is far from Calvin's own theology). In another line, a more or less Marxist reading of John of the Cross makes him a humanist impeded by the dogmas he accepted (Manuel Ballestero, *Juan de la Cruz. De la Angustía al Olvido. Análisis del fondo intuido en la 'Subida del Monte Carmelo'* [Barcelona: Ediciones Península, 1977], 165).

44. This was the age-long practice of the Church before the Reformation; see Beryl Smalley, *The Study of the Bible in the Middle Ages* (Oxford: Clarendon, 1940).

CHAPTER EIGHT

1. *R.*, 1.
2. *The Vision of the Trinity*, 77–81.
3. *S. C.*, n. 63.
4. *S. T.*, 1, q. 20, a. 1.
5. *S. T.*, 1, q. 37, a. 1.
6. *R.*, 2.
7. 1, q. 37, a. 2.
8. See *A.*, 2:chap. 9, n. 3; *C.*, st. 7, nn. 5, 9.
9. *F.*, st. 4, n. 17.
10. *A.*, 2:chap. 24, n. 4.
11. Ibid., chap. 16, n. 9.
12. Ibid., chap. 26, n. 5.
13. *N.*, chap. 12, n. 3.
14. Ibid., 2:chap. 1, n. 1.
15. *A.*, 3:chap. 14, n. 2; *N.*, 2:chap. 30, n. 2; *C.*, st. 4, n. 1; st. 33, n. 3.
16. *C.*, st. 15, n. 6.
17. Ibid, st. 38, nn. 3–4; *R.*, 8.
18. *S. T.*, 1, q. 2–26 (God), q. 27–43 (the three Persons).
19. *The Vision of the Trinity*, chap. 3, pp. 57–86.
20. *R.*, 2.
21. Ibid., 4.
22. Direct studies of the first Person are impossible, since the Father manifests himself only through the Word and the Spirit: see Louis Bouyer, *Le Père Invisible* (Paris: Le Cerf, 1976).
23. *A.*, 2:chap. 22, n. 5.
24. *C.*, st. 5, n. 4.
25. Ibid., st. 39, n. 6.
26. *F. (B)*, st. 4, n. 17. Version (A), at st. 4, n. 17, is practically the same; yet it seems less clear, due to the absence of the word "aspiration."
27. *A.*, chap. 14, n. 2.
28. Mother Julian, *The Showings* (or, *Revelations of Divine Love*), chap. 58; George H. Tavard, *Woman in Christian Tradition*, 144–46.
29. *A.*, 1:chap. 2, n. 4; *Tobias*, 6:14–22.
30. Book of Wisdom, Ch. 8 Verse 13; John 1:1–2
31. *A.*, 1:chap. 4, n. 8.
32. Ibid., chap. 5, n. 8.
33. Ibid., chap. 13, n. 11; see chap. 4, above.
34. Ibid., chap. 14, n. 2.
35. *A.*, 2:chap. 16, n. 1.
36. *A.*, 2:chap. 15, n. 4.

37. Ibid., chap. 29, n. 6.

38. Ibid., chap. 11, n. 9; *Song of Songs*, 2:4.

39. Ibid., chap. 1, n. 2; 3:chap. 13, n. 5.

40. *N.*, 1:Declaration, n. 2.

41. Chap. 14, n. 1.

42. *N.*, 2:chap. 24, n. 4.

43. Ibid., chap. 4, n. 2.

44. Ibid., chap. 5, n. 2.

45. Ibid., chap. 10, n. 4.

46. Ibid., chap. 12, n. 3.

47. Ibid., chap. 5, n. 1.

48. *A.*, 2:chap. 22, n. 5; 3:chap. 44, n. 4; *N.*, 2:chap, 19, n. 4.

49. *N.*, 2:chap. 1, n. 1.

50. Ibid., chap. 19, n. 9.

51. *A.*, 1:chap. 13, n. 4.

52. *N.*, 2:chap. 7, n. 5.

53. *A.*, 2:chap. 7, n. 2; n. 11.

54. Ibid., 3:chap. 31, n. 5; n. 7.

55. *N.*, chap. 21, n. 3; chap. 23, n. 4.

56. *A.*, 1:chap. 13, n. 4.

57. *C.*, st. 13, n. 11.

58. Ibid., st. 39, n. 6.

59. This is suggested by Huot, *Lectures*, 139–40.

60. St. Bernard, *Sermon 15 on the Song of Songs*; Heinrich Suso, *Life*, chap. 45, where the piety of Elsbeth Stagel, a disciple of Suso, is reflected. Latin translations of the Rhineland mystics were published in Cologne by Laurentius Surius: Tauler in 1548, Ruysbroeck in 1549, Suso in 1555. The *Theologia mystica* of Harphius (a Franciscan who joined the Brethren of the Common Life, d. 1477) went through several editions beginning in 1538. Furthermore, the *Institutiones*, a compilation excerpted from the mystics of the Rhineland and Flanders, most probably composed by St. Peter Canisius, and included among the works of Tauler, had been translated and published in Spanish in 1551. See Orcibal, *La 'Montée du Carmel' a-t-elle été interpolée?*, 21–26.

61. See *The Way of a Pilgrim, and The Pilgrim Continues on his Way* (New York: Harper, 1954), an anonymous writing of the nineteenth century; for a contemporary interpretation of this devotion, see Arthur Vogel, *The Jesus Prayer for Today* (New York: Paulist, 1982).

62. E.g., *L.*, n. 45, to Leonora de San Gabriel (Simeon, 1615).

63. *L.*, n. 30, to María de Jesús (Simeon, 1595).

64. "*Jesus Maria*," in *L.*, n. 40, to an unidentified Carmelite nun (Simeon, 1609); "May Jesus Maria be with Your Reverence," to Nicolás de Jesús-María

(Doria), *L.*, n. 34 (Simeon, 1601).

65. As in *L.*, n. 22, addressed to Anne of Jesus (Simeon, 1579). Clearly, John's practice is not uniform.

66. *L.*, n. 20 (Simeon, 1576).

67. *C.*, st. 1, nn. 1–2.

68. Ibid., n. 4.

69. *C.*, st. 1, n. 2.

70. Ibid., st. 13, n. 10.

71. Ibid., st. 36, n. 1.

72. Ibid., st. 5, n. 1.

73. *A.*, 1:chap. 2, n. 4.

74. Ibid., chap. 4, n. 5.

75. Proverbs 8:4–6; 18–21.

76. *A.*, 1:chap. 4, n. 8.

77. This is Huot's suggestion (*Lectures*, p. 139, note 150). That John was influenced by Luis de León's *The Names of Christ* (1583) when he ended his commentary on the *Canticle* with the evocation of the name of Jesus (Huot's idea) seems extremely doubtful; it is in any case difficult to determine whether Luis intended to trace a progression from the first name (*pimpollo*, root) to the last (which may be the thirteenth: *Jesus*, as in the 1593 edition, or the fourteenth: *Cordero* (Lamb), as in the posthumous edition of 1595; see *Obras Completas Castellanas*, BAC, 1959.

78. *A.*, 2:chap. 15, n. 4.

79. Ibid., chap. 16, n. 7.

80. Ibid., n. 9.

81. Ibid., chap. 29, n. 6.

82. *N.*, 2:chap. 4, n. 2.

83. Ibid., chap. 24, n. 3.

84. Ibid., chap. 5, n. 1.

85. *C.*, st. 35, n. 4.

86. Ibid., st. 36, nn. 1–2.

87. Ibid., st., 3, n. 9.

88. Ibid., st. 13–14.

89. Ibid., n. 5.

90. Ibid., st. 39, n. 6.

CHAPTER NINE

1. John 1:3; *C.*, st. 8, n. 3; st. 13–14, n. 5.

2. *Sin arrimo y con arrimo:* n. 12 in Simeon, 82–83.

3. Thérèse of Lisieux does not translate John's poem; starting from his

first line, she writes her own piece, a *"Glose on the divine according to St John of the Cross"*; see Thérèse de Lisieux, *Poésies* (Paris: Le Cerf, 1979). On Thérèse and John of the Cross, see Jean-François Six, *Thérèse de Lisieux au Carmel* (Paris: Le Seuil, 1973), 72–77, 200–208.

4. This text has apparently not been identified: Alonso mentions no version of it; see Eulogio, *San Juan de la Cruz*, 250–51.

5. See chap. 13, below.

6. Huot de Longchamp, *Lectures*, 156–60, where the author discusses the exact meaning of *hermosura* (beauty) in the *Canticle* and the *Living Flame*. Brenan rates this poem very low: "The development attributed to San Juan is quite different and so poor that, even if he wrote it—and it is not in his usual style or diction—it seems better to omit it" (*St. John of the Cross*, 129). Florisoone sees here no more than a "poetic game" (*Esthétique et Mystique*, 162–63, note 39). These judgments are unnecessarily negative. Alonso cites a secular model of this poem (*Poesía Española*, 239–42), yet he admits that the piece *a lo divino* may well be from John's pen (*La Poesía*, 88–90).

7. *Tras de un amoroso lance*, n. 6 in Simeon, 58–59.

8. *Complete Poetical Works of Francis Thompson* (New York: Modern Library, 1913), 88–93.

9. See the text, presumably incomplete, in Alonso, *Poesía Española*, 242–44.

10. See *A.*, 2:chap. 2, n. 1; *C.*, st. 13–14, n. 23.

11. *C.*, st. 16, n. 5; see chap. 7, above.

12. Alonso, *Poesía Española*, 245–47, with the remarks in *La Poesía*, 43–48, 148–49.

13. *A.*, 2:chap. 22, n. 5.

14. Sor Juana Inés de la Cruz, *Obras Completas* (Mexico: Porrua, 1975), 412–16.

15. See chap. 8, above.

16. See Florisoone's reflections, *Esthétique et Mystique*, 86–87.

17. No. 15 and 16 in Simeon, 86–87.

18. See chap. 8, above.

19. *S.*, nn. 7, 16, 25 (Simeon, 125–27).

20. *S.*, n. 26 (pp. 127–28).

21. See *Justification*, 49–69.

22. op. cit., pp. 104–6. N. 106 in *Sayings of Light and Love* rings with a Lutheran peal: "All the goodness that we have is lent to us, and God holds it as his own." But John adds a remark that Luther would not make: "God works, and his work is God" (Simeon, 138). This text is cited according to the manuscript of the *Archivo Silveriano* of Burgos (Simeon, 135, n. 5). The BAC edition, followed by Kavanaugh and Rodriguez, gives it another

form: "God and his work is *(sic)* God" (BAC, 1291; Kavanaugh and Rodriguez, *Collected Works*, 676, where it is listed as *Maxims on Love*, n. 29). The exact authenticity of all the maxims has not been ascertained.

23. *S.*, n. 58 (Simeon, 132).

CHAPTER TEN

1. *F.*, annotation to st. 1.

2. Garcilaso's works comprise three eclogues, two elegies, five *canciones* or songs, one "epistle," some forty sonnets, and a few minor pieces.

3. In fact, Dante's rhyme varies considerably, going from the *aba* sequence to *bab*, then *aaa* and *aca* in the first twelve lines of Canto 23; there are many editions: I have used Dante Allighieri, *La Divina Commedia* (Milan: Bietti, 1977).

4. *F.*, st. 1, n. 2.

5. Leviticus 25:8–54.

6. Acts 2:1–4.

7. Galatians 3:28: on the theological implications of this verse, see George H. Tavard, *Woman in Christian Tradition* (Notre Dame University Press, 1973).

8. *C.*, Prologue, n. 1.

9. *"The Mystery of the Holy Spirit,"* in *Downside Review*, vol. 68, 1950, pp. 255–70.

CHAPTER ELEVEN

1. *F.*, Prologue, n. 1.

2. Ibid., Prologue, n. 4.

3. These categories are borrowed from Louis Hjelmslev, *Prolégomènes à une Théorie du Langage* (Paris: Editions de Minuit, 1971), 65–79.

4. This principle is given several formulations, e.g., *Forma completa est in subjecto secundum conditionem subjecti* (*S. T.*, 111, q. 63, a. 5, ad 1); it appears at times in the negative: the soul has no capacity to receive (*A.*, 1:chap. 8, n. 2).

5. *F.*, st. 3, nn. 26–58.

6. Ibid., st. 2, nn. 21, 31.

7. Ibid., st. 1, n. 3. Does the ending of the next quote *(en temple de vida divina)* hide a play of words, *temple* meaning *disposition*, and also a *temple*, church, or chapel of the Knights Templar? The Segovia carmel was close to such a temple, the chapel of which has survived to this day.

8. *S. T.*, I, q. 35, a. 2; q. 36, a. 4; see St. Augustine, *On the Trinity*, Book 15, chap. 26, n. 47 (NAPNF, 3:255).

9. *F.*, st. 1, n.9; st. 3, n. 58.

10. *C.*, st. 34, n. 1; *F.*, st. 1, n. 3.

11. John 14:16; see 14:26; 16:7.

12. *F.*, st. 2, n. 1.

13. Ibid., n. 19.

14. *F. (B)*, st. 2, n. 20.

15. Ibid., n. 14; the reference to the stigmata (Galatians 6:17) is not in version (A).

16. Ibid., st. 3, n. 52.

17. This does not imply that memory should be cultivated for its own sake: the lessons of the *Ascent*, 3:chaps. 1–15, remain valid. One may suspect that John of the Cross would not have appreciated, had he known them, the methods of memory-expansion practiced in the humanistic and scientific studies of his time, not least in the schools of the Society of Jesus: we do not know if he was exposed to them at the school of Medina del Campo; see Jonathan Spence, *The Memory Palace of Matteo Ricci* (New York: Viking, 1984). Matteo Ricci, who tried to impress the Chinese mandarins with his mnemotechnical methods, entered China proper in September 1583, while John was prior in Granada.

18. *F.*, st. 4, n. 17.

19. Ibid., st. 1, n. 3.

20. Ibid., n. 13.

21. Ibid., n. 14.

22. Ibid., n. 4; Judges 13:20.

23. *F.*, st. 1, n. 13; John of the Cross does not list the degrees of love at this point, as he does elsewhere (seven degrees: *A.*, 2:chap. 2, n. 10, in contrast with the seven beasts of Revelation 12:3; *C.*, st. 17, nn. 2.3, in relation with the seven gifts of the Holy Spirit; ten degrees: *N.*, 2:chaps. 19–20, in keeping with the *De decem gradibus amoris Dei et proximi*, of Helwicus Teutonicus—Helwich of Germar, O. P.—which was mistakenly ascribed to Thomas Aquinas. St. Bernard had listed four degrees in his *De diligendo Deo*, but also three, five, and ten elsewhere (Etienne Gilson, *La Théologie Mystique de saint Bernard* [Paris: Vrin, 1947], 110–11, 200); Orcibal remarks that the seven degrees are also in Ruysbroeck, whereas Richard of St. Victor, Harphius, Tauler, count only nine, and Honorius of Autun fifteen (op. cit., p. 213, n. 2); concerned about an inconsistency in the Johannist writings, Orcibal suggests (*La 'Montée du Carmel' a-t-elle été interpolée?*, 212–14) that chaps. 19–20 were inserted by another hand, possibly from John's own notes; yet this hypothesis is not necessary: the scale of degrees of love, even when mentioned and used by John of the Cross, was convenient, but not normative.

24. F., st. 1, n. 9.

25. Ibid., n. 8.

26. Ibid., st. 2, n. 32.

27. Ibid., n. 8.

28. *Autobiography*, chap. 29.

29. F., st. 2, n. 12.

30. Ibid., n. 9.

31. The Copernican revolution was only at its beginnings at the time of John of the Cross: Nicholas Copernic (1473–1543) had his *De Revolutionibus* published in 1543; but his views spread very slowly. It is likely that John either was not acquainted, or did not agree, with them.

32. F., st. 2, n.10.

33. See chap. 7, above.

34. F., st. 3, n. 7; *Song of Songs*, 7:2.

35. F., st. 3, n. 8.

36. See F., st. 1, n. 12.

37. F., st. 2, n. 30.

38. Ibid., st. 1, n. 30.

39. Ibid., n. 27.

40. F (B)., st. 1, n. 33.

41. See Hyacinthe Héring, *De Amplexu Reservato (Angelicum)*, vol. 28, 1951, pp. 3–35.

42. See Eckhart, *Sermon on "Intravit Jesus in Templum,"* in Raymond Blakney, ed., *Meister Eckhart* (New York: Harper, 1957), 156–60; Suso: *Life*, chap. 49.

43. F. (B)., st. 1, n. 33.

44. The meaning of the word *state* in spiritual literature has evolved. In Bonaventure's language *status* designated a high point of experience, corresponding rather well with what John is describing. In the seventeenth-century "French school," *état* will be a stable experience of participation in God. I take the word in this sense here.

45. F., st. 1, n. 7.

46. *Song of Songs*, 1:2; St. Bernard, *Sermon 7 on the 'Song of Songs'*, n. 2.

47. St. Augustine, *Confessions*, 13, chap. 9, n. 10.

48. F., st. 1, n. 11.

49. Ibid., n. 12.

50. Ibid., n. 13.

51. Ibid., st. 2, n. 2.

52. Ibid., n. 3.

53. Ibid., n. 2.

54. Ibid., n. 3.

55. Ibid., n. 4.

56. *F. (B)*, st. 3, n. 8; see 2 Macc. 1:19.

57. *F. (B)*, st. 2, n. 10; Mark 4:30–32.

58. *F.*, st. 1, n. 24.

59. Ibid., n. 25. Version (B) keeps the singular through the sentence (st. 1, n. 31).

60. 1 Peter 2:4; on Denys, see von Balthasar, *La Gloire et la Croix*, vol. 2/1, pp. 163–92.

61. *F.*, st. 1, n. 22.

62. *F. (B)*, st. 3, n. 10.

63. Ibid., st. 2, n. 32.

64. Ibid., n. 34.

65. *F.*, st. 2, n. 15.

66. Ibid., n. 16; 1 Kings 19:12.

67. *F.*, st. 2, n. 7; wisdom: st. 1, n. 14; spouse: st. 3, n. 26; beloved: st. 3, n. 67; darling: st. 3, n. 68.

68. *F.*, st. 4. n. 4.

69. Ibid., n. 13.

70. See Ruysbroeck, *The Spiritual Espousals*, Book 3, chap. 6 (Eric Colledge, ed. [New York: Harper, n.d.], 185).

71. Robert Michel, *Vivre dans l'Esprit: Marie de l'Incarnation* (Montreal: Editions Bellarmin, 1975), 325.

72. *F. (B)*, st. 2, n. 20.

73. *C. (B)*, st. 38, n. 6; see chap. 13, below.

74. *F.*, st. 2, n. 19.

75. Ibid., st. 3, n. 2.

76. *F. (B)*, st. 3, n. 3.

77. *F.*, st. 2, n. 19.

78. *F. (B)*, st. 3, n. 2.

79. *F.*, st. 3, n. 6.

80. *F. (B)*, st. 3, n. 6.

81. Ibid., n. 12.

82. *F.*, st. 3, n. 13.

83. Ibid., n. 14.

84. Ibid., n. 17.

85. Ibid., st. 1, n. 4; "All the movements of such a soul are divine" (st. 1, n. 9).

86. *F.*, st. 3, n. 67.

87. Ibid., n. 68.

88. *F. (B)*, st. 4, n. 4; see note 31, above.

89. *F.*, st. 4, n. 5.

90. Ibid., n. 6.

91. Ibid., n. 7.

92. Ibid., n. 10.

93. Ibid., n. 9.

94. Ibid., n. 16.

95. Ibid., n. 17.

96. *C.*, st. 38, n. 3; *S.*, n. 105 (Simeon, p. 138); see Morel, *Le Sens de l'Existence*, 2:229–56; on some christological implications of this definition of the human, see Tavard, *Images of the Christ* (Washington: University Press of America, 1982), 95–119.

97. On the principle of personhood in Trinitarian theology, see Tavard, *The Vision of Trinity*, pp. 74–78.

98. On symbol in theology, see Tavard, *La Théologie parmi les sciences humaines*, pp. 82–90.

99. This is the point where the oriental theology of the "divine energies" ("palamism") would fit a Trinitarian experience of the Johannist type; as John of the Cross writes, "God works, and his work is God" (*S.*, n. 106).

CHAPTER TWELVE

1. Baruzi, *Saint Jean*, 16–47. "Let us recall," Baruzi concluded concerning all the Johannist writings, "that we are confronted with a ruin" (p. 47). This is an exaggeration. As is shown, among others, by Eulogio, the work is sufficiently well preserved for careful study of its form and doctrine. The most radical negation of the Johannist authorship of *Canticle (B)* was made by Philippe Chevallier, *Le Cantique spirituel de saint Jean de la Croix* (Bruges: Desclée de Brouwer, 1930); Philippe Chevallier, *Le Texte définitif du Cantique spirituel* (Solesmes: Abbaye, 1950). Generally, though not universally, subsequent French critics have tended to doubt the authenticity of version (B), whereas Spanish scholars have tended to defend it. Kavanaugh and Rodriguez do not include version (A) in their translation, unlike Allison Peers, who translates both versions. Karol Wojtyla prefers to quote only passages that are common to both texts. (This statement, however, has been omitted in the English translation: *Faith according to Saint John of the Cross* [San Francisco: Ignatius, 1981], 28; see the Spanish translation, *La Fe según San Juan de la Cruz* [BAC, 1979], 15). See the well-balanced discussion by Roger Duvivier, *La Genèse*, xxxv–lxxix, who considers authentic the passages of (B) that are related to the annotations of the Sanlúcar manuscript, while admitting that there are other interpolations.

2. Alonso, *La Poesía*, 152–53.

3. By the same token Huot de Longchamp (*Lectures*, 420) rejects the value of the annotations in the Sanlúcar manuscript (p. 418). Eulogio thinks that these annotations are not only authentic but are even from John's own

pen (*San Juan de la Cruz*, 386–88). The graphological argument, however, remains tenuous.

4. Eulogio, *San Juan de la Cruz*, 282–371.

5. Ibid., 379.

6. Jean Krynen, *Le Cantique Spirituel de saint Jean de la Croix commenté et refondu au XVIIe siècle: un regard sur l'histoire de l'éxégèse du Cantique de Jaén* (Salamanca: Universidad, 1948). According to Krynen, the interpolator would have been Agustino Antolinez (1554–1626), Augustinian, archbishop of Santiago, who wrote a commentary on the *Spiritual Canticle* (Angel Custodio Vega, ed., *Amores de Dios y el Alma, por Fray Agustino Antolinez* [Madrid: El Escorial, 1956]). This theory has not been followed.

7. Theologians are often also poets in the patristic and medieval tradition. The separation of theology and poetry seems to have followed the invasion of theological method by rationalism in the course of the nineteenth century.

8. As is the case with the English translations of Thompson (*The Poet and the Mystic*, 173–77) and Nicholson (in Brenan, *St. John of the Cross*, 148–61), who follow the early editions of Rome (1627, in Italian) and of Madrid (1630). Duvivier studies version (A), including the new st. 11 (which he calls 10bis) with some reservation, apparently shared by no one else, as to the authenticity of the stanza: "One would receive it with less reticence if it was found in the same situation among older witnesses than the Rome and Madrid editions" (*Le Dynamisme existentiel*, 44).

9. See chap. 3, above.

10. Presumably in keeping with the idea of death through love, which is so prominent in the commentary on the *Living Flame*; see chapter 11.

11. I still follow the dating of Simeon, op. cit.

12. George H. Tavard, "The Holy Tradition," in Leonard Swidler, ed., *Dialogue for Reunion* (New York: Herder and Herder, 1962), 54–88; George H. Tavard, "The Meaning of Scripture," in Leonard Swidler, ed., *Scripture and Ecumenism. Protestant, Catholic, Orthodox and Jewish* (Pittsburgh: Duquesne University Press, 1965), 59–73.

13. A strictly literal translation would say: "See *that* sickness / Of love, *that* is not healed, / except with the presence and the image," where "that" renders the Spanish *que*. If, in the English language, such a sentence is not correct, the customs of the Castilian dialect allow it and even make it particularly evocative. Yet some editors have corrected it by adding a verb to the first *que*:

mira que *es* la dolencia	see that *it is* the sickness
de amor, que no se cura,	of love, that is not healed,
sino con la presencia	except with the presence
y la figura.	and the image.

(James Maurice Kelly, *The Oxford Book of Spanish Verse. XIIIth–XXth century* [Oxford: Clarendon, 1965], 154).

14. See note 2, above.

15. See chapter 13.

16. The question has been raised whether John of the Cross could have been influenced by some Muslim mystics of mozarabic Spain. Miguel Asin Palacios argues for the influence of Ibn 'Abbâd de Ronda (a city of Andalusia, southwest of Granada); Ibn 'Abbâd, a mystic of the "night," lived in the fourteenth-fifteenth centuries (*Saint John of the Cross and Islam* [New York: Vantage Books, 1981]). In his biography of the saint, Bruno de Jésus-Marie also explains that when John of the Cross arrived in Granada there lived in the city a Muslim woman who was known as a great mystic: "la Mora de Ubeda," a disciple of al-Ghazzali. She is known through the notes of a Muslim pilgrim in quest of mystical experience and doctrine, "El Mancebo de Arévalo" (*St. John of the Cross* [New York: Sheed and Ward, 1932], 253–58). Yet one thing is certain: John never alludes to such persons or their doctrines.

CHAPTER THIRTEEN

1. See chap. 12, n. 1, above.

2. Thus Lucinio del SS. Sacramento wishes to defend "the Carmelite school" against its adversaries (BAC, p. 946).

3. This need not imply that the one is better than the other. Judgments of this kind insert into the debate theological criteria that are alien to John of the Cross.

4. Some authors, especially theologians and philosophers, have studied John of the Cross in the light of a theory on these relations (Garrigou-Lagrange, *Perfection chrétienne et contemplation selon s. Thomas d'Aquin et s. Jean de la Croix* [Saint-Maximin: Editions de la Vie Spirituelle, 1923]; Jacques Maritain, *The Degrees of Knowledge* [New York: Scribners, 1959], 310–83).

5. Huot de Longchamp, *Lectures*, 420 (capitalization by the author).

6. *C.*, st. 39, n. 6.

7. *C. (B)*, st. 40, n. 7.

8. *A.*, Prologue, n. 2.

9. *C.*, Prologue, n. 4.

10. This is precisely what worries those authors for whom this would contradict the previous attitude of John of the Cross before the mystery of participation in God. But the exploration of a new point of view need not imply a contradiction.

11. This description follows the edition by Simeon; it is regrettable that no uniformity in numbering the paragraphs has been reached among editors and translators.

12. *C. (B)*, arg., n. 1.

13. Ibid., n. 2.

14. See Roques, *L'Univers dionysien*.

15. The classical work is by Jean-François Bonnefoy, *Une Somme bonaventurienne de théologie mystique: le 'De Triplici Via'* (Paris: Librarie Saint François, 1934).

16. García de Cisneros (1455/56–1510), *Ejercitatorio de la vida espiritual*; Francisco de Osuna, *Third Alphabet*, Letter T (tractate 18), chaps. 2–3, pp. 480–89; Teresa of Avila, *Autobiography*, chap. 4.

17. *C. (B)*, arg., n. 2.

18. Ibid., st. 22, n. 3.

19. Ibid., st. 37, n. 2.

20. Ibid., st. 10, n. 1–3; *A.*, 2:chaps. 13–14; *N.*, 1:chaps. 9–10; *F.*, st. 3, nn. 30–33.

21. *C. (B)*, st. 14–15, n. 2.

22. Ibid., st. 14–15, n. 2.

23. *C. (B)*, st. 14–15, n. 29. John does not quote the entire verse of Rev. 3:20; this is frequent in his writings; see Vilnet, *Bible et Mystique*, 45–51.

24. *C. (B)*, st. 22, nn. 4, 5.

25. Ibid., st. 23, n. 1: "In this high state of spiritual marriage...."

26. Ibid., st. 40, n. 3.

27. *C.*, st. 40, n. 4.

28. *C. (B)*, st. 36, n. 1.

29. Ibid., st. 38, n. 1.

30. Ibid., st. 39, n. 2.

31. Thus Huot, *Lectures*, 417–20.

32. *C. (B)*, st. 39, n. 1.

33. The English poet Wordsworth was fond of the Lake District, in the county of Cumberland; the French poet Lamartine composed a famous poem on "The Lake."

34. *C.*, st. 37, n. 5.

35. *De Regno Dei*, n. 19 (*Obras de San Buenaventura*, BAC, vol. 3, 1947, p. 690).

36. See George H. Tavard, "St. Bonaventure as Mystic and Theologian," in Margaret Schatkin, ed., *The Heritage of the Early Church. Essays in honor of Georges Vassilievitch Florovsky* (Rome: Tipografia P. U. G., 1973), 289–306.

37. *Sermon on 'In diebus suis placuit Deo,'* in Blakney, *Meister Eckhart*, 212, 214; see above, chap. 5, n. 12.

38. Eric Colledge, *The Spiritual Espousals*, op. cit., p. 186.

39. See chap. 8, n. 60, above.

40. *C. (B)*, st. 38, n. 5; see Thomas Aquinas, *S. T.*, 1, q. 12, a. 1: ... *beati Dei essentiam videant.*

41. *C. (B)*, st. 38, n. 3.

42. Ibid., n. 5.

43. *S.*, n. 58 (Simeon, p. 132).

44. *C. (B)*, st. 38, n. 5.

45. Ibid., n. 6. This brings up the point that concerned Anne of Jesus when she found that the French Carmelite sisters practiced a "metaphysical piety" focused on God's being, whereas the Spaniards held to a more christocentric devotion. Although the Carmels of France felt the influence of Cardinal de Bérulle, the initiator of the "French school of spirituality," inspiration for such a type of piety could already be drawn from the Johannist writings, which harmoniously combine the two attractions (see L. Van der Bossche, *Anne de Jésus* [Bruges: Desclée de Brouwer, 1958]). For Vilnet, John speaks here "only as a good theologian, who knows how to use the Bible" (Vilnet, *Bible et Mystique*, p. 231); Vilnet concludes that this passage is unauthentic; moreover, according to him, these texts of Revelation are "totally ignored in the works of John of the Cross," with an exception in *F.*, st. 2, n. 19, where Rev. 2:17 is quoted (*Bible et Mystique*, 230). But this is obviously a circular argument. Vilnet generally opposes the authenticity of version (B) for the reason that this version has modified the way in which biblical citations are presented in version (A); this again is not a convincing argument.

46. *C. (B)*, st. 38, n. 9.

47. Ibid., st. 11, n. 3.

48. Ibid., n. 4.

49. Ibid., n. 8.

50. Ibid., n. 10.

51. Ibid., st. 9–10.

52. The three texts in questions are *C. (B)*, st. 11; *C. (A)*, st. 35, n. 3, and its parallel, *C. (B)*, st. 36, n. 5.

53. *C. (B)*, st. 11, n. 10.

54. Version (B) of the *Living Flame* presumably dates back to the time when John lived at La Peñuela, before his last illness, that is, in August-September 1591, though this cannot be absolutely certain. Chevallier induces from this date that John maintained to the end of his life the doctrine of *C. (A)*, *F. (A)* and *(B)*, which would be contrary to that of *C. (B)* (*Saint Jean de la Croix, Docteur des Ames* [Paris: Aubier, 1959]), 214–15. Yet this is a vicious circle, since the problem is precisely to know whether there is a contradiction or simply a complementation between the two versions of the *Canticle*. The contradiction has not been established.

55. *C. (B)*, st. 27, n. 1.

56. *Prayer of a soul taken in love*, in *S.*, n. 26 in Simeon, p. 128 (n. 25, in Kavanaugh and Rodriguez, *Collected Works*, 668–69).

57. *C. (B)*, st. 40, n. 7.
58. *F. (B)*, st. 4, n. 17.

INDEX

Adam, 240
Advice, 177–78
After a transport of love (poem), 93
agapè, 170
A little shepherd (poem), 140, 173–76
alhumbrados, 78
Alonso, Dámaso, 42, 217
Almodóvar, 118
Alphonsus X, 5, 20
Alzon, Emmanuel d', ix
Aminadab, 127, 236
anagogy, 81
analogy, 81, 83, 111–13
Andalusia, 53, 56, 118, 128, 159
angels, 93–4
Anne de Jesus, 3, 131
annunciation, 29, 59, 210
appropriatioàns, 196–97, 215
Arévalo, 6, 127
Aristotle, 103, 110, 202
Ascent of Mount Carmel, 2, 32, 37,
   41, 56–7, 59, 61, 63, 65, 67, 69,
   81–2, 84, 86–7, 93, 95–7, 103,
   105–7, 109–11, 115, 131–32, 134–
   35, 144, 146–49, 152–54, 165, 167,
   169, 171, 173, 175, 178, 186, 194,
   230–31, 235, 239
attributes of God, 28, 82, 84, 90–1,
   108, 123, 141, 152–55, 207–14,
   234–5, 237, 243
Avila, 1, 7, 12

Babylon, 30, 33–4
Baeza, 118, 173
baptism, 240–41
Baruzi, Jean, 217, 229
Beas de Segura, 118, 173
beauty of God, 29, 82, 91, 94, 118,
   122–26, 155, 164, 166, 210–11,
   237, 244–45
beginners, 109–10, 115, 226, 232

Beloved, the, 46–8, 51, 55, 57–9, 93,
   95, 107, 115, 117, 119–20, 123–26,
   130, 137–57, 167, 171, 175, 187–
   88, 190, 200, 212, 223–25, 235–37,
   246, 248
Bérulle, ix
Bible (books of the):
   O.T.: Jonas, 86
         Proverbs, 146, 153
         Revelation, 236, 243
         Song of Songs, 38, 45, 47, 49,
            59, 69, 102, 125, 127, 134–
            35, 140, 145, 147–48, 173,
            182, 200
         Tobias, 145–48, 153
         Wisdom, 145–48, 151–56,
            196, 207, 234, 237
   N.T.: Mark, 228
         Matthew, 228
         Luke, 20
         John, 25, 138, 146
         Acts, 187
         Galatians, 188
         I John, 27, 138
         2 Peter, 206
Bl. John Duns Scotus, 28
Bl. John Ruysbroeck, 77, 208, 241
Bl. John-Martin Moye, ix

Calced Carmelites, 1, 12, 55
Castile, 46, 128, 160
Cautions, 177–78
Charles V, 6
Chevallier, Philippe, 229
cherub, 199
Christ, 10, 34, 45, 64, 68, 84, 91,
   114–15, 147–48, 151, 173–79,
   180, 244
church, 99, 102, 131, 135–36, 230–
   36, 247
Cloud of Unknowing, the, 76–7

coincidence of opposites, 78, 216
creatures, 20, 27–8, 81–6, 109, 111–
  13, 121, 125, 144, 152, 155–57,
  164, 178, 186, 195, 200–1, 204,
  213, 225–26, 241
creed, 62, 98, 100–1, 103–4, 110,
  113–14
cross of Jesus, 155, 174

Dante, 182–83
Dark Night (commentary), 59, 61–8,
  85–8, 94–5, 130–35, 141, 144, 147,
  235, 239
Dark Night (poem), 1, 16, 53, 56–9,
  68, 81, 93–4, 140, 171, 181–2
degrees of love, 198–99
degrees of spiritual life, 122–23
deification, 108, 204, 206
Deity, 215
Denys, 76, 114, 142, 206, 232
direction of conscience, 132, 194
divine unity, 208
Divinity, 118, 140
Discalced Carmelites, 53, 55
drawing of the Crucified, 41, 174, 176

Eckhart, 241
Elijah, 33, 207
El Calvario, 37, 56, 118, 173
entrance to contemplation, 235, 238
Entréme (poem), 11–2, 54–6, 68,
  71–2, 93
Erasmus, 114
eternity, 78, 124–27, 157, 185, 208,
  228–46
eucharist, 9, 20, 48, 93
Eulogio de la Virgen del Carmel, 78,
  218
Eve, 49, 240
evening knowledge, 81, 125, 180, 213

faith, 62–3, 66, 70–1, 75, 88, 93–115,
  135, 154, 162–63, 166
Filioque, 195–96
fine point of the soul, 202
Following a loving impulse (poem),

168–73
Fontiveros, 6, 17–8, 127
For all the beauty (poem), 93–4, 140,
  163–68
formal locutions, 106
Fountain (poem), 2, 15–20, 30, 39,
  51, 93
Francisca de la Madre de Dios, 117–
  20, 122
Francisco de los Apostoles, 12

García Jiménez Cisneros, Francisco,
  233
Garcilaso de la Vega, 6–7, 16, 38, 41,
  43, 45, 59, 128, 181–82
German de San Matthias, 7–8
Gideon, 127
God, 20–6, 62, 71, 73, 77–8, 81–4, 91,
  97–8, 107, 111–15, 125, 141–42,
  148, 153, 157, 164, 168, 174–76,
  179, 195, 204–14, 234–5, 243–46
God the Father, 17, 20–4, 87, 125,
  137–39, 143–45, 153, 161, 180,
  187, 198, 203, 207–8, 246
Gonzalez de Mendoza, Pedro, 53,
  118
Granada, 118, 173, 181, 218

Harphius, 77
Hilton, Walter, 77
Holy Scripture, 98–99, 110, 131,
  134–36, 227, 230–31
Holy Spirit, 3, 20, 84, 90, 104, 124,
  134, 138–43, 161, 163, 170, 188–
  90, 194–200, 203–12, 215–16,
  237, 246
Honorius of Autun, 28
hope, 31–2, 45, 93–4, 97–8, 105–6,
  115, 124, 162, 169, 172, 228, 233,
  248
Huot de Longchamp, Max, 218, 230
hylomorphism, 202

incarnation, 20–28, 87, 93, 115–16,
  175, 234–37
inquisition, 136

Jerome de San José, 119
Juana Inés de la Cruz, 174
justification, 66, 114

kingdom of God, 205–6
Krynen, Jean, 218

Lamartine, 240
Lateran Council IV, 111–12
Latin vulgate, 126–27
learned ignorance, 73, 76–7
León, Luis de, 6, 126
letters of John of the Cross, 177
light, 62–3, 71, 91, 96–7, 100, 103, 111, 141, 162, 175–86
lira, 8, 57, 181–82, 189
Living Flame of Love (commentary), 2, 88, 90, 110, 132–35, 141, 145, 155, 161, 164, 176, 181–94, 200, 203, 208, 215, 229, 235, 245–46
Living Flame of Love (poem), 28, 72, 108, 131–32, 140, 161, 163, 181–91, 223–24, 296
love, 3, 20, 27, 31, 68, 73, 76, 81, 86–9, 93–8, 104–106, 109–10, 114, 122, 132–40, 146, 162–63, 168–72, 194, 198–206, 223, 225, 242
Luther, Martin, 114–15, 178–79

Madrid, 1
Magdalen of the Holy Spirit, 65
Medina del Campo, 6, 12, 45, 59, 65, 127–8
memory, 45, 97–8, 105, 130, 197
mystical death, 31, 64, 86, 89, 156, 176, 105–6, 210, 216, 223–26, 245
meditation, 67
morning knowledge, 81, 125, 155, 180, 213, 237

name of Jesus, 149–50, 230, 246
nature, 46–47, 50, 59, 87, 89, 91, 100, 106, 121, 123, 125, 156, 224–25, 236, 246

Nicholas of Cusa, 11, 77–8
night, 11, 58–62, 66, 71, 75–6, 79, 88–9, 91, 94, 97–8, 103–4, 109–13, 161–62, 170
night of sense, 63–4, 72, 81–2, 88, 133, 149, 161, 175
night of spirit, 64, 67, 72, 85–6, 133, 161, 175
nudity, 125–26

opposition of contraries, 79–82, 84–5, 87–90, 96, 154, 162
original justice, 240–41
Osuna, Francisco de, 76, 233

participation in God, 212, 215–16, 244–45, 248
passive intellect, 102–5
pelagianism, 170
pentecost, v, 187
Peñalosa, Ana de, 131, 133, 193, 197
Philip II, vii–viii
Piacenza, chapter of, 2
presence of God, 9, 243–45
prologues of the commentaries, 2–3, 6, 131, 133–34, 230–35

Raymon Lull, 20–1
redemption, 28
revelation, 99–102, 110
resurrection, 32, 86, 174, 185, 244
Rhineland mysticism, 202, 241–43
Richard of St Victor, 137, 139
Romance on Babylon (poem), 1–2, 29–35, 39, 51, 140
Romance on the Incarnation (poem), 1, 20–7, 31, 51, 87, 93, 95, 138, 143–44, 148, 157, 173, 190
Rupert of Deutz, 28

Salamanca, 241
Sanlúcar (MS), 53
Sayings of light and love, 32, 118–20, 177–79, 242, 244
Sebastián de Córdoba, 6–7, 181
Segovia, 174

seraph, 199
sexuality, 202
Silverio de Santa Teresa, x
Simeon, 29
Simeon de la Sagrada Familia, x
sin, 28, 82, 96, 114, 163, 178–79, 240
Sion, 30–33
sketch of Mount Carmel, 41, 62, 65
Solomon, 45
Spiritual Canticle (commentary A),
    1, 59, 73, 83, 88–9, 96, 101, 107,
    118, 131–35; spiritual senses,
    102–3, 136, 165–67
Spiritual Canticle (commentary B),
    89–90, 101, 120, 124, 130, 178,
    208, 229–46
Spiritual Canticle (poem), 1–4, 16,
    28, 35, 37–51, 56–7, 59, 72, 75, 94,
    100, 117–36, 140, 160, 163, 171,
    177, 180–83, 188–89, 217–28
spiritual marriage, 45, 48, 75, 90, 97,
    104, 107–8, 122, 125, 149, 228,
    230, 232–38
St Anselm, 28
St Augustine, 26–7, 97, 137–39,
    142, 152, 170, 195–96, 203–4
St Bernard, 76, 149, 203
St Bernardin of Siena, 150, 152
St Bonaventure, ix, 17, 45, 76, 80–1,
    109, 114, 232, 240–1
St Francis Borgia, viii
St Francis of Assisi, 199
St Francis of Sales, ix
St Gregory the Great, 76, 114
St Ignatius Loyola, viii
St Mary of the Incarnation, 208
St Paul, 102, 104, 188, 197
St Peter of Alcantara, viii
St Teresa of Avila, viii, 7–8, 55–6, 61,
    63, 76, 118, 147–48, 199, 233
St Thérèse de Lisieux, 160
St Thomas Aquinas, 25, 80–1, 84,
    95–6, 98, 103, 114, 138–39, 141–
    42, 195
St Vincent Ferrer, 149
substantial locutions, 106–7, 114

successive locutions, 103, 106
suffering, 28, 86, 89
Surius, 77, 149, 242
symbolism, 10, 75, 83, 94, 102, 109,
    124, 126, 133–36, 147, 150, 156,
    161, 173–74, 190–1, 195–99,
    215–16

Tauler, 77, 149
Theologia Germanica, 114
Thompson, Francis, 168
three ways, 63, 83, 231–35, 238
todo-nada, 32–3, 62, 65–7, 73, 78–9,
    92, 95, 145–47, 169, 171
Toledo, 1–4, 7, 13, 21, 38, 45, 53,
    55, 119, 190, 219, 228
Trinity, 17, 20–8, 93, 113, 133, 137,
    140–43, 156–57, 161, 190, 195,
    198, 207, 212, 215–16, 241

union to God, 58, 62, 68, 75, 78, 85,
    89, 97, 105–8, 111–12, 120, 130,
    142, 146–47, 153–54, 169–70,
    176, 204–6, 230, 235
unknowing, 54–5, 66, 68–73, 75–9,
    93, 95, 109, 113, 115

Vatican Council II, 247
Virgin Mary, 25, 39, 59, 150–1, 174,
    210
vision of God, 101–2, 234–35, 242–
    43

William of St Thierry, 76, 114
Without support and with support
    (poem), 159–63
Word of God, 20, 86–7, 108, 123, 137–
    38, 143–48, 151, 153, 155, 161,
    173–75, 179–80, 188, 195, 198–
    200, 203, 208, 210–14, 234, 246
Wordsworth, 240
wound, 31, 46–7, 119, 122, 175,
    184–85, 196–99, 204

Yepes, Juan de, 5, 17, 44–5, 65, 128,
    160